Contents

RELIABILITY DATA BANKS

RELIABILITY
DATA
BANKS

Edited by

A. G. CANNON

and

A. BENDELL

ELSEVIER APPLIED SCIENCE
LONDON and NEW YORK

ELSEVIER SCIENCE PUBLISHERS LTD
Crown House, Linton Road, Barking, Essex IG11 8JU, England

Sole Distributor in the USA and Canada
ELSEVIER SCIENCE PUBLISHING CO., INC.
655 Avenue of the Americas, New York, NY 10010, USA

WITH 25 TABLES AND 136 ILLUSTRATIONS

© 1991 ELSEVIER SCIENCE PUBLISHERS LTD
Chapter 7 © 1991 US Government
Chapter 10 © 1991 IAEA

British Library Cataloguing in Publication Data

Reliability data banks
  1. Engineering equipment. Reliability. Data banks.
  I. Cannon, A. G. II. Bendell, A.
  025.0662000452

ISBN 1-85166-513-7

Library of Congress Cataloging-in-Publication Data

Reliability data banks / edited by A. G. Cannon and A. Bendell.
    p. cm.
  Includes bibliographical references and index.
  ISBN 1-85166-513-7
  1. Reliability (Engineering)—Data bases. I. Cannon, A. G. II. Bendell, A.
TA169.R437   1991
620′.00452′0285574—dc20   90-42119
                                                                      CIP

Special regulations for readers in the USA

Printed in Great Britain by Galliard (Printers) Ltd, Great Yarmouth

List of Contributors

A. Bendell
Department of Mathematics, Statistics and Operational Research, Nottingham Polytechnic, Burton Street, Nottingham NG1 4BU, UK

P. Bockholts
TNO Division of Technology for Society, PO Box 342, 7300 AH Apeldoorn, Laan van Westenenk 501, Apeldoorn, The Netherlands

A. G. Cannon
2 Colletts Close, Corfe Castle, Dorset BH20 5HG, UK

the late S. Capobianchi
Commission of the European Communities, Joint Research Centre, Ispra Establishment, 21020 Ispra (Va), Italy

A. Cross
National Centre of Systems Reliability, AEA Technology, SRD, Wigshaw Lane, Culcheth, Warrington WA3 4NE, UK

K. Kamimura
Plutonium Fuel Division, Tokai Works, Power Reactor and Nuclear Fuel Development Corporation, Tokai-mura, Ibariki-ken 319-11, Japan

H. E. Knee
The Centralized Reliability Data Organization Reliability and Human Factors Group, Engineering Physics and Mathematics Division, The Oak Ridge National Laboratory, Oak Ridge, Tennessee 37831, USA

L. J. B. Koehorst
TNO Division of Technology for Society, PO Box 342, 7300 AH Apeldoorn, Laan van Westenenk 501, Apeldoorn, The Netherlands

L. Lederman
International Atomic Energy Agency, Wagramerstrasse 5, PO Box 100, A-1400 Vienna, Austria

S. Masuda
Plutonium Fuel Division, Tokai Works, Power Reactor and Nuclear Fuel Development Corporation, Tokai-mura, Ibariki-ken 319-11, Japan

H. Mizuta
National Space Development Agency of Japan, 2-4-1, Hamamatu-cho, Minato-ku, Tokyo 105, Japan

H. Procaccia
Direction des Etudes et Recherches, 25 Allée Privée—Carrefour Pleyel, 93206 Saint-Denis, Cedex 1, France

B. Stevens
National Centre of Systems Reliability, AEA Technology, SRD, Wigshaw Lane, Culcheth, Warrington WA3 4NE, UK

K. Takahasi
Plutonium Fuel Division, Tokai Works, Power Reactor and Nuclear Fuel Development Corporation, Tokai-mura, Ibariki-ken 319-11, Japan

B. Tomic
International Atomic Energy Agency, Wagramerstrasse 5, PO Box 100, A-1400 Vienna, Austria

H. J. Wingender
PO Box 1313, D-8755 Alzenau, Germany

T. Yamaguchi
Plutonium Fuel Division, Tokai Works, Power Reactor and Nuclear Fuel Development Corporation, Tokai-mura, Ibariki-ken 319-11, Japan

1

Reliability

A. Bendell

Department of Mathematics, Statistics and Operational Research,
Nottingham Polytechnic, Burton Street, Nottingham NG1 4BU, UK

1.1 INTRODUCTION

From washing machines to weapons systems, from chemical plants to smelters, from electric shavers to space shuttles, the need for some concept of reliability is now commonplace.

This book is concerned with the consequential establishment, development and use of reliability data bases world-wide as a means of supporting and developing the need to know about the reliability of modern systems. Its primary function is to demonstrate successful case studies based on some of the most important reliability data bases on the world scene. Data bases from the UK, The Netherlands, the FRG, France, Italy, the USA and Japan are covered, as well as principles of the establishment and use of reliability data bases. The aims are partly to map potential sources of data, to show what has been and can be achieved, and to capture the current position and thus to clarify the future. The authors and editors wish to thank all those who co-operated in the making of the book and apologise for those important data bases which, because of space and other considerations, have been excluded.

1.2 WHAT IS RELIABILITY? WHY WANT RELIABILITY? PRINCIPLES OF ACHIEVING RELIABILITY

The achievement and assessment of reliability has always been an implicit aspect of engineering practice since the earliest times. Reliability in the form of continued existence or functioning is an important characteristic of all engineering systems.

The movement towards quantification and the construction of a theory for reliability, however, is relatively young. Although the exact age of reliability theory is subject to some dispute, there is general agreement that it has not yet celebrated its 40th birthday. This is borne out by the first appearance of the main journals in the field: the *IEEE Transactions on Reliability* first appeared in 1951, *Technometrics* in 1959, *Microelectronics and Reliability* in 1961 and *Reliability Engineering* in 1980.

In a similar way, the major reliability books—Bazovsky,[1] Lloyd and Lipow,[2] Zelen (ed.),[3] Barlow and Proschan,[4] Gnedenko *et al.*[5] and Shooman[6]—did not start appearing until the 1960s. In the 1970s and 1980s many other major textbooks have appeared. It is interesting, however, that the subject of reliability data bases has not previously been systematically treated in such a book.

The important early papers which established the basic characteristics of what is now established as reliability theory and of the problem of systems reliability predictions were those by von Neuman,[7] Moore and Shannon[8] and Birnbaum *et al.*[9]

Interest in the study of reliability is a response to the need to try and answer such questions as:

(1) How reliable is this system, or what is its probability of surviving a specified number of hours?
(2) Which is the most reliable of a number of possible designs for a system?
(3) Is it worth introducing redundancy into a design in case a component fails?
(4) How is the field performance of an item affected by its conditions of use?
(5) What will be the warranty, maintenance and logistic support costs for the system in the field?
(6) Can we improve the reliability and throughput of the system?

The achievement of reliability is of paramount concern for modern systems, as also is the need to assess reliability to aid such achievement, to choose between opposing designs and products, and to assess the requirements for logistic support, spares holdings, etc. The principles of achieving reliability are those of good engineering. Designs should be based on fitness for purpose and should be examined using the structured tools available to designers. The product and the processes of its manufacture should be optimised, making use of approaches such as the Taguchi method which has, in recent years, made such an impact on world industry.

Taguchi methods are an efficient prototyping methodology based upon the minimum number of prototypes or trials necessary to identify the main effects or factors which may affect the robustness or quality of the system or product. One's aim is to choose the specification for such control factors which provide greatest robustness against uncontrollable noise effects. This book, however, is not about good design. For further information on Taguchi methods, the reader is referred to Taguchi and Wu[10] and Bendell *et al.*[11]

Moving beyond design, reliability is to be achieved by ensuring well-controlled production processes. Statistical process control and quality control methods employ statistical sampling methods to ensure that production processes do not drift gradually out of tolerance without such deviation being observed. Again, this is outside the scope of this book, and the interested reader is referred to, for example, Mortimer.[12]

Reliability achievement in the field is based upon good practice in installation, operation and maintenance of equipment. This area is by its nature much closer to the content and purpose of this book, as many reliability field data which exist in reliability data bases originate (and indeed must originate) from on-site maintenance records in industrial plant. Accordingly, aspects of this part of reliability achievement will be dealt with by the guest authors later in the book.

1.3 QUANTIFYING RELIABILITY

Reliability of a component of age t ($t \geq 0$), denoted by $R(t)$, is defined here, as elsewhere in reliability work, as the probability that the item is still operating satisfactorily at that age. $R(t)$ is taken to be monotonically non-increasing with $R(0) \equiv 1$, $R(\infty) \equiv 0$. Related functions to this reliability or survivor function are the distribution function of time to failure

$$F(t) = 1 - R(t)$$

its derivative the probability density function of time to failure (strictly, in mathematical terms, if it exists everywhere)

$$f(t) = F'(t)$$

and the hazard function, age-specific failure rate or failure intensity

$$h(t) = f(t)/R(t)$$

It is possible to show that

$$R(t) = \exp\left[-\int_0^t h(x)\,dx\right] \qquad f(t) = h(t)\exp\left[-\int_0^t h(x)\,dx\right]$$

Also of potential interest in reliability work is the cumulative hazard

$$H(t) = \int_0^t h(x)\,dx$$

and the moments of the time to failure distribution (if they exist), in particular the mean time to failure (MTTF)

$$E(t) = \int_0^\infty tf(t)\,dt = \int_0^\infty R(t)\,dt$$

The folklore of reliability engineering[6,13] suggests that for many real items of equipment the hazard function takes the 'bathtub' shape shown in Fig. 1.

It is common to restrict attention to specific classes of life or time to failure distributions defined in terms of the above functions. Of greatest practical interest are classes of distributions which in some sense correspond to wearout or ageing, such as the class of distributions with increasing hazard or failure rate (IFR), for which $h(t)$ is increasing in t, as at the end of the bathtub curve.[4] Of course, dual classes for the above can be defined by reversing the direction of monotonicity or

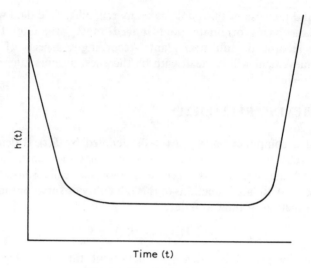

Fig. 1. The 'bathtub curve'.

inequality, to describe the life distributions of items that improve with age (the start of the bathtub).

Interest in the reliability literature (and especially amongst reliability engineers) has concentrated largely upon the one-parameter exponential density for time to failure:

$$f(t) = \frac{1}{\phi} \exp(-t/\phi) \qquad R(t) = \exp(-t/\phi) \qquad h(t) = \frac{1}{\phi}$$

$$E(t) = \phi \qquad \text{var}(t) = \phi^2 \qquad \phi > 0 \tag{1}$$

as its constant hazard corresponds to random failure or the central section of the bathtub curve.

Despite, for example, Shooman's[6] early warning, it is still apparently true that many reliability engineers assume a constant hazard or age-specific failure rate unless there is strong evidence to the contrary (see, for example, Refs 13–16), and this often causes serious error.[17,18] Indeed, reliability data are often presented implicitly based upon this assumption,[19–22] and as we shall see later the administration of reliability data banks often shares this approach.[23–26] To the mathematician, the assumption of exponentiality corresponds to specifying a Markov process, in this case a simple Poisson process, for the component.[27] If upon failure the component is repaired and has an independent exponential repair time distribution, the alternating renewal process so generated forms a simple two-state Markov process. Apart from the absence of an obvious wearout mechanism and the belief that failures may occur 'at random', say from environmental extremes, some justification for the use of the exponential distribution in systems is its arising as a limit.[5,28]

The other distributional form given increasing prominence in the literature is the

Weibull distribution, named after Weibull but originally derived by Fisher and Tippett.[29] For this

$$f(t) = \frac{\beta}{\phi}(t/\phi)^{\beta-1} \exp\left[-(t/\phi)^{\beta}\right] \qquad R(t) = \exp\left[-(t/\phi)^{\beta}\right] \qquad h(t) = \frac{\beta}{\phi}(t/\phi)^{\beta-1}$$

$$E(t) = \phi\Gamma(1 + \beta^{-1}) \qquad \text{var}(t) = \phi^2\{\Gamma(1 + 2\beta^{-1}) - [\Gamma(1 + \beta^{-1})]^2\} \quad \phi > 0, \beta > 0 \tag{2}$$

The hazard function is monotonically increasing in t if $\beta > 1$ (corresponding to ageing, wearout or the third section of the bathtub curve), whereas it is monotonically decreasing if $\beta < 1$ (corresponding to initial or burn-in failures, or the first section of the bathtub). If $\beta = 1$, the distribution reduces to the exponential one.

The simplicity of the form of the hazard and its ability to model any section of the bathtub curve partially explain the popularity of the Weibull distribution in reliability work, as does its relationship to extreme value theory.[30] One of its disadvantages is that standard methods of estimation are inconvenient; maximum likelihood estimation, for example, requires iterative solution.[31] However, alternative explicit estimation methods are available; Refs 30 and 32 give extensive bibliographies.

In particular, simple graphical estimation methods exist[33-35] and the appropriate special graph papers are commercially available (e.g. Chartwell 6572-3). Another disadvantage of the Weibull distribution, relative for instance to the gamma function, is the complexity of results in renewal theory to which it leads.[36] It should be noted that, in general, its mean and variance are not explicit, requiring tables or algorithms for the gamma function.

The exponential and Weibull distributions described above are respectively one- and two-parameter distributions. The fit to data can often be improved substantially by the addition of an extra threshold parameter $\alpha > 0$ so that each t in the right-hand sides of $f(t)$, $R(t)$ and $h(t)$ is replaced by $(t - \alpha)$.

1.4 THE METHODS OF SYSTEMS RELIABILITY SYNTHESIS

The early papers on reliability by von Neuman,[7] Moore and Shannon[8] and Birnbaum *et al.*[9] established the mathematical basis for the evaluation of the reliability of complex systems of components from knowledge of component reliability, and for the construction of reliable systems from relatively unreliable components. A methodology for the computation of systems reliability from component reliability is necessary as, in most cases, data on the reliability of complete systems or sub-systems are virtually non-existent, and the complexity of the system and its often high reliability precludes the estimation of systems reliability by life tests on identical systems on time and cost criteria. This point is given emphasis by the steady increase in the reliability of many components and thus systems through time.

Although for single components for which life testing would be prohibitively long, the solution is accelerated life testing (i.e. life testing in environments more severe than those in which the component is expected to operate), this possibility is not available for complex systems. Accelerated testing was originally devised to provide failed components to be analysed so as to improve design. However, there is no guarantee that the basic physical processes of failure encountered under excessively severe environments should be the same as those which would be encountered under long-term exposure to a normal environment. This is likely to happen only when there is a single predominant mode of failure, which is unlikely for complex systems.

To be able to evaluate systems reliability from knowledge of component

Alternative representations of system structure.

Reliability network

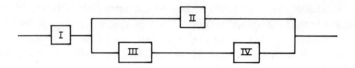

Structure function
('1' denotes operating state, '0' denotes failed state)

	component			system
I	II	III	IV	
1	1	1	1	1
1	1	1	0	1
1	1	0	1	1
1	1	0	0	1
1	0	1	1	1
1	0	1	0	0
1	0	0	1	0
1	0	0	0	0
0	1	1	1	0
0	1	1	0	0
0	1	0	1	0
0	1	0	0	0
0	0	1	1	0
0	0	1	0	0
0	0	0	1	0
0	0	0	0	0

Boolean representation
Hindrance function:
(A_I denotes failure of component I, F denotes system failure)

$$F = A_I + A_{II}(A_{III} + A_{IV})$$

Admission function:
(B_I denotes operation of component I, R denotes system operation)

$$R = B_I(B_{II} + B_{III}B_{IV})$$

Fig. 2.   Alternative representations of systems structure.

reliabilities it is necessary to possess information about the structure of the system; specifically, which combinations of component failures result in system failure or, equivalently, which combinations of operating components result in system operation. With the basic binary definition of reliability and the usual implicit assumptions of the basic systems reliability model, there are a number of equivalent representations of this aspect of system structure. These are notably the structure function or truth table, the reliability network, or logic or block-diagram, and the Boolean hindrance or admission functions. A fault-tree representation may also be employed.

As an example of their application in the basic systems reliability model, we show in Fig. 2 these equivalent representations for a simple system which will work only if component I and either II or (III and IV) work.

It is apparent from the figure that the implicit assumptions which make these representations equivalent—apart from the assumptions that the system has a single function, the system's structure is static and components and system can each only take one of two states—are that component and system operation is instantaneous, the order of component failures does not affect the state of the system, and there is one unambiguous and homogeneous failure mode—failure to operate (failure to idle is impossible). With these assumptions, simple numerical bounds of known accuracy can be put on the system's reliability for given component reliabilities by making use of the Inclusion–Exclusion Theorem and Bonferroni's Inequality.[13,27]

1.5 NEED FOR RELIABILITY DATA

It follows from the above arguments that there is a need for reliability data at the part or component level to be extracted from field records of the installation, and used to allow us to predict and compare the reliabilities of complete systems based upon knowledge of the system structure in terms of its components or parts.

Study of the collection, validation, storage, handling and use of such data is the purpose of this book.

REFERENCES

1. Bazovsky, I., *Reliability Theory and Practice*. Prentice-Hall, Englewood Cliffs, NJ, 1961.
2. Lloyd, D. K. & Lipow, M., *Reliability: Management: Methods and Mathematics*. Prentice-Hall, London, 1962.
3. Zelen, M. (ed.), *Statistical Theory of Reliability*. University of Wisconsin Press, Wisconsin, 1963.
4. Barlow, R. E. & Proschan, F., *Mathematical Theory of Reliability*. John Wiley, New York, 1965.
5. Gnedenko, B. W., Bielajev, J. K. & Solovier, A. D., *Mathematical Methods of Reliability Theory*. Academic Press, New York, 1965 (English edition 1970).
6. Shooman, M. L., *Probabilistic Reliability: An Engineering Approach*. McGraw-Hill, New York, 1968.

7. von Neuman, J., Probabilistic logics and the synthesis of reliable organisms from unreliable components. *Automata Studies, Ann. Maths Studies,* Vol. 34. Princeton University Press, Princeton, NJ, 1956, pp. 43–98.

8. Moore, E. F. & Shannon, C. E., Reliable circuits using less reliable relays. *J. Franklin Inst.,* **262** (1956) 191–208, 281–97.

9. Birnbaum, Z. W., Esary, J. D. & Saunders, S. C., Multi-component systems and structures and their reliability. *Technometrics,* **3** (1961) 55–77.

10. Taguchi, G. & Wu, Y., *Introduction to Off-Line Quality Control.* Central Japan Quality Control Association, 1985.

11. Bendell, A., Disney, J. & Pridmore, W. A., *Taguchi Methods: Applications in World Industry.* IFS Publications, 1989.

12. Mortimer, J., *Statistical Process Control.* IFS Publications, 1988.

13. Lomnicki, Z. A., Some aspects of the statistical approach to reliability (with discussion). *J. R. Statist. Soc., B,* **136** (1973) 395–419.

14. Bourne, A. J., *Reliability Assessment of Technological Systems.* Systems Reliability Service, UKAEA, 1973.

15. Cottrell, D. F., Dormancy effects on non-electronics. *Proc. Annual Reliability and Maintainability Symp.* IEEE, 1977, pp. 7–11.

16. Dorey, J., Reliability data derived from Electricité de France operating experience: example of the pumps. *Proc. 2nd National Reliability Conf., Birmingham, Vol. 1.* National Centre of Systems Reliability (UKAEA), 1979, 3A/2/1-8.

17. Yasuda, J., Correlation between laboratory test and field part failure rates. *IEEE Trans. Reliab.,* **R-26** (1977) 82–4.

18. Moss, R. Y., Modelling variable hazard life data. *Proc. 28th Electronic Components Conf., Anaheim.* IEEE, 1978, pp. 16–22.

19. Kujawski, G. F. & Rypka, E. A., Effects of 'on–off' cycling on equipment reliability. *Proc. Annual Reliability and Maintainability Symp.* IEEE, 1978, pp. 225–30.

20. Gibson, M. R., Field data from the chemical industry. *Proc. 2nd National Reliability Conf., Birmingham, Vol. 1.* National Centre of Systems Reliability (UKAEA), 1979, 2B/2/1-8.

21. Snaith, E. R., Can reliability predictions be validated? *Proc. 2nd National Reliability Conf., Birmingham, Vol. 2.* National Centre of Systems Reliability (UKAEA), 1979, 6B/1/1-10.

22. Henley, E. J. & Kumamoto, H., *Reliability Engineering and Risk Assessment.* Prentice-Hall, Englewood Cliffs, NJ, 1981.

23. George, L. L., Re-evaluation of the Air Force Actuarial System. *Proc. Annual Reliability and Maintainability Symp.* IEEE, 1978, pp. 7–10.

24. Silberberg, S., American nuclear power plant operational data compilation system—use of the system by Electricité de France. *Proc. 2nd National Reliability Conf., Birmingham, Vol. 1.* National Centre of Systems Reliability (UKAEA), 1979, 2B/1/1-6.

25. Holmberg, G. & Markling, G., From failure report to part failure rate, reliability data collection and evaluation for monitoring equipment. *Proc. 3rd European Data Bank Seminar, Bradford.* National Centre of Systems Reliability (UKAEA), NCSR R-24, 1980, pp. 271–93.

26. Colombo, A. G. & Jaarsma, R. J., Statistical methods for the European reliability data bank. *Proc. 3rd Reliability Data Bank Seminar, Bradford.* National Centre for Systems Reliability (UKAEA), NCSR R-24, 1980, pp. 157–73.

27. Feller, W., *An Introduction to Probability Theory and its Applications,* Vol. 1, 3rd edn. John Wiley, New York, 1968.

28. Feller, W., *An Introduction to Probability Theory and its Applications,* Vol. 2, 2nd edn. John Wiley, New York, 1971.

29. Fisher, R. A. & Tippett, L. H. C., Limiting forms of the frequency distribution of the largest or smallest member of a sample. *Proc. Cambridge Phil. Soc.,* **24** (1928) 180–90.

30. Mann, N. R., Point and interval estimation procedures for the two-parameter Weibull and extreme-value distributions. *Technometrics*, **10** (1968) 231–56.
31. Archer, N. P., A computational technique for maximum likelihood estimation with Weibull models. *IEEE Trans. Reliab.*, **R-29** (1980) 57–62.
32. Mann, N. R., Schafer, R. E. & Singpurwalla, N. D., *Methods for Statistical Analysis of Reliability and Life Data*. John Wiley, New York, 1974.
33. Kao, J. H. K., A graphical estimation of mixed Weibull parameters in life testing of electron tubes. *Technometrics*, **1** (1959) 389–407.
34. Kao, J. H. K., A summary of some new techniques on failure analysis. *Proc. 6th National Symp. Reliability on Reliability and Quality Control*, USA, 1960, pp. 190–201.
35. King, J. R., *Probability Charts for Decision Making*. Industrial Press, New York, 1971.
36. Cox, D. R., *Renewal Theory*. Methuen, London, 1962.

2

Principles of Reliability Data Bases

A. Bendell

Department of Mathematics, Statistics and Operational Research, Nottingham Polytechnic, Burton Street, Nottingham NG1 4BU, UK

2.1 PURPOSES

There are many justifications for the collection and storage of plant reliability data. These include quality monitoring or improvement programmes, ascertaining compliance with safety requirements, system availability requirements, economic criteria and legislation restrictions. Further, the collection of such data may facilitate the identification of optimum maintenance and replacement decisions, logistic and spares provisioning decisions and design decisions, as well as providing continuing feedback to the system.

However, as elsewhere, *it is important at the beginning of a collection exercise to identify clearly the primary purposes.* A collection scheme which is ideal in satisfying certain objectives or criteria may well be far from ideal in satisfying others. Many of the practical problems which have arisen historically with collection schemes, and unfortunately continue to arise in certain cases, can be associated with *lack of clear objectives*, or of extensive enough objectives, at the design of the data collection. As one cannot squeeze out of the data more information than has been collected, it is essential to know what one wishes to know at the outset of the exercise.

By its nature, *data collection itself implicitly makes assumptions* about the nature of the failure or other process. Bendell and Walls[1] described in some detail how the usual oversimplified assumptions on which reliability data collection and analysis are based are frequently in error, so that historical data collection schemes and data banks have summarised the data in a form which is not too appropriate for their structure. Aspects such as trend or lack of homogeneity in the data were included in the discussion. Walls and Bendell[2] provided extensive illustrations of this effect and made recommendations relevant to future data collection exercises.

It is, of course, true that subsidiary justifications for data collection will, and usually do, occur retrospectively once the data collection scheme is in operation. These windfalls can be of immense value in satisfying information needs which may arise, or in providing unexpected insight into the physical systems. That is why it is essential to have a clear justification for data collection in mind at the start of the exercise. As there are advantages in making a data collection exercise *as broad and robust as possible*, it is important to be aware of what information one is inadvertently excluding at the point of collection. This leads to the question of what to collect.

2.2 CONSTRUCTION

Historically, many reliability data banks have been established on a *fault-count* or *window* basis. The majority of data bases in this book are of that form. The collection of reliability data at all, even in this form, was a major step forward and has been of immense use. Indeed, on occasion, there has been no alternative but to collect data in this format, if any data at all are to be obtained.

However, such collection on a number-of-faults-within-a-period basis in reality implies implicit assumptions which the data are unlikely to meet. The incorrectness of these assumptions can then imply that estimates and forecasts based on the reliability data collected will be seriously in error. The most basic implicit assumptions are those of a constant fault-rate or exponentiality, a lack of trend or no-growth (a homogeneous Poisson process), a lack of serial correlation between interfailure times, a lack of heterogeneity, a lack of outliers or rogues, and a lack of dependence between failure times or common-cause failures.

To investigate such assumptions, and to provide more correct estimates and forecasts of reliability, it is necessary instead to base reliability collection on an *event basis*. This requires that the actual failure times or fault times of components or equipment are recorded, as well as other events in time such as maintenance actions, preventive replacements, shutdowns, start of observation, etc. The penalty for this, of course, is that considerably more data storage is required in the computer files or manual systems supporting the data collection activities. Perhaps because of this, there were historically many reliability data banks (such as the SRS system) which, although collecting the data on an event basis, entered it into the system on a summarised fault-count or failure-count form. This was unfortunate, as what does not go into the computer system cannot come out.

Two other aspects of the construction of data bases must be stressed. First, to dimensionalise or scale the phenomenon of failure, it is essential to collect information on the *population at risk*, which necessitates a systems description and site census. This, in itself, is always time-consuming, difficult and full of surprises. On an event basis, it is, in addition, very complex, with new units or parts coming into service, failing, being withdrawn for temporary periods, etc. It is important to withstand the consequent pressure to summarise information from the data at an early stage in the data system collection rather than at a late stage.

The other essential aspect is that frequently in data collection exercises insufficient attention is given to the *data format*. This is a return to the previous point about the importance of making minimal assumptions at the start, but even if one is working on an event basis, frequently essential information is neglected. On the other hand, there is a trade-off between what one can collect and the costs involved, and here there is a great need for a cost–benefit analysis of what one is to collect. As one is often extracting information from already existing record systems, such as job cards, from other parts of the organisation or outside, there are also limited possibilities before increases occur in the costs involved. This becomes more complicated when multiple sites and multiple organisations are involved and there is a need for a unified data collection set-up. An interesting example of this type of effect was presented by Marshall *et al.*[3] in regard to an MOD-funded electronic component data base. In that particular case, it took a working group several months of intense effort to approach an agreed format, incorporating the collection and transmission of soft system background description data. An essential aspect of the data format is the extent and nature of *protocols* for data collection, data transmission, etc. It is unfortunate that documentation here is all too often absent.

2.3 DATA ACQUISITION

Even incorrectly designed data collection is a complex activity, which should be regarded as *continuing and subject to continual monitoring* rather than as a routine clerical activity or a one-off and *ad hoc* procedure. As the extraction of reliability data is usually very much a secondary activity, with the initial recording of the data on job cards and the like being at least partly for very different purposes, it should not be surprising to note that frequently such reliability data are based on incomplete records and are full of errors. The folklore of reliability data collection talks of perhaps 10–20% of *errors in recorded field data.* Whether this is an underestimate varies, but the nature and magnitude of even isolated errors can imply major distortions of subsequently derived results. The *incomplete record* problem is a major one, but unless identified at an early stage of collection there is little that can be done about it. Even if such a problem is identified, it is necessary to track back to those who know the equipment and its use, and this, unless carried out very soon after the incident, is unlikely to be very successful. In contrast, the problem of collection errors, although perhaps of much greater importance, is such that *if the will exists something can be done about it.* Indeed, it should, for whereas incomplete records can prevent the accumulation of sufficient reliability data for analysis purposes, the collection errors will not prevent the analysis but may lead to results that are *severely misleading.*

The current state and extent of collection errors in recorded reliability data is extremely bad. In principle, there is little difficulty in reducing the magnitude of this effect, by careful *data validation at data entry*, as exists as a routine facility on many commercial data base packages. Unfortunately, such an approach is infrequently practised, although simple analytical and graphical methods to check for, and identify, abnormal behaviour in reliability and other data are well known.[1] Of course, in addition, the standard validity checks, for example on whether a numerical value falls within a permitted range, should also be applied. There is some movement in the reliability area towards this limited precaution, but it has been remarkably slow, and the more sophisticated methodologies for initial data checking are almost entirely absent. By the time the data have entered automatic storage it is, of course, too late. Even if errors are subsequently discovered, it is no longer possible to track back to their source and exploit the personnel's recent memory.

Another aspect of data base construction and data acquisition is a question of the *level of aggregation*, and the associated problems of *data combination*. For example, what are the natural groupings of valves for reliability data analysis purposes? If insufficient, nominally identical, valves are available, should they be grouped on the basis of additional characteristics or on diffuse environments, or on the basis of fluids carried or level of stress from the system?

Data combination methods for sparse data over a grid of alternative characteristics have been proposed over an extensive period. There is early work by Martz and Waller,[4] and also a number of papers, of perhaps limited use, generated by the Ispra team.[5,6] The methods typically assume constant fault rates but suffer from a number of other disadvantages including lack of strict validity! The methods usually described are of a so-called, but suspect, Bayesian nature. There is, however, potential for more correct development of methodology in this area.

As a penultimate point related to reliability data acquisition, it is worth reiterating that collection of such data should not be seen as a one-off exercise. Once collected, the intrinsic value of such data is likely to be revisited, if not continuously in sight, over many years. The implication, therefore, is that *careful documentation* of the collection process and of the data collection is worthwhile, and that such collection should be seen in terms of *entry to a data base*.

Although automatic data collection is now becoming more common, especially in production, this does not necessarily assist the data analyst. Measurement and production equipment, incorporating automatic data capture, typically collects data not in the form required by the data analyst, and for other purposes. Often it also collects too much, and frequently does not store it. Such data may also be inconsistent with data acquired from other production equipment. To date, problems of specification and data validation remain unsolved for some automatic collection.

2.4 PHYSICAL IMPLEMENTATION

The physical implementation of reliability data bases varies enormously, as illustrated by the range of systems described in this book: from manual to microcomputer and mainframe systems, and from the use of excellent multipurpose commercial data base packages for personal computers to purpose-built and sometimes archaic mainframe structures. There is, by their nature, always a lag in the data contents, methodology and technology of reliability data bases, as it takes time to establish such a base and accumulate data. With the rapid pace of technical development, by the time this has taken place, the base could be accused by a purist of being out of date. Large mainframe-based systems have suffered from this effect to a greater extent than the emerging microcomputer-based systems, as they have not been so accessible to developments in commercial data base packages. The advantages of such packages is in the easy manipulation and validation of data. The disadvantage is, however, that they will not normally be perfectly appropriate or convenient for any one reliability data bank application.

There is a distinction between the storage of data in a computer data file and the storage of data in a computer data base. Although a data base may be a file or a set of files storing data, the main difference is that the files may be accessed for a number of different applications (as opposed to a file of data designed and optimised purely for one application). This difference is easily seen by considering the example of a telephone directory. Imagine a computer file storing all the names, addresses and telephone numbers in ascending order as they appear in the directory. This then would only be efficient and useful for extracting data by names. What about extracting the names and telephone numbers of persons living in a particular street, or the names and addresses of all persons with a telephone number starting with the digits 89? The storage of the telephone directory as a computer data base may mean having a number of sorted files or a series of indices, or even some more complex structure, to permit a number of applications such as these extractions. The important fact is that the data base can be accessed for different applications in different ways. The programs accessing the data base may be regularly used or of an *ad hoc* nature and run only once. It is therefore not usually sensible to optimise the data base for any specific single application, as this may adversely affect some other task.[7-9]

In the general design of a data base it is normal to design the structure of the data base independent of any particular applications. There are two concepts used in the creation of a computerised data base:

(a) Logical data model: This refers to the interrelationships of data fields, and when determined and constructed this represents an 'application-oriented view of the data base'.
(b) Physical data base: This refers to the actual storage medium used. The design of the physical data base will usually be concerned with disk and tape read–write constraints, the amount of main memory available, etc. (Fig. 1).

The translation from the logical data base to the physical data base is governed by the *data base management system* (DBMS). The DBMS handles the conversion necessary to link the two. Thus each individual application program requires knowledge of only the logical data model to operate and is therefore independent of the structure of the physical data base. This is called *logical data independence*.

There are three generally recognised data models used in data base design: hierarchical, network and relational. Each may be particularly appropriate for different purposes.

(a) *Hierarchical*: Data fields within records are related by a 'family tree-like' relationship. Each level represents a particular attribute of the data. An example is presented in Fig. 2a.

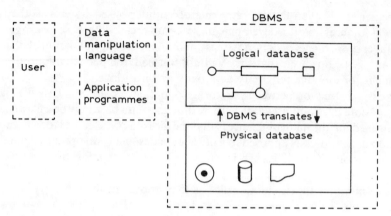

Fig. 1. Data base environment.

(b) *Network*: This is similar to the hierarchical model; however, each attribute can have one or more parents (Fig. 2b).

(c) *Relational*: This data model is totally different from either (a) or (b). The model is constructed from tables of data elements which are called relations (Fig. 2c).

The relational data base is generally more flexible than the hierarchical and network models. The fact that there is no predefined logical structure means that many different relationships can be catered for by simply combining tables.

   Most data bases are used to store large amounts of data. Data entry, and data base administration in general, can be time-consuming tasks. Hence error checking and data validation are important aspects of ensuring the integrity of any data base. Most commercial data base packages provide the facility to define acceptable ranges, values or types of data which can be entered.

Example:

Component type	Date installed	Fault	Action

Component type: AA9999, e.g. RC 1006
      Validation: First two characters are alpha (letters) only and next four are numeric only.

Date installed: 99/99/99, e.g. 25/06/83
      Validation: All characters are numeric and date is a valid one, e.g. not 39/20/82.

Fault: Code AA, e.g. BO = burnt out
      Validation: Check all characters are alpha only. Could also check against list of all possible fault codes depending upon length of list.

Action: Code AA, e.g. RP (repair) or RR (replace)
      Validation: Simply only RP or RR is accepted. This kind of validation ensures a high level of data base integrity.

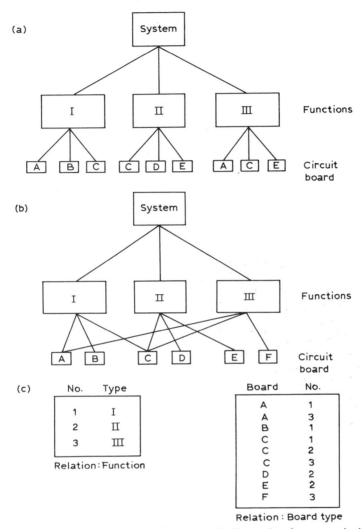

Fig. 2. (a) Example of a hierarchical data base. (b) Example of a network data base. (c) Example of a relational data base.

Commercial data base packages facilitate the production of reports, summary statistics and the addressing of queries. Most standard data base packages also provide an 'easy-to-use' data manipulation language to permit users to design and produce their own reports simply and quickly.

2.5 DEVELOPMENT AND OPERATION

Managing a large reliability data base is a complex operation requiring considerable staff and resources, as is illustrated later in the book. However, even a small reliability data base can be of immense value, but again the management effort should not be neglected. This is particularly the case during the period of its establishment and rapid build-up of data holding. Although this process of data acquisition is, by its nature, a continuous and continuing process, if the data are to be kept up to date and relevant, it is particularly difficult in the early stages. During these stages, problems in data recording entry and validation will come to light, and data base redesign is likely to be necessary, at least in minor respects.

The analysis of reliability data results in information about the data structure which should be fed back into the collection process and data base structure and organisation. This should be seen as a continuing operation. It is for this reason that collection exercises should not be seen as in discrete stages, rather than continual. It is bad policy first to collect all the necessary reliability data, and then to analyse them, as the analysis is obtained too late to alter the collection mechanism. Rather, initial analysis should be taking place as soon as the first data are obtained. In this sense, pilot studies are worthwhile but are no substitute for continual monitoring.

REFERENCES

1. Bendell, A. & Walls, L. A., Exploring reliability data. *Quality Reliab. Engng Int.*, **1** (1985) 37–52.
2. Walls, L. A. & Bendell, A., The structure and exploration of reliability field data; what to look for and how to analyse it. *Proc. 5th Nat. Reliab. Conf.*, Birmingham, 1985, 5B/5/1-17.
3. Marshall, J. M., Hayes, J. A., Campbell, D. S. & Bendell, A., An electronic component data base. *Proc. Advances Reliab. Technol. Symp.*, National Centre of Systems Reliability (UKAEA) and Bradford University, 1988.
4. Martz, H. F. & Waller, R. A., An exploratory comparison of methods for combining failure-rate data from different data sources. Rep. LA7556-M5, Los Alamos Scientific Laboratory, 1977.
5. Colombo, A. G. & Jaarsma, R. J., Combination of reliability parameters from different data sources. *Proc. 4th EuReDatA Conf.*, Venice, 1983.
6. Colombo, A. G. & Saracco, O., Bayesian estimation of the time-independent failure rate of an item taking into account its quality and operational constraints. *Proc. 4th EuReDatA Conf.*, Venice, 1983.
7. Hanson, O., *Essentials of Computer Data Files*. Pitman, London, 1985.
8. Robinson, H., *Database Analysis and Design*. Chartwell Birattl, 1981.
9. Ullman, J. D., *Database System*. Computer Science Press, 1982.

3

Analysis Methodologies

A. Bendell

Department of Mathematics, Statistics and Operational Research,
Nottingham Polytechnic, Burton Street, Nottingham NG1 4BU, UK

3.1 RESTRICTIONS OWING TO DATA BASE ASSUMPTIONS

As indicated in Chapter 2, assumptions made in the design of the data base, such as a restriction to a fault-count structure, severely affect the analysis of data. Further, the validity of any analysis that is possible is dubious if the assumptions are not valid. In this chapter we discuss both the analysis methods that can be applied in various circumstances and the investigation of the validity of the assumptions on which they are based.

3.2 CONSTANT FAULT-RATE OR FAILURE-RATE METHODS

Constant fault rate corresponds to the exponential distribution described in Chapter 1, as $h(t)$ is constant in eqn (1) of Section 1.3. This often is the basis for much of relability theory, including Markov, fault-tree and failure modes, effects and criticality analysis (FMECA) calculations. Many reliability data bases are based on this assumption, and fault-tree and FMECA calculations frequently employ data from such sources. We shall not describe the Markov, fault-tree and FMECA methods in any detail here, and the reader is referred to, for example, British Standard BS 5760[1] and Billington and Allen.[2]

What we shall describe in this section are some basic analysis methods for data of this type, rather than the use of such data within more complex system analysis methodologies. Space even for this is limited here; a much fuller and, alas, more complex account has been given by Mann *et al.*[3]

Much of the discussion of the next section, which considers data analysis in the context of the Weibull distribution, is also of interest for the exponential distribution, as it represents a special case. However, we briefly mention in this section one or two aspects of data analysis explicitly for the exponential distribution, in the context of an example of breakdowns on a worm conveyor.

TABLE 1
'Breakdowns' of a Worm Conveyor (Data Collected 1981–1984)

Event number i	Time between failure (days) t_i	Date of event				Event number i	Time between failure (days) t_i	Date of event		
0	—	1	7	80		32	2	22	6	82
1	0	1	7			33	27	19	7	
2	1	2	7			34	26	14	8	
3	1	3	7			35	0	14	8	
4	3	6	7			36	1	15	8	
5	7	13	7			37	3	18	8	
6	2	15	7			38	0	18	8	
7	7	22	7			39	158	23	1	83
8	20	11	8	PM		40	13	5	2	
9	8	19	8			41	2	7	2	
10	17	5	9			42	8	15	2	
11	91	5	12			43	17	3	3	
12	1	6	12			44	5	8	3	
13	31	6	1	81		45	44	21	4	
14	85	1	4	PM		46	24	15	5	
15	24	25	4			47	29	13	6	
16	29	24	5			48	48	4	7	
17	31	24	6			49	33	6	8	
18	2	26	6			50	14	20	8	
19	25	21	7			51	6	26	8	
20	51	10	9			52	1	27	8	
21	31	11	9			53	21	17	9	
22	9	20	9			54	6	23	9	
23	37	27	10	PM		55	9	2	10	
24	17	13	11			56	35	6	11	
25	55	7	1	82		57	93	7	2	84
26	18	25	1			58	29	8	3	
27	11	5	2			59	41	18	4	
28	47	24	3			60	40	28	5	
29	7	31	3			61	20	17	6	
30	32	2	5			62	13	30	6	
31	49	20	6			End	—	30	6	

The data in Table 1 show the dates of 'breakdowns' of the worm conveyor over the period 1980–1984. A constant failure rate is physically reasonable as an initial hypothesis in this context, and was, in fact, applied. Rewriting the expression for $R(t)$ in eqn (1) of Chapter 1, we have

$$\ln \frac{1}{R(t)} = \frac{t}{\theta}$$

Based upon data, the sample equivalent to the reliability function $R(t)$ for any failure time t is the proportion of inter-breakdown periods exceeding t; here

$$r(t) = \frac{n_t}{62}$$

where n_t is the number of periods exceeding t. Thus one may plot $\ln(62/n_t)$ against t (or $62/n_t$ against t on log × linear graph paper) to (i) confirm the appropriateness of the exponential distribution and (ii) estimate the parameter θ. In fact, systematic adjustments to the value of $r(t)$ are often introduced. These are discussed in more detail in the context of the Weibull distribution in the next section. However, for a sample size as large as it is here, 62, these make little difference (except to retain one additional point on the graph), and we shall ignore them.

In Fig. 1, we show the graph of $\ln(62/n_t)$ against t for the data. That this graph is suggestive of scatter about a straight line through the origin confirms the appropriateness of the initial hypothesis of an exponential distribution. An estimate of θ can be obtained by putting a line approximately through the centre of the data points and taking the reciprocal. This may be done most satisfactorily by least-squares regression techniques, and other methods such as median regression are sometimes used;[4,5] but it is frequently sufficient, given the ambiguities in the data and the rest of the analysis, simply to fit a straight line by eye. Such a line is shown in Fig. 1, and yields an estimated hazard of

$$1/\hat{\theta} \simeq \frac{3\cdot 23}{75} \simeq 0\cdot 043 \text{ days}^{-1}$$

so that the mean time to failure (MTTF)

$$\hat{\theta} \simeq 23\cdot 22 \text{ days}$$

The alternative to the above exploratory graphical technique would be a formalised

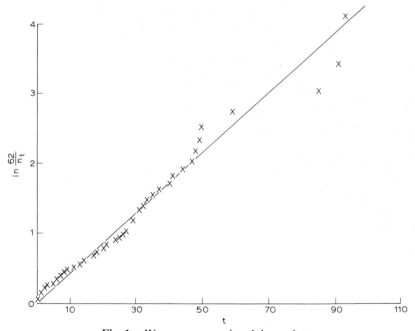

Fig. 1. Worm conveyor breakdown data.

TABLE 2
Number of Breakdowns per Month

Number of 'breakdowns'	0	1	2	3	4	5	6	7
Number of months	13	20	10	2	1	1	0	1

goodness-of-fit test, such as the χ^2 or Kolmogorov–Smirnov, together with an estimation procedure for θ. For the exponential distribution, unlike the Weibull distribution we shall discuss below, such estimation is very convenient, and many estimation methods including maximum likelihood imply that the mean

$$\bar{t} = \frac{1}{62} \sum_i^{62} t_i$$

is an estimator of θ. Here this yields

$$1/\hat{\theta} = \frac{62}{1544} \simeq 0{\cdot}040 \, \text{days}^{-1} \qquad \hat{\theta} \simeq 24{\cdot}90 \, \text{days}$$

which is very close to the graphical estimate. However, exploratory graphical techniques have many advantages, such as in indicating the nature of any departure from the hypothesised distribution.

Another way of considering exponential failure data is to make use of the relationship that exists between the exponential and Poisson distributions. If the times between failures are independent and identically distributed with the exponential distribution, then the number of failures in a given period t has the Poisson distribution with probability function

$$f(x) = \frac{e^{-t/\theta}(t/\theta)^x}{x!} \qquad x = 0, 1, 2, \ldots$$

This relationship is useful if the times between failures are not known in detail but only the number of failures in given unit periods, and it may, in any case, be more convenient to work with. Indeed, the data in Table 2 were originally analysed in this form.

Special graph papers are available for studying supposedly Poisson data, but will not be discussed here. Goodness-of-fit tests and standard estimation methodologies can again be applied. However, a simple property of the Poisson distribution does provide an intuitive feel for the appropriateness of this distribution, and hence of the exponential, for a given data set. This is that the mean and variance of the distribution are both equal to t/θ, so that one can compare the sample mean and variance to see how far from equality they are.

For the worm conveyor data, from Table 1 the number of 'breakdowns' per month is found to have the distribution shown in Table 2. This gives

$$\bar{x} = \frac{\sum x}{n} = \frac{62}{48} = 1{\cdot}2917 \qquad \hat{\sigma}^2 = \frac{\sum (x - \bar{x})^2}{n - 1} = \frac{87{\cdot}917}{47} = 1{\cdot}8706 \qquad \frac{\sigma^2}{\bar{x}} \simeq 1{\cdot}448$$

Thus the data are seen to be somewhat over-dispersed for the Poisson distribution, and the month with seven 'breakdowns' is somewhat suspicious. As it turns out, this is the first month under study, so that these data may well be inappropriate for the steady state. Recomputing $\bar{x}$ and σ^2 without these seven events we obtain

$$\bar{x} = \frac{\sum x}{n} = \frac{55}{47} \simeq 1\cdot1702 \qquad \hat{\sigma}^2 = \frac{\sum(x - \bar{x})^2}{n-1} = \frac{54\cdot6383}{46} \qquad \frac{\hat{\sigma}^2}{\bar{x}} = 1\cdot015$$

which is much more satisfactory. Thus this exploratory approach has identified a suspect group of data, which upon elimination leaves the remaining data looking consistent with the Poisson and hence with the exponential distribution. It should be noted, however, that a conventional χ^2 goodness-of-fit test would conclude that the data were consistent with a Poisson distribution without eliminating the first month's data.

3.3 NON-CONSTANT FAULT-RATE METHODS; THE WEIBULL DISTRIBUTION

Apart from constant failure rate, the next most usual assumption in reliability data bases and analysis is that the times to failure or times between failure are independent and identically distributed (i.i.d.). This means that there are no trends nor cycles in the plant or other reliability field data from which the data base is constructed. Of the distributional forms then applied, the Weibull distribution is the most common in reliability work (see Section 1.3).

3.3.1 Probability Plotting

Simple graphical estimation methods can be used for the Weibull distribution, in the form of plotting on Weibull probability paper (particularly in the case of uncensored data), and hazard plotting (which is particularly useful in the censored case). In this section we consider first Weibull probability plotting. For simplicity, we restrict attention to uncensored data, although simple adjustments can be introduced in the case of censoring.[6] However, if censoring is present, the hazard plotting techniques developed by Nelson[7] and based upon ln × ln graph paper are computationally simpler.

There are many good references on Weibull probability plotting.[3,8-10] Similarly to our procedure in the exponential case, the basic idea is to transform suitably the expression for $R(t)$ in eqn (2) of Chapter 1 so that a linear function of the parameters is obtained. Thus

$$\ln\left[\ln\frac{1}{R(t)}\right] = \beta \ln t - \beta \ln \theta$$

Hence a plot of the sample equivalent of $\ln[\ln(1/R(t))]$ against $\ln t$ should

(i) confirm the appropriateness of the Weibull distribution by identifying approximately a straight-line relationship;

(ii) provide estimates of the parameters β and θ from the gradient of the plot and from its intercept; and

(iii) identify whether the exponential special case of the Weibull distribution applies, i.e. whether $\beta \simeq 1$.

As in our discussion of the exponential case, a systematic adjustment is usually made to the sample equivalent of $R(t)$. The various adjustments commonly employed have been reviewed and compared by Mann et al.,[4] largely based upon the paper of Kimball.[11] For any failure age t the direct sample equivalent to $F(t) = 1 - R(t)$ would be to use i_t/n, where n is the total number of failures and i_t is the observed number of failures up to and including time t. One adjustment that is commonly used[10] is $i_t/(n + 1)$. Mann et al.[3] instead tentatively deduced from their comparisons that the adjusted form $(i_t - \frac{1}{2})/n$ is best. However, the basis for this conclusion is very limited (e.g. it is only based on samples of six observations), and investigation suggests that the common adjusted form $i_t/(n + 1)$ and possibly even the unadjusted form i_t/n are sometimes preferable. The results of Hinds et al.[12] also indicated that the form $(i_t - \frac{1}{2})/n$ is good, but those authors also used Bernard's approximation to median rank $(i_t - 0.3)/(n + 0.4)$, although this is theoretically very dubious. In practice, it is not necessary to calculate the $\ln[\ln(1/R(t))]$ values, as appropriate Weibull probability paper is commercially available. Two common forms are Chartwell 6572 and 6573. Examples of these are shown in Figs 2 and 3. The difference is that the horizontal axis representing age at failure is ln three-cycle on Chartwell 6573, whereas that on 6572 is only ln two-cycle. The basic plotting method on each of these two papers is the same, although parameter estimation for θ varies. As illustration, we consider the following small data set:

		Times to failure (h)		
903	783	1 450	1 390	1 002
734	933	686	1 121	504

This is shown plotted on each of the two types of Weibull paper in Figs 4 and 5, based upon the adjusted sample form $P(t) = i_t/(n + 1)$. The value of $P(t)$ is plotted on the vertical axis against t on the horizontal. The plotting positions are shown in Table 3.

To fit a straight line to the probability plot, the same considerations apply as in the exponential case. Often it is sufficient to fit by eye. To do this accurately, median regression ideas are often used to ensure that half the points are above and half the points are below the line. Following Ferrell,[5] this can be done iteratively, working at alternate ends of the data. Lines have been fitted to the data in Figs 4 and 5. Estimation of θ is essentially the same on each of the papers, whereas that of β differs. To estimate θ use is made of the fact that

$$F(\theta) = 1 - R(\theta) = 1 - e^{-1} = 0.6321$$

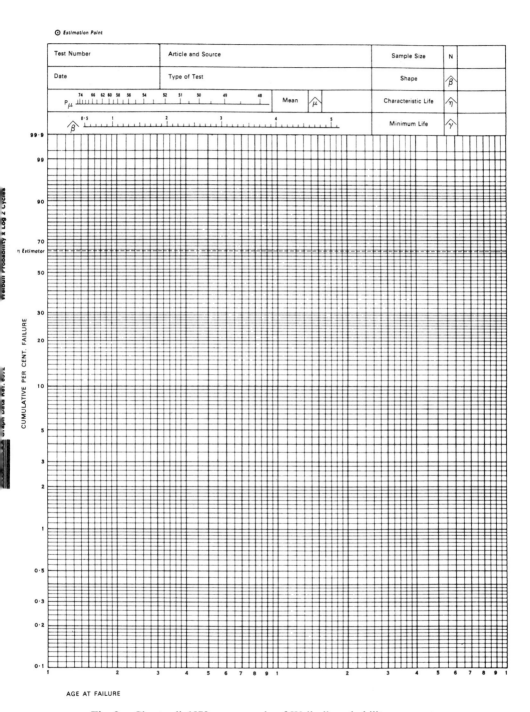

Fig. 2. Chartwell 6572, an example of Weibull probability paper.

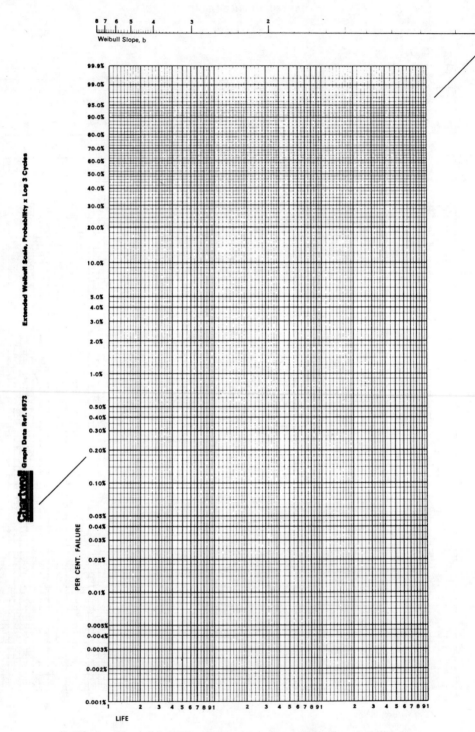

Fig. 3. Chartwell 6573, another example of Weibull probability paper.

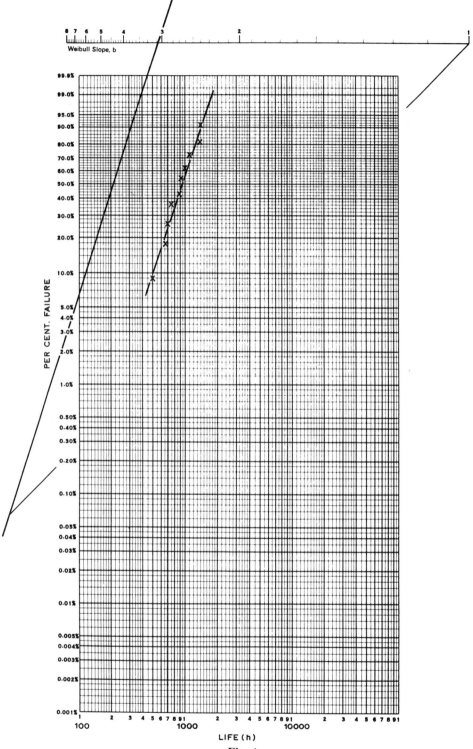

Fig. 4

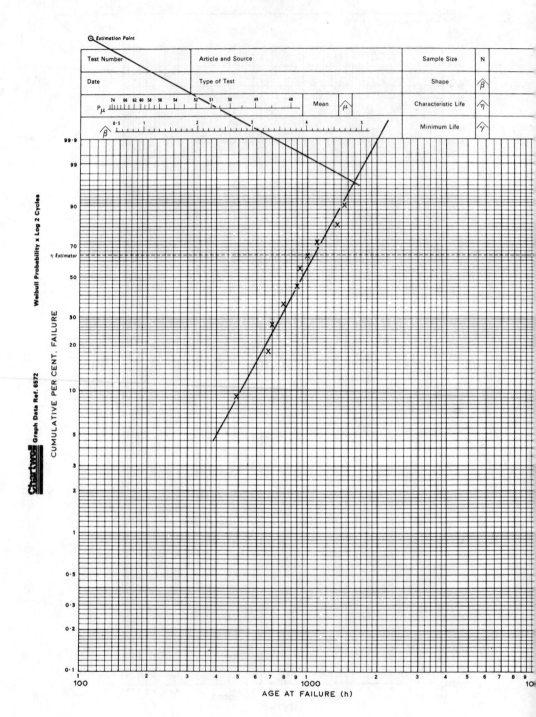

Fig. 5

TABLE 3
Calculation of Plotting Position

t	$i_t/11$	Percentage
504	0·090 909 =	9·09
686		18·18
734		27·27
783		36·36
903		45·45
933		54·55
1 002		63·64
1 121		72·73
1 390		81·82
1 450		90·91

for all β. Thus, on Chartwell 6572 (Fig. 5), a horizontal line labelled 'η estimator' is marked at 63·21% on the vertical scale. To estimate θ, one reads across to the fitted line and reads down to the horizontal scale. Thus, from Fig. 5, $\theta = 1050$ h. The procedure for Chartwell 6573 is identical (except that the 63·21% horizontal line is not labelled).

To estimate β on Chartwell 6572 it is necessary to drop a perpendicular from the labelled estimation point to the fitted line, as in Fig. 5. The intercept of this line with the β scale yields the estimate of β. Here $\hat{\beta} \simeq 3\cdot1$. On Chartwell 6573 (Fig. 4) it is instead necessary to draw a line parallel to the fitted line which passes through the tick on the left-hand side of the page. The intercept of the line with the 'Weibull slope, b' scale provides the estimate of β. Here $\hat{\beta} \simeq 3\cdot1$. On Chartwell 6572, an estimate of the mean lifetime can conveniently be obtained from the intercept of the perpendicular with the $P\mu$ scale. This gives the percentage failed at the mean lifetime as 50·5%. Identifying this value on the vertical scale, reading across to the line and down, yields the mean lifetime $\hat{\mu} = 990$ h. The standard deviation of lifetime can be obtained approximately as $(\hat{\theta} . A)$ where A is obtained (by interpolation) from the following table:

β	1·0	1·5	2·0	2·5	3·0	3·5	4·0	5·0
A	1·0	0·61	0·51	0·37	0·32	0·28	0·25	0·21

It is also possible to superimpose confidence intervals onto the Weibull probability plots, but we do not describe this here as their usefulness is limited. (A good reference to this is King.[10])

What is worth looking at, however, both as an aspect of direct usefulness in interpreting data on Weibull probability paper and as a further insight into the exploratory approach of data analysis, is the meaning of non-linearity in Weibull plots. There are four main reasons why such non-linearity may occur.

(i) *Sampling error*, i.e. the random sample of failure times, especially if it is small, may be unrepresentative of the population from which it is drawn.

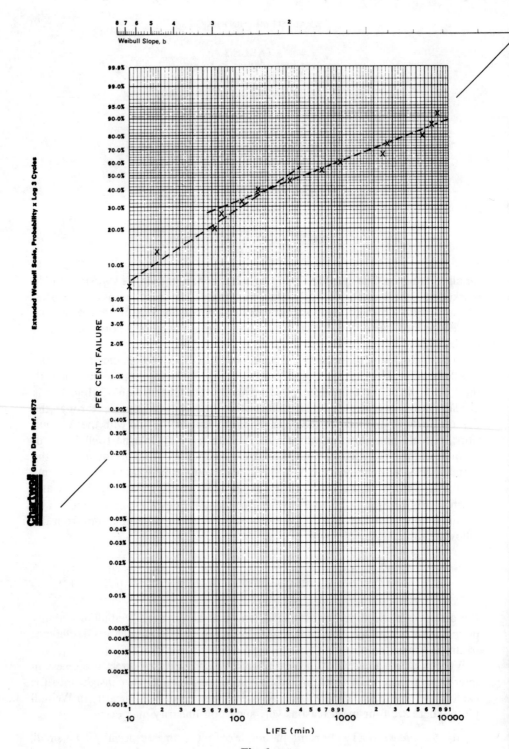

Fig. 6

(ii) *Mixed Weibull effects*, i.e. two or more failure modes with different time to failure distributions occur in the data.

(iii) *Using the wrong probability paper*, i.e. the distribution is not Weibull.

(iv) *The presence of a threshold parameter, γ*, i.e. failures *cannot* occur before some time threshold or minimum lifetime γ, and each t on the right-hand sides of eqn (2) in Chapter 1 needs to be replaced by $(t - \gamma)$.

It is usually assumed[10] that sampling error does not lead to systematic non-linearity, say a relatively smooth curve, that may be mistaken as associated with one of the other causes such as a non-Weibull distribution. However, although perhaps intuitively unlikely, it is apparent that this can occur. For small samples, unfortunately, it appears to be a significant danger.[13]

The occurrence of mixed Weibull effects has been discussed not infrequently in the literature, for example, by Kao[8] on electron tubes. In this, this interpretation of the probability plot is difficult and it is best to fit lines locally for each failure mode. Particularly with more than two failure modes, 'steps' may occur between the main linear trends, if the data are plotted on a single probability plot. The number of modes corresponds to the number of main linear trends. The relative frequencies of the various modes may also be obtained from the probability plot.

If a non-Weibull distribution is plotted on Weibull probability paper, systematic curvature should result. The data shown in Table 4 and plotted in Fig. 6 (using the adjustment $i_t/(n + 1)$) are an example on the times to failure caused by electric

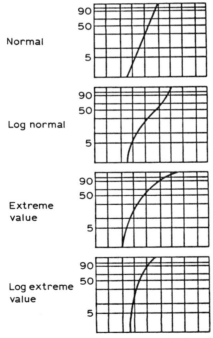

Fig. 7. Diagram showing how various alternative distributional forms appear on Weibull probability paper.[10]

TABLE 4
Times to Failure (min)

10	19	65	73	116	166	322	654	969	2 450	2 732	5 764	6 010	7 935

breakdown in solid tantalum capacitors exposed to a severe overvoltage. The data, in fact, give a good fit to a log-normal distribution, but on Weibull paper provide a shallow S shape, which might be mistaken for two intersecting straight lines, as is shown. Figure 7, adapted from King,[10] shows how various alternative distributional forms should appear on Weibull probability paper, apart from sampling error. The question remains as to how to distinguish mixed effects, from an alternative distribution, as they may look similar. *The real point is that the plots only point to features in the data so that the reliability analyst should go back to the physical context of the data and examine it.* Could this equipment have multiple failure modes, and if so what are they? Is the physical mechanism such that we would expect a different distributional form from the Weibull? However, as a rule of thumb, on the basis of empirical evidence King[10] suggested that a convex plot to the horizontal axis may be a good clue to mixed Weibull effects, whereas a concave plot is a good clue that the Weibull distribution is inappropriate.

There remains the question of determining the minimum lifetime before failure is possible. The existence of a non-zero threshold parameter complicates all forms of Weibull analysis, including probability plotting. Many authors, including King,[10] have suggested the estimation of θ by the time to first failure (i.e. the smallest time to failure), so that the smallest time to failure is subtracted from all subsequent failure times. Mann et al.[3] instead suggested a trial-and-error method of identifying the appropriate value of θ from the Weibull probability plot. The method is to decrease the estimate of θ if the curve plotted is concave upwards and to increase it (although not above the time to first failure) if the curve is concave downwards. As an illustration, we consider an example (from Mann et al.[3]) of six aluminium specimens of the same type placed on test in a corrosive environment with additional stress. Failures were observed at 3·45, 5·00, 5·90, 7·30, 8·60 and 10·20 days. In the plot labelled I in Fig. 8 the raw failure data are plotted, based on the adjusted form $(i_t - \frac{1}{2})/n$. In the second plot, II, $\gamma = 3·00$ was subtracted from each observed failure time before the plot was made, and in the final plot, III, the reduced value $\gamma = 1·00$ was subtracted.

Figure 8 serves to illustrate the fact that, in particular, plots which are concave to the horizontal axis might be the result of a non-zero threshold parameter, rather than a non-Weibull distribution. Another clue to the presence of a non-zero threshold may be if the analysis ignoring the threshold parameter throws up an exceptionally large estimate for β, say in excess of 3·5. (See Moss's contribution to the discussion of Lomnicki's paper.[14])

3.3.2 Hazard Plotting

If failure data consist of failure times of failed units and running times of unfailed units, the data are incomplete and are called *censored*, and the running times are

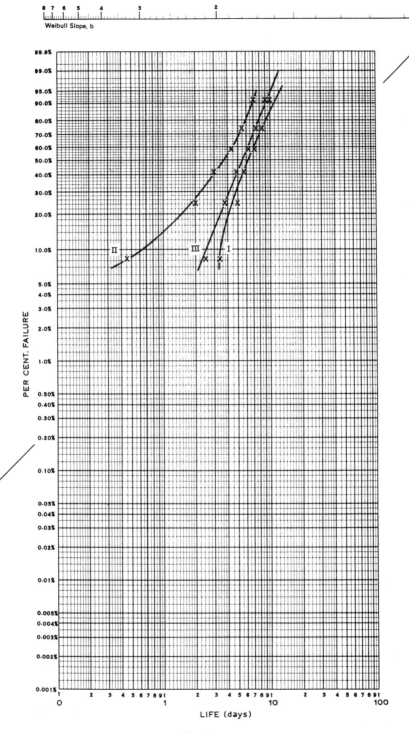

Fig. 8

called *censoring times*. If the unfailed units all have the same censoring time, which is greater than the failure times, the data are *singly censored*, and may be analysed by conventional probability plotting. If unfailed units have different censoring times, the data are *multiply censored*. This may arise as a result of units being put on test at various times but being taken off together, by units being removed from study because of some extraneous cause or mode of failure not under investigation, or from the use of field or plant data which consist of failure times for failed units and differing current running times for unfailed units.

For multiply censored data, the hazard plotting techniques developed by Nelson[7] are computationally simpler to use than the probability papers. Just as probability papers transform the Weibull cumulative distribution function $F(t)$ so that a linear function of the parameters is obtained, so too does hazard plotting transform the Weibull cumulative hazard function $H(t)$ to give a linear function of the parameters. Although special hazard plotting papers are available (e.g. from TEAM), the straightforwardness of the transformation in the Weibull case means that ordinary graph paper can be used. Thus, as

$$H(t) = \int_0^t \frac{\beta}{\theta}\left(\frac{t}{\theta}\right)^{\beta-1} dt = \left(\frac{t}{\theta}\right)^{\beta} \qquad \ln H(t) = \beta \ln t - \beta \ln \theta$$

or equivalently

$$\ln t = \frac{1}{\beta} \ln (H(t)) + \ln \theta$$

Hence a plot of $\ln t$ against the sample equivalent of $\ln (H(t))$ should, as with probability plots,

(i)   confirm the appropriateness of the Weibull distribution by identifying approximately a straight-line relationship;
(ii) provide estimates of the parameters β and θ from the gradient of the plot and from its intercept; and
(iii) identify whether the exponential special case of the Weibull distribution applies (i.e. whether $\beta \simeq 1$).

In addition, hazard plotting provides some information on the behaviour of the failure rate which is not conveniently available from probability plots.

To obtain the sample equivalent of $\ln (H(t))$, it is necessary to compute the sample hazard value for each failure time t. This is

$$\left(\frac{\text{number of failures at } t}{\text{number of exposed just before } t}\right)$$

and the sample cumulative hazard is the sum of such terms for all failure times up to and including t. Assuming independence, simultaneous failures are of negligible probability, so that the sample hazard may be written as $(1/K)$ or $(100/K)\%$, where K is the number of units with a failure or censoring time greater than (or equal to) the failure time t.

An illustration of the computation involved, taken from Nelson,[7] is shown in

TABLE 5
Generator Fan Failure Data and Hazard Calculations

Number (K)	Hours	Hazard	Cumulative hazard	Number (K)	Hours	Hazard	Cumulative hazard
1 (70)	4 500^a	1·43	1·43	36 (35)	43 000		
2 (69)	4 600			37 (34)	46 000^a	2·94	18·78
3 (68)	11 500^a	1·47	2·90	38 (33)	48 500		
4 (67)	11 500^a	1·49	4·39	39 (32)	48 500		
5 (66)	15 600			40 (31)	48 500		
6 (65)	16 000^a	1·54	5·93	41 (30)	48 500		
7 (64)	16 600			42 (29)	50 000		
8 (63)	18 500			43 (28)	50 000		
9 (62)	18 500			44 (27)	50 000		
10 (61)	18 500			45 (26)	61 000		
11 (60)	18 500			46 (25)	61 000^a	4·00	22·78
12 (59)	18 500			47 (24)	61 000		
13 (58)	20 300			48 (23)	61 000		
14 (57)	20 300			49 (22)	63 000		
15 (56)	20 300			50 (21)	64 500		
16 (55)	20 700^a	1·82	7·75	51 (20)	64 500		
17 (54)	20 700^a	1·85	9·60	52 (19)	67 000		
18 (53)	20 800^a	1·89	11·49	53 (18)	74 500		
19 (52)	22 000			54 (17)	78 000		
20 (51)	30 000			55 (16)	78 000		
21 (50)	30 000			56 (15)	81 000		
22 (49)	30 000			57 (14)	81 000		
23 (48)	30 000			58 (13)	82 000		
24 (47)	31 000^a	2·13	13·62	59 (12)	85 000		
25 (46)	32 000			60 (11)	85 000		
26 (45)	34 500^a	2·22	15·84	61 (10)	85 000		
27 (44)	37 500			62 (9)	87 500		
28 (43)	37 500			63 (8)	87 500^a	12·50	35·28
29 (42)	41 500			64 (7)	87 500		
30 (41)	41 500			65 (6)	94 000		
31 (40)	41 500			66 (5)	99 000		
32 (39)	41 500			67 (4)	101 000		
33 (38)	43 000			68 (3)	101 000		
34 (37)	43 000			69 (2)	101 000		
35 (36)	43 000			70 (1)	115 000		

^{a} Denotes failure.

Table 5. The n failure and censoring times are ordered in the sample from smallest to largest, without regard to whether they are censoring or failure times. Conventionally, the failure times in the list are marked with an asterisk (a) to distinguish them from the censoring times. (If some censoring and failure times have the same value they should be put in the list in random order.) The appropriate K values are obtained by numbering the times in reverse order, and the sample hazard and cumulative hazard values are calculated. The appropriate hazard plot for these data is shown in Fig. 9.

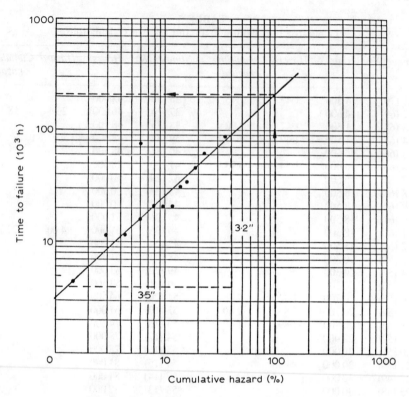

Fig. 9. Hazard plot for the data of Table 5.

From Fig. 19 the estimated gradient is measured as $1/\beta \simeq 3 \cdot 2/3 \cdot 5 = 0 \cdot 91$, yielding $\hat{\beta} \simeq 1 \cdot 1$. To estimate θ, we use the fact that when $H(t) = 100\%$, $\ln H(t) = 0$, so that $\ln t = \ln \theta$, or $\theta = t$. Thus $\hat{\theta}$ is obtained by reading up from 100%, and reading across to the time scale. In this case, this yields $\hat{\theta} = 210\,000$ h.

The choice of the appropriate hazard plot to use—Weibull as discussed above, or normal, log-normal, etc.—may be based on engineering judgement or experience. However, Fig. 10 (adapted from Nelson[7] and King[10]) provides some indication of how to choose an appropriate distribution and plot by initially plotting on linear graph paper and observing shape. Details of the alternative hazard plots to the Weibull have been given by Nelson[7] and King.[10] Similar complications concerning the incorrect choice of distribution, the presence of multiple failure modes, threshold parameters and sampling error apply with hazard plotting as with probability plotting, and care is again needed. Nelson[7] recommended that in fitting a line to a hazard plot to estimate parameters, the fitted line should be based primarily on the centre part of the data. Grouped data may be treated by equal spacing over the group's range. Only part, not all, of the data might be plotted, but a minimum of 20 data points is recommended, and all the data should be used in the cumulative hazard calculations.

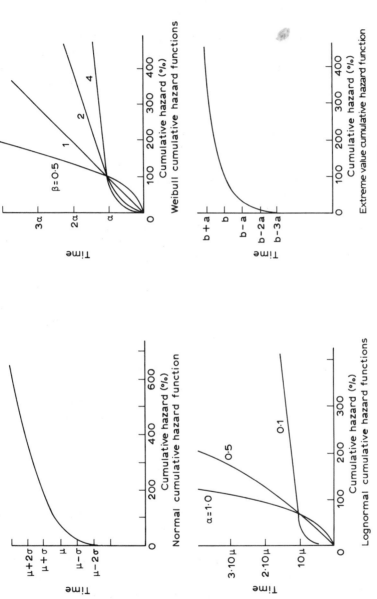

Fig. 10. Cumulative hazard plots for various distributions.[7,10]

Finally, we note that in hazard plotting

(i) cumulative hazard values can, of course, be greater than 100%; and
(ii) it is implicitly assumed that if the unfailed units *were* run to *failure*, their failure times would be statistically independent of their censoring times.

Although we have concentrated in this chapter so far on the Weibull and exponential distribution, because of their importance in reliability work, much that we have described transfers readily to other distributions and their associated probability papers. King[10] is a useful and easy-to-read text on these.

3.4 MORE GENERAL DATA STRUCTURES

The data structures assumed in the previous section cover the intrinsic forms of most reliability data bases in current use. However, because of the nature of physical plant, maintenance procedures and failure reporting, reliability data are intrinsically very complicated, with varying and complex data structures. There is, of course, no opportunity to explore these in detail here. However, common data structures do exist within particular industries and technologies, and knowledge of these can and should be exploited in constructing a data base. In terms of analysis, a first step, *provided that the data have been recorded in adequate detail*, is to *explore* the data, to investigate the appropriate structure for analysis. A flow chart for this purpose, with an indication of the analysis methods to apply in varying circumstances, is adapted from Walls and Bendell[15] (Fig. 11). How to do this *exploratory data analysis* and the methods to apply to analyse the data in terms of the structures found were described by Bendall and Walls.[16]

Figure 12, also reproduced from Walls and Bendell,[15] illustrates how such exploratory analysis typically reveals deficiencies in data base construction. The figure is based upon all available source documents from the Systems Reliability Service data base, and indicates that the data sources typically show trend and serial correlation (SC) which is not captured in the summarised data held in the computerised data base.

Although advanced methods exist, the current standard practice in reliability analysis is largely 'black box' in nature. Unfortunately, methods tend to be applied on an *algorithmic basis*, with little attention to the validity of the intrinsic assumptions, the homogeneity of the data under consideration, or to the sensitivity of the results to assumptions, data errors and the like. The reasons for such a sorry state of affairs must be largely traceable to the *lack of initial education* and the *lack of support* for reliability studies within industry. This is a subject which I believe to be of major importance to the future of the British industry. Although relatively simple techniques, such as those described in the earlier sections, can provide vital simplified information, if one wishes to understand the nature and magnitude of the reliability problem it is criminally dangerous to apply them on a routine algorithmic, black-box basis. Plenty of evidence of the dangers involved has been given by Walls and Bendell,[15] and in much other

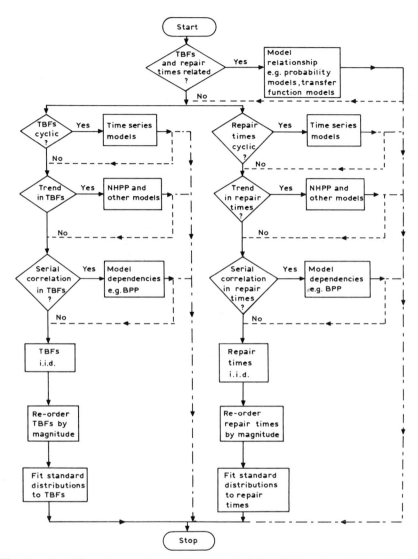

Fig. 11. Possible exploratory route through reliability TBF and repair time data.[15]

published work. However, the real evidence is the horror stories that many experienced reliability engineers can relate. The care that is necessary, and is to be expected of a professional engineer in all his duties, should, and must, be expected also in the collection and analysis of reliability data. Care is the antithesis of the black-box application of statistical methodologies.

The analysis of data which exhibit anything like the full complexity of structures that can be present in reliability work is a complex subject and is not described in detail here. However, the reader is referred to reviews of new methods in reliability analysis by Bendell[17] and Lawless.[18] Of particular interest are reliability growth

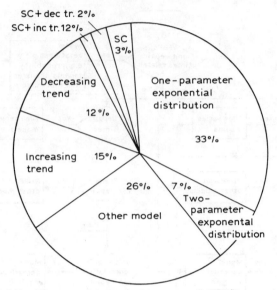

Fig. 12. Nature and extent of structure in SRS source data.

models,[19,20] time series methods,[21-24] multivariate methods,[25,26] proportional hazards modelling[27,28] and Bayesian methods.[29]

Multivariate techniques have received little discussion in the reliability literature, although they were suggested for this some time ago by Buckland.[25] Although their actual application is still in its early stages, the initial work reported in Libberton *et al.*'s[26] study is very promising.

It is also noteworthy that such methodologies are being investigated for their applicability to the software reliability analysis problem, both within the Software Reliability Modelling project under the UK Alvey programme and within the REQUEST project under the European ESPRIT programme. Such methods acknowledge the multi-dimensional nature of reliability data when all the characteristics of components and failures are taken into consideration, and attempt to identify and interpret the patterns arising in the consequential multi-dimensional space.

In contrast, *time series methods* have been proposed and implemented on reliability data almost exclusively by Professor Nozer Singpurwalla and his co-workers, at the George Washington University in the USA. Time series methodology is another well-established branch of statistical techniques, which makes few intrinsic assumptions about the data being modelled and which attempts to explain patterns in consecutive time between failures (or other quantities). Some of the more interesting studies are those of Singpurwalla[21,22] and Crow and Singpurwalla.[30] Walls and Bendell[24] pointed out, however, that reliability data typically contain more inherent variability than in other application areas to which time series analysis has long been successfully applied, and that developments of methodology will be necessary in this area.

Proportional hazards modelling is an extremely promising method for incorporating the effects of explanatory variables into reliability analysis; for dealing successfully with sparse, non-homogeneous data which are heavily censored, as is typical of reliability field data; and for identifying the appropriate structure. Also, it is, in itself, a data combination method which can achieve aggregation without assuming identical behaviour for dissimilar conditions or groups of equipment. Although originally proposed for reliability, as well as medical applications, by Cox,[31] it has been much more extensively applied in the medical field. The reliability references are poor, but the technique has much promise in this area and the team at Nottingham Polytechnic are having major success with its application.[28,32]

Bayesian methods may well have much to offer, particularly in the analysis of small data sets, but in the reliability area have often been misapplied. As in other application areas, naive, misinformed, allegedly Bayesian arguments have often been propounded by those without the background and experience to appreciate the subtlety of the statistical arguments. It is the practice, not the theory, of Bayesian methodologies which currently leaves most to be desired in reliability analysis.

REFERENCES

1. British Standard BS 5760, *Reliability of Systems, Equipments and Components*. British Standards Institution, London.
2. Billington, R. & Allen, R. N., *Reliability Evaluation of Engineering Systems*, 1982.
3. Mann, N. R., Schafer, R. E. & Singpurwalla, N. D., *Methods for Statistical Analysis of Reliability and Life Data*. John Wiley, New York, 1974.
4. Johnson, L. G., The median ranks of sample values in their population with an application to certain fatigue studies. *Ind. Math.*, **2** (1951) 1–6.
5. Ferrell, E. B., Probability paper for plotting experimental data. *Ind. Quality Control*, **XV**(1) (1958).
6. Bompas-Smith, J. H., *Mechanical Survival: The Use of Reliability Data*. McGraw-Hill, New York, 1973.
7. Nelson, W., Hazard plotting for incomplete failure data. *J. Quality Technol.*, **1**(1) (1969).
8. Kao, J. H. K., Graphical estimation of mixed Weibull parameters in life testing of electron tubes. *Technometrics*, **1** (1959) 389–407.
9. Kao, J. H. K., A summary of some new techniques on failure analysis. *Proc. 6th Nat. Symp. Reliab. Quality Control in Electronics*, 1960, pp. 190–201.
10. King, J. R., *Probability Charts for Decision Making*. Industrial Press, 1971.
11. Kimball, B. F., On the choice of plotting positions on probability paper. *J. Am. Statist. Assoc.*, **55** (1960) 546–60.
12. Hinds, P. R., Newton, D. W. & Jardine, A. K. S., Problems of Weibull parameter estimation from small samples. *National Reliability Conf., Nottingham*. National Centre of Systems Reliability (UKAEA), 1977, NRC 5/3/1-32.
13. Walls, A. & Bendell, A., Human factors and sampling variation in graphical identification and testing for the Weibull distribution. *Reliab. Engng* (1984).
14. Lomnicki, Z. A., Some aspects of the statistical approach to reliability (with discussion). *J. R. Statist. Soc., B*, **136** (1973) 395–419.
15. Walls, L. A. & Bendell, A., The structure and exploration of reliability field data; what to look for and how to analyse it. *Proc. 5th Nat. Reliab. Conf.*, 1985, 5B/5/1-17.

16. Bendell, A. & Walls, L. A., Exploring reliability data. *Quality Reliab. Engng Int.*, **1** (1985) 37–52.
17. Bendell, A., New methods in reliability analysis. *Proc. Euroconf., Copenhagen*, 1986.
18. Lawless, J. F., Statistical methods in reliability (with discussion). *Technometrics*, **25** (1983) 305–55.
19. Duane, J. T., Learning curve approach to reliability. *IEEE Trans. Aerospace* (1964) 563–6.
20. Crow, L. H., On tracking reliability growth. *Proc. Annual Reliability and Maintainability Symp.*, 1975, pp. 438–43.
21. Singpurwalla, N. D., Estimating reliability growth (or deterioration) using time series analysis. *Naval Res. Logistics Quart.*, **25** (1978) 1–4.
22. Singpurwalla, N. D., Analysing availability using transfer function models and cross-spectral analysis. *Naval Res. Logistics Quart.*, **27** (1980).
23. Singpurwalla, N. D. & Soyer, R., Assessing (software) reliability growth using a random coefficient autoregressive process and its ramifications. *IEEE Trans. Software Engng*, **SE-11** (1985) 1456–64.
24. Walls, L. A. & Bendell, A., Time series methods in reliability. *Proc. 9th ARTS*, Bradford, April 1986 (to appear in *Reliab. Engng*).
25. Buckland, W. R., Reliability of nuclear power plants. Statistical techniques for analysis. *Task Force on Problems of Rare Events in the Reliability of Nuclear Power Plants.* Commission of the European Communities, Joint Research Centre, Ispra, 8–10 June 1976, CSNI Rep. 10, 1976.
26. Libberton, G. P., Bendell, A., Walls, L. A. & Cannon, A. G., Reliability data collection and analysis for automatic fire detection systems on a large industrial site. *Proc. Seminar on Data Collection and Analysis for Reliability Assessment.* Inst. Mech. Engrs, 1986.
27. Kalbfleisch, J. D. & Prentice, R. L., *The Statistical Analysis of Failure Time Data.* John Wiley, Chichester, 1980.
28. Wightman, D. W. & Bendell, A., The practical application of proportional hazards modelling. *Reliab. Engng*, **15** (1986) 29–55.
29. Colombo, A. G. & Saracco, O., Bayesian estimation of the time-independent failure rate of an item, taking into account its quality and operational constraints. *Proc. 4th EuReDatA Conf.*, 1983.
30. Crow, L. H. & Singpurwalla, N. D., An empirically derived Fourier series model for describing software failures. *IEEE Trans. Reliab.*, **R-33** (1984) 176–83.
31. Cox, D. R., Regression models and life-tables (with discussion). *J. R. Statist. Soc.*, B, **34** (1972) 187–220.
32. Bendell, A., Proportional hazards modelling in reliability assessment. *Reliab. Engng*, **11** (1985) 175–83.

4

Some Achievements due to the Development of Data Banks

A. G. Cannon

2 Colletts Close, Corfe Castle, Dorset BH20 5HG, UK

4.1 INTRODUCTION

Data banks are the modern expression of a process that has been an occupation of man from time immemorial. The earliest collections of records are of Chinese or Egyptian origin. The prime requirements of such records are that they are based on fact and are accessible to those who need them. These requirements have remained unaltered but the mechanisms whereby the end product is achieved have advanced considerably. In fact, the changes over the period that this review covers have been considerable and dramatic.

Let us first look at the stimuli that promote the decision to process data. The word 'process' is used here deliberately as it is a much more useful concept than that of the permanent data bank. Processing conveys the idea of dynamics, which is essential in present-day needs. Information, however it is gathered, must be processed to provide a service to the 'customer' within a time-scale that is suitable to him and his system, whether this is a plant, aircraft, reactor or oil rig. Information must be gathered, ordered and analysed from the plant, and processed and stored for immediate output as required. During recent decades, several industries (e.g. the aircraft, North Sea oil recovery, nuclear and chemical industries) have benefited greatly by the examination of records on their operations, all motivated initially by the need to achieve a level of safety of operation as laid down by some form of legislation. A brief review of the needs and achievements of some of these industries follows. In all cases, the advantages accruing to the nation at large and to the operators in particular are plain, and perhaps we at times have all been grateful for the efforts of the staff concerned.

43

4.2 THE NUCLEAR INDUSTRY

The nuclear industry is involved in a continual process of extrapolation to extend our present knowledge of the properties of the materials and of the functioning of the equipment concerned.

The legislation which founded the nuclear industry in the UK required it to adopt standards of safety which had not been previously specified. From the performance of the industry, it would appear that it has gone a very long way to meeting these requirements, as can be seen from its very good safety record and the good availability and reliability of both reactor and chemical plant. One of the reasons for this is the collection, analysis and interpretation of data covering the past operational performance of items of plant. These records have permitted precise figures for reliability/availability to be derived within the environment in which items are being operated, i.e. taking account of the materials being processed, the conditions in which they are working, the methods of operation, the methods of maintenance, etc. This information has allowed the optimisation of the maintenance system itself, often resulting in a considerable saving in cost and manpower. It has pointed to fallibilities of the operational system and indicated the direction for improvement.

Such data provide an invaluable feedback to improve design, and underwrite the basis for diversity or redundancy to circumvent identifiable weaknesses in the system. All this has been achieved at minimal increased cost to the operations. Little additional operational effort has been required and no special system of data recording has been set up. Use has been made of existing records, such as maintenance job cards, operator log-books, permits to work, stores requisitions, data logging systems and computer files. The information when collected together leads to figures of system reliability for items of plant and clearly indicates the overall reliability expectancy of the plant, and of course its hazard potential, an essential part of nuclear plant operation.

4.3 AIRCRAFT INDUSTRY

The UK Civil Aviation Authority, over a considerable number of years, has required the logging of information on the safety of aircraft operation. In addition, it has required precise details to be kept of tests and calibrations of equipment, and of the results of maintenance of aircraft systems. During this period, the figures have been examined, interpreted and applied, in a similar way to that outlined above for the nuclear industry, i.e. they have been used as a feedback to improve maintenance and design, and to influence and improve operation. In the aircraft industry, one can also point to a continuous improvement in the performance of the machines and a continuous reduction in the hazard potential. It is suggested that this is, in no small way, the result of the collection and analysis of data from normal operations and maintenance. However, the information is also used for design purposes. The Ministry of Defence at Swanton Morley has one of the largest operational data banks of its type, devoted entirely to reports of the performance of service and civil aircraft in operation throughout the world. This data bank provides an on-line service to manufacturers, as an aid in improving performance. Press reports in recent months have demonstrated how contractors to the Ministry of Defence have been able to show in operation their contractually required reliability performance and thus receive bonus payments on that account. All of this based on a disciplined data collection system.

4.4 ELECTRONICS INDUSTRY

Partly because of the control systems which come from the requirements of the electronics industry, and which permit definition of the exact conditions in which a particular component will be expected to operate, it has been possible to define very clearly the test procedures which are required to measure the performance of these components. Test rigs have been set up to carry out this work and very extensive data are available in the form of MIL SPEC 217 A, B, C, D, E, etc., among many others. The Reliability Analysis Centre publishes data on the performance of systems in the electronics industry; this to some extent is special information and to some extent is field data. Although this information is specially derived and has cost a considerable amount of money in experimental facilities, it is still necessary to derive information from plant operation to check it, and especially to ensure that no other factors are operating which may invalidate the experimental data. Recently, cases of this have arisen in the nuclear industry and the chemical industry, where the performance of items of equipment was not meeting conditions as one might have expected from the experimental results. In fact, differences of performance, in some cases of an order of magnitude, were noted. Had data not been collected from plant records one would not have been aware of this. Not only did the data indicate the difference in performance but it also gave sufficient information to indicate why this difference in performance was present.

4.5 CHEMICAL INDUSTRY

Much work has been done over the past decade or so in the chemical industry in collecting information from existing records, with the aim of improving the performance of the plants under investigation. The UK 1974 Health and Safety Act points the way towards the future and indicates that for a definable high-hazard plant there will be a need for some form of safety documentation. This safety documentation sets the scene for the safe performance of the plant and it is possible that the Factory Inspectorate will need to establish a procedure to ensure that these safety requirements are met. One way of achieving this is by using maintenance records, operator log-books, etc., to give figures of reliability/availability; these records will then indicate when the system is not meeting its design requirements. Although this statement looks to the future, some firms have been carrying out this process in limited areas for a very long time, and indeed the Factory Inspectorate have long required this type of investigation, for example, for pressure vessels and for lifting tackle.

4.6 DATA

Although, at first, data analysis was safety motivated, it has now reached the stage where the main consideration is system viability. In fact, the process of development now takes the form of assessments to determine whether or not a system will be economic and how the relevant items should be arranged for most benefit. In all the cases mentioned above there is one major common feature—the basis for the decisions taken derives from the collection and analysis of validated relevant data derived from records specifically required for that purpose. In other industries, this state of affairs has not always been the norm. In fact, for most of the first decade or so of some processes, the information of interest owed its existence to very different reasons. For example, one source of information was job cards (i.e. the instructions to an artisan), upon which were often also recorded the action that had been taken to rectify a specified fault. That this type of data was used was partly a result of cost and partly urgency, in that information was required 'yesterday'. In the early days, more because few believed that this information had anything of value, it was necessary to prove the point, and analysis methods had to be developed, and specifications had to be derived, to cover the detail of information required to fit a particular need. These considerations led to a number of parallel developments in the computer programming field and in data structure systems. These will be separately reviewed.

4.7 COMPUTATIONAL CONSIDERATIONS

Any programming system for data handling must be able to accept the information in the form most suitable for the requirements of the customer; the data must be stored in such a way that they are readily accessible and can be retrieved for processing, either within the computer or by other means; and the system must be able to answer any of the questions which may be asked of it. Consideration of these factors has led to two definable approaches. The first approach, which is now, for various reasons, increasingly used, is where the data system is designed after thorough analysis of the components of the plant system under consideration. This process is at first very labour intensive and expensive, but when complete is an investment for the system life. The alternative approach is to arrange the data storage to handle the component descriptions as they arise from the data retrieval system. This was the approach used during the years when computer systems were under development, before data management programs were available. Such systems had great difficulties when it was found that the procedural rules accepted at earlier stages were inadequate for the task expected of them; for example, the numerical coding needed extension. Nevertheless, these methods at least started a number of data banks with a minimum of effort and a minimum of computational tools.

Data base management systems are now so advanced that they take in their stride the handling of words and numbers. In many cases, however, the claims made of them are much ahead of their capability, and are often statements of expected ability. Computer programmers come in two forms: those who translate often literally and those who understand the language. The latter make startling differences to the efficacy and speed with which a given objective is achieved. In the earlier days of the three decades of development under consideration, data bases were exclusively installed on mainframe computers, for these had the capacity for handling the megabytes of information necessary. Minicomputers now have data base management systems capable of meeting many of these requirements, and even microcomputers are adequate for some purposes.

It is not always necessary or indeed wise to computerise all data processing; in fact, unless the data base is a commitment of considerable size and of some duration, perhaps approaching permanency, it is not possible to justify either the expense or time necessary. Manual processing has a part to play, especially if the investigation is approached using well-thought-out and well-designed forms to prompt and guide the operators.

4.8 DATA NEEDS OR REQUIREMENTS

A choice may arise of requirement or necessity. Can one specify what is required or has one to make do with what is available? Let us look at the second question first. What information is available, which is relevant? There may be a problem of lack of data, or of which data to select. Job cards, permits to work, clearance certificates, stores requisitions and sometimes stores indents all have a part to play—they are interrelated in the context of plant maintenance and thus reliability. If job cards are produced and kept they are a valuable if crude source. In conscientiously operated systems, a job card will be produced for each event which involves an operation on a component of the system. At this juncture, careful consideration must be given to which items it is necessary to follow. One is mostly not interested in services, e.g. water, gas or electricity hardware. The main interest is probably electrical, electronic or mechanical, so these items can be used as a point of initial selection and the number of cards which must be examined can be greatly reduced. Other items may be put to one side, for various reasons, and this should be done in the interests of economy of both time and effort. The information on job cards can be categorised into several forms, such as failures, surveillance, calibration and checking. The first type gives an immediate indication of the spares requirements, repair times, etc. The second permits an optimisation of process inspections, for if at each of several inspections nothing was found amiss then there is a case for review of the frequency, aimed at reducing that frequency. Stores requisitions provide a first-order check that the repair claimed was in fact of the nature described. Permits to work and other documents provide a back-up in a similar cross-checking way. All of this information can be collected using portable computer terminals which communicate with a processing unit as part of a main system centrally placed on a given site, or by using one of the interim systems described later in this chapter.

Further details of any incident or event may be obtained by discussion with the staff concerned, but this must be carried out in a non-incriminating atmosphere, otherwise the person concerned may be placed on the defensive, either for himself or for his colleagues. No information about an event that is not documented in some form should be included in the permanent records.

The above discussion touches on the approach to data collection from the viewpoint of the use of existing data. In fact, it is postulated that the data that are used exist for reasons other than reliability. With the co-operation of all concerned the data collection method can be refined to any desired extent. One can design a form that replaces the job card which requests all the detail of information required up to any level of sophistication. However, complicated forms are not easy to understand; also, plant personnel are committed in other directions on the process and may not have the time available, and cost is important. These early approaches have now given birth to the present-day dedicated systems described later.

4.9 OTHER FACTORS WORTHY OF CONSIDERATION

The details gleaned by the procedures described above provide a picture of operation of an item which is a distillation of its performance in the environment which prevailed during the period covered by the observations.

What does this really amount to in terms of information that may be of value in the subsequent examination? This may be stated as a list of types of question to guide the investigator in making a decision on what information to examine, and the extent of detail required, as follows:

If corrosion or erosion played a part, were the irritants within the system or from elsewhere?

Which staff were on duty at the time? Are there any indications of any peaks of faults at any time? Is this periodic in nature? What other stresses were present and do they affect the picture in a statistically significant manner?

Do staff understand their function? Are operating instructions adequate? Are the training needs met?

Cases are on record where repetitive faults can be caused by a lack of understanding of the item's needs or often by merely replacing a failed item without consideration being given to the possibility that other components may be near failure. Data will be able to help in the diagnosis of many plant ills, even including operator-induced failure.

In certain research investigations it may be necessary to ask what factors may contribute to the performance observed.

To summarise, extremely simple examinations and recording of data in the fashion described above can provide factual information from which plant systems can be optimised. The level of sophistication of these simple results depends upon planning insight, and, above all, on co-operation from all concerned.

4.10 STAFFING

The effort for this work need not be prohibitive in terms of either personnel or cost. Studies can be successful, provided supervision is adequate, using relatively inexperienced staff. Sandwich course students have been successfully employed in the UK in this role. This has advantages, for such staff are often able to bridge the shop-floor–management divide. Proper and adequate instruction, briefing and introduction, as well as choice of person, are essential. The order of result is that one student has the potential to examine 10 item histories over a period of 4 years in 6 months. With experience, of course, a more accurate assessment of a given situation can be made. Quality and availability of data are paramount. Such investigations will highlight events that are unexpected, or perhaps unpleasant, but in these circumstances should not lead to recriminations, unless this is of paramount importance. Unfortunately, success or failure of these exercises depends on the maintenance of confidentiality.

4.10.1 Factors to be Investigated

Much has been said above concerning the needs of data; some of the underlying concepts that have developed from the study of reliability will now be considered. Let us now look at some terms in everyday use, which are examined in much more detail in other chapters.

Reliability is the ability of an item of equipment to perform its design function when required, and as often as required. Alternatively, and for calculational purposes, it may be said to be the probability that the system or item will meet its specification during operation when required, as often as required and as designed (of course, in the environment for which it was designed). Typically, one might expect mechanical components to exhibit fault rates in the region of 10^{-2}–10^{-3}, and seldom better. Electronic components that have been 'burnt in' can approach 2–3×10^{-6} in a well-controlled and well-set-up system. Human fallibility can be as low as 10^{-2} or even worse, dependent upon circumstances.

A closely related concept to reliability is availability. This is the probability that an item of equipment is able to function as and when required, in the way required, and as accurately or as precisely as required. Availability therefore includes the concept of reliability to function during the time the system is not only on-line but on standby or is otherwise not functioning. Concepts of maintenance for a system on standby or not functioning can be very different from those for the on-line case. The necessity arises for checking from time to time that the system is available, i.e. will function, etc., when called upon. This leads to a different maintenance and testing regime from that required for on-line surveillance.

Reliability growth is the increase/decrease of reliability of an item during the life of the system of which it forms part. This is in some ways a diagnostic tool for investigating the overall performance of a plant. In the early stages of commissioning, it is expected that the increase of reliability should be dramatic, as the system operators, maintenance staff, and mechanical, electrical and instrument components settle down, and initial faults of construction, omission, commission, etc., are ironed out. Typically, an observer will see a period of constant failure rate after commissioning, which represents the useful life of the system, but to maintain this state care and attention to records and maintenance are necessary, together with adequate staff training and liaison, so that as time progresses more is learnt of the entire system.

We will now consider the factors which affect the overall performance. Human factors, common cause and common mode failures, and software reliability are among the more important.

Human factors relate to the study of the performance of the human operator. This is difficult to grasp. Studies on what motivates human beings and on how to direct these motivations towards the desired effect have led to the development of a very considerable body of information which enables one to improve most situations, but all is far from being completely under control. There is little doubt that the person is the least reliable of all the items making up a system. Having said that, however, he has properties that no other system yet offers. He is at his worst when required to perform routine repetitive functions, and at his best when interpreting situations that have been well studied.

It is logical to link software reliability with human factors, because it is a study of the means whereby software faults can be reduced to an acceptable minimum by following a clearly defined routine. The main concern involves programming errors. It has been found that cross-checking by experts working independently but in parallel is a considerable help, and other useful routines and disciplines have been developed.

Common mode and common cause fault systems are always spoken of together but are very different. Oddly, they are often confused. The best way to describe common mode failure is by example. If we observed, in a survey of valves of a particular type (e.g. gate valves) but of various sizes, distributed throughout sites widely dispersed in the country, that the gates were suffering fatigue failure, this is likely to be a common mode of failure. However, there are reservations, as the thresholds differ, because of the various component sizes and thicknesses, differing flow rates, and possibly differing materials. As a result, the modes may not be all the same.

Common cause failure, however, is easier to diagnose, although some of the underlying reasons are at times insidious. As the term states, the observed failures are caused by the same factors. Possible reasons include improper construction materials, overstressed materials, improper use, etc. Common cause failures can arise as a result of calibrations being done by the same person at the same time throughout a period of operation. The time factor could mean that the calibration is done when the system is at a particular part of its cycle of operation, which could include, for example, a peak period of power supply. Also, checking instruments may not have been adequately calibrated, or the person concerned may have been unwell or suffered a bereavement, for example.

Methods for the reduction of these types of faults have been extensively developed, and most are simple to implement. Checking should not always be done either by the same person or by using the same checking equipment, nor at the same time of day or part of a cycle. A change of person reduces the risk of personal problems influencing the result. Another contributor to this family of faults can be the use of faulty procedures; for example, at one time it was common practice to clean relay contacts with solvent, until it was realised that impurities in these solvents were causing corrosion of the very contacts it was desired to clean. The reduction of fire risks stimulated the development of silicone and tri-butyl-phosphate lubricants, which can be successful if used specifically as instructed by the manufacturers. However, as it is common for contracts to be placed on a competitive tender basis, where the cheapest bid is accepted, several disasters resulted from this process because cheap raw materials were supplied, whereas those materials that were required for the successful application were produced to a higher specification and therefore much more expensive. Hence, it is necessary to produce an adequate specification of what is required, backed up by a check that the specification is understood where the process of acquisition is critical.

One must be clear on the purpose of the study, and have an understanding of the factors which might be involved and which need to be studied. Proper instruction of the data collecting staff concerned is essential; perhaps more essential is the briefing of the staff who will operate the installation under study. An appraisal must be made of the likely adequacy of the available information to meet the requirements, backed by sufficient analytical and validation facilities. The following question then needs attention: what facilities are necessary to provide adequately the result desired? It may not be necessary to resort to a sophisticated computer handling system. Hand logging of the results in simple cases can be adequate and cheapest. Personal computers have a part to play at the next level of complexity, and the largest computers available may be used in the most complicated data bases.

It is not possible to put a cost on data collection projects because of the vast range of topics which may be involved. It has been shown that, where projects are geared to specific cases of demonstrated need, returns out of all proportion to the costs are achievable. The authors are aware of cases where the effort cost for a 6-month investigation was recovered in a week's production of the improved system. This included delaying a redesigned plant by 4 years. As an indication of cost, some of the larger data systems represent overall investments of several million pounds sterling, and smaller ones may cost a few thousand pounds sterling.

There are three published 'standard texts' on these types of investigation. These indicate the advantages and limitations of this approach to plant investigation, which has now become known as probabilistic risk assessment. The first is the Rasmussen investigation in the USA into the safety of water reactors. This is the most quoted, although it contains some curious derivations. Figures supplied by organisations from various countries were all regarded as of equal merit, and little effort was given to trying to match like conditions of services with like operations elsewhere. Figures differing by as much as three orders of magnitude were apparently averaged. This is the more surprising when one considers the large amount of analytical tool development which went on in parallel and which is highly regarded today.

The second of these investigations on reactors was undertaken by the Gesellschaft für Reaktorsicherheit in the FRG. This was a very thoroughgoing investigation, which collected information from organisations in various countries and analysed these results using the most acceptable techniques available. The conclusions are difficult to summarise but we will content ourselves by picking out one of them: the report stated that the break of a relatively small pipe in a reactor system could possibly lead to a loss of coolant accident, and went on to say that there was such a paucity of information on these systems that nothing further that was definitive could be concluded. The author chaired a subsequent international group set up to recommend values for pipe reliability. From eight nations represented in that group it was not possible to assemble anything but a very mediocre data sample, although there must be many thousands of miles of pipework in the world. Several vital services are dependent upon it, for instance water, gas and oil, including North Sea operations.

The third such investigation, which is in two parts, demonstrates the advantages of obtaining data from data banks. The Canvey Island (UK) investigation represents the case of an assessment of the hazard to a community of a chemical/oil complex which very nearly surrounds it. The investigation was required to answer the question: 'Was there any greater hazard to this community than to similar other communities in the UK?' The first part of the investigation used data from various data systems but not from the sites and arrived at a figure of hazard ratio of about four to the disadvantage of the community. A later investigation using data from the sites allowed this figure to be reduced to two.

There have been many other investigations, mostly by private concerns aimed at specific projects, which are very useful indicators of the efficacy of the methods and indicative of the value of data stores. Two related projects are mentioned below.

The OREDO scheme run in the Norwegian sector of the North Sea aims to provide a data book of the most likely performance reliabilities of a very wide range of components used in the rigs and platforms in that zone and operated by a broad contributing spectrum of firms. This information is required to be used as a data source for submissions to the Norwegian Petroleum Directorate, to cover the safety of operations in that sector. When one bears in mind that the NPD has laid down rigid probabilistic requirements for any definable incident, then the implications of such measures are clear: not only have the operators to design to meet these probabilities but also they must organise their operations to ensure that these reliabilities are ensured.

In recovery of oil and gas from North Sea operations, the economic viability of most drilling finds is assessed by using reliability/availability methods. The development of a well depends on an assessment of its probable continuing economic viability.

It is now fair to say that some members of most industry categories make use of reliability/availability techniques. The examples above represent, therefore, a small sample from the whole. Other industries involved include the motor industry, the electrical generation industry, shipping and defence (land, sea and air).

5

FACTS: Most Comprehensive Information System for Industrial Safety

L. J. B. Koehorst & P. Bockholts

TNO Division of Technology for Society, PO Box 342, 7300 AH Apeldoorn, Laan van Westenenk 501, Apeldoorn, The Netherlands

5.1 INTRODUCTION

FACTS (Failure and ACcident Technical information System) is a data bank containing technical information about incidents with hazardous materials that have occurred in the processing industries, during storage and transport, during use or during waste treatment of chemicals. Major as well as minor accidents and near-misses are included. The aim of the data bank is to give an insight into how and why events happened, which mechanisms played a role and to provide lessons.

FACTS contains data that have been derived from analysis of the available documents. At present, the data base contains more than 15 000 cases, most of which are from the last 30 years. The amount is rapidly growing, and a large variety of queries are possible.

FACTS includes the following facilities:

—general or very specific information about incidents can be retrieved, through a completely flexible search profile;
—information can be analysed focusing on a variety of incident characteristics;
—incident causes can be identified;
—coupling with other data bases is possible;
—data from individual incidents can be obtained;
—copies from original incident documents/reports can be obtained;
—abstracts from confidential reports are available.

5.2 THE TNO ORGANIZATION

TNO, The Netherlands Organization for Applied Scientific Research, was established legally in 1930 with the aim of ensuring that applied scientific research is put to the service of the community in the most efficient manner possible. TNO is a fully independent, nonprofit-making applied research organization.

TNO's major target group is trade and industry, small and medium-sized firms in particular. Other important target groups are central and local authorities, private organizations, societies, foundations and individuals. In some cases, collective research is carried out for specific branches of industry.

TNO consists of eight divisions, each with its own specific field of research: Building and Metal Research, Industrial Products and Services, Technology for Society, Technical Scientific Services, Nutrition and Food Research, Health Research, National Defence Research, and Policy Research and Information. The divisions comprise 35 institutes in total, which are either branch or discipline oriented. It is common practice for TNO to form teams of experts drawn from various institutes for the execution of projects that require a multi-disciplinary approach.

5.2.1 The Department of Industrial Safety

This department belongs to the division 'Technology for Society'. In Fig. 1 the main activities of the department and the mutual relations of applications and subjects are shown.

The Department of Industrial Safety is more specifically involved in:

—safety studies, with special attention to economics and environmental consequences;
—the development and improvement of economic, physical and decision models, to design inspection, maintenance and safety procedures;

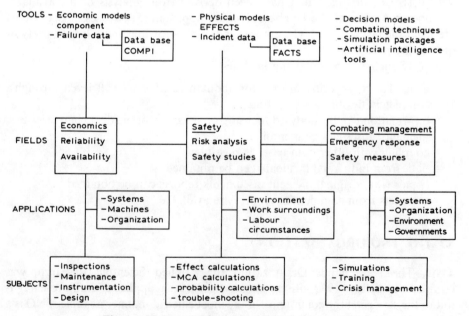

Fig. 1.   Main activities of the TNO departments.

—risk analysis and risk management, to investigate the risks of industrial activities to human beings and the environment;

—data collection from component failures and incidents;

—development of artificial intelligence systems;

—development of combating management procedures.

It is impossible to carry out these studies or analyses without the availability of a very clear picture of accident case histories. Realistic analysis will require a large number of case histories.

TNO is therefore engaged in collecting all known national and international incident data. Technical information about incidents with hazardous materials in the manufacture, production, storage, transshipment, transport, use, application and waste-processing sectors are stored in FACTS. Because there is steady development in industrial processes, it is necessary to keep information about incidents that have occurred up to date. In this way it is possible to recognize general trends as the result of changes in production processes and legislation.

Studies by this department that incorporate the use of FACTS deal with:

—liquefied petroleum gas/liquefied natural gas (LPG/LNG) storage systems;

—backgrounds of some major LPG accidents, such as those in Mexico and Bhopal;

—human failure;

—cause identification;

—accident analysis in the chemical industries.

5.3 LOOKING BACK ON THE START OF FACTS

In our industrial society, the use of dangerous equipment and materials is rapidly increasing. Because of the existing knowledge of the properties and characteristics of such equipment and materials, and expertise, only few incidents occur. Nevertheless, investigations should be continuously made to avoid the occurrence of incidents that are a potential hazard to people and the environment.

Reduction of effects and consequences by adequate preventive actions also constitutes an important field for research. Analysis of historical data on incidents may contribute substantially to an increasing degree of safety of activities that use hazardous materials. Avoidance and prevention of incidents with chemicals is essential, particularly in very densely populated countries.

5.3.1 The Reason for the Setting-up of FACTS

It became clear in the 1970s that a need had arisen for more structured information about incidents with hazardous materials. This need was felt by government and industry alike. TNO carried out safety analyses for both, which showed the necessity for a data bank containing incident data. By order of the Ministry for Social Affairs and Employment and the Ministry for the Environment, TNO designed a data bank in close co-operation with Dutch industry and the above ministries.

5.3.1.1 Definition of Aim and Applications of FACTS

The aim of FACTS is to collect incident data to give insight into the cause and course of incidents with hazardous materials, so that something may be learnt from history, and may thus contribute to safety through the initiation of avoidance and preventive actions.

The following applications can be specified: applications to

—quantify the risk of particular industrial activities and their justification;
—identify trends, and increase knowledge on probabilities;
—verify models, scenarios and probabilities that are used in risk analysis;
—develop event trees;
—investigate causes, circumstances and consequences of industrial accidents.

5.4 INFORMATION HANDLING

FACTS contains information that can generally be described as data on incidents that occurred during the handling of hazardous materials. This general description involves the following factors.

5.4.1 Information Sources

The field in which FACTS is used is so comprehensive that suitable information for FACTS is not limited to a single source. The information sources used to collect incident data can be divided into six categories.

(1) Organizations with internal reporting systems. Conditions of strict anonymity apply to data derived from these sources. Police, fire brigades and labour inspectorates are the major supplying bodies.
(2) Companies supply data under conditions of strict anonymity.
(3) Literature and other publications, annual reports, symposia, etc.
(4) Magazines and periodicals dealing with industrial safety, risk management and loss prevention.
(5) Cuttings from newspapers are used as signals for obtaining appropriate information.
(6) Information from organizations who represent FACTS in their country. FACTS agencies exist in the following countries: the UK, Spain, Italy, the USA and Norway.

It goes without saying that information from six different sources may present substantial differences. Certain sources supply more general information (newspapers); other sources, such as police inspectorates, give very detailed information. The time between the moment an incident occurs and publication of information about the incident may also vary. Publication of analyses and evaluations from major incidents sometimes takes several years. This delayed information, however, is added in FACTS to the already available information. In this way, a continuous updating of information is being carried out.

5.4.2 Type of Information

The criteria for the inclusion of an event in FACTS are:

—danger and/or damage to the nearby population and the environment;
—existence of acute danger of wounding and/or acute danger to property;
—processing, winning, transport, research, storage, transshipment, use/application and waste treatment activities;
—events that can be classified as 'near-misses'.

Incidents with nuclear materials or incidents that occur during military activities are not included in FACTS.

When an incident has occurred consistent with the above-mentioned incident profile, incident data are collected through the various information sources. A discrepancy between the frequency of incidents occurring and the number of those incidents that are recorded must be accepted as a matter of fact. Incidents with minor consequences are not recorded at all. Incidents with some consequences will be incidentally recorded. Only incidents that involve severe damage or danger will be published, analysed and documented. The recording of the intermediate field (on a scale of seriousness) is incomplete and may depend on social relevance, industrial firms' organization and other factors. Some of these factors change from time to time.

A picture of the available information compared with what actually happens is given in Fig. 2.

The available data are of a varying nature. The structure of FACTS has been chosen in such a way that it must be possible to handle all these different types of information. In cases where the collected information contains contradictions, all individual information items will be stored. No judgement is made about which is right or wrong. Interpretations based on the collected information will also not be added to this information.

To gain maximum profit from the collected information, high demands are made

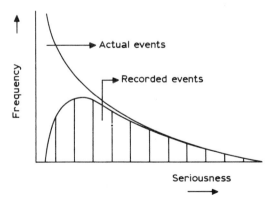

Fig. 2. Relationship between the number of accidents and their seriousness.

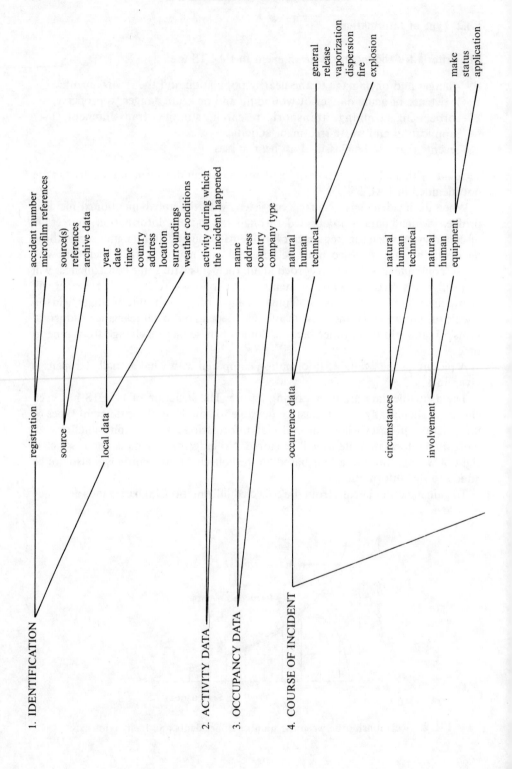

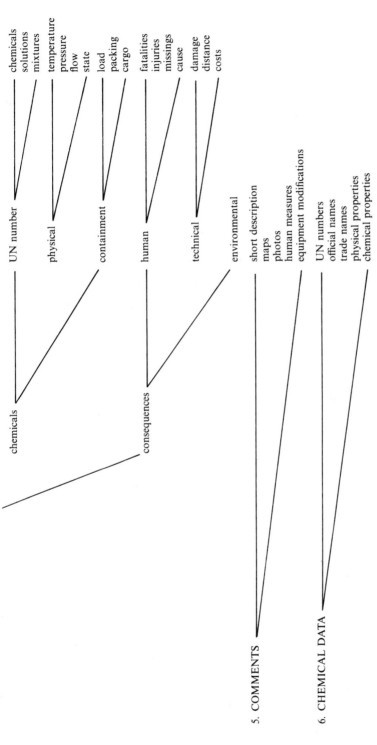

Fig. 3. Schedule of attributes and values.

with regard to the way the information is stored. It is important

   —to store the information in a readable way;
   —to store the information such that it becomes possible to find each piece of information;
   —to have the option of adding freshly available information at any time;
   —that the stored information contains exactly the same data as the original information, no more and no less.

From the available information, data are used that give insight into

   —the cause of the incident;
   —the course of the incident;
   —the consequences to human beings, the environment and equipment.

To ensure systematic storage of information, the data are divided into several categories of keywords, by which the incident data are coded.

5.4.3 Model for the Coding of Incident Data

A starting point for the coding of incidents is the possibility of gaining access to the information in various ways. The original information is described and coded through the use of keywords and free text. The combination of keywords and free texts results in a summary of the original information which is read step by step. This model offers the possibility of coding the most variable information in an unambiguous way. Each keyword can be used as a search item. Keywords may be attributes and values. The values can be considered as a subdivision of the attributes. (For examples of attributes and values, see Fig. 3.) The values are hierarchically structured, as shown in Fig. 3. The structure of the values is illustrated in four branches. The others have been omitted to keep the flowchart readable.

    The available data are divided into a number of categories, as shown in Fig. 3. Data referring to the course of an incident (group 4) are the most important, because they indicate what actually happened in the incident. For this purpose, each incident is subdivided into a sequence of occurrences and the relevant attributes are recorded for each individual occurrence. This action is the actual model for the coding of incident data. The model is based on a time-scale with intervals that correspond to the various occurrences that may be identified in an accident. Each occurrence often contains additional information concerning people, equipment, circumstances, technical data, etc. This information is described by using the appropriate attributes with their values. If the correct value is not available or not precise enough, free text may also be used.

    The recording of each accident is carried out in a number of lines (Fig. 4), related to the amount of available data. The first column indicates type (= attribute) of information (see also the list of abbreviations in the Appendix). The second column contains the values, which give more detailed information about the part to which the attribute is referring. The number of attributes and values is large, about 1500, but limited. To allow for greater specificity, the use of free text is also permitted. This constitutes the third column, which also contains the numerical data.

ATTRIBUTE	VALUE	TEXT
ACC #		305
FILM		1980-001-1051 TO 1052
SOURCE		LIT.
SDESCR		AMMONIA PLANT SAFETY VOL. 12
ADDRSS	FRANCE	LIEVEN, PAS DE CALAIS
ADATE		1968 0821
TIME		1220
ACTIVE	TRANSSHIPMENT	ONLY PRESS IN TANKER AND STORE EQUALIZED
LOCTN	FACTORY YARD	
DNAME		SOCIETE CHIMIQUE DE LA GRANDE PAROISSE
DTYPE	CHEMICAL	
DCHEM	AMMONIA	
ENCIR	TEMPERATURE	22/C
CAUSE	TECHNICAL FAILURE	STRESS CORROSION
1. OCCUR	FATIGUE	BY NOT SUPPORTING OVERHANG
2. OCCUR	CORROSION	STRESS
3. OCCUR	CRACK	CIRCUMFERENCE
EQINV	WELD	
4. OCCUR	BURST/RUPTURE	
EQINV	TANK	
EQAPPL		CONSTRUCTED FOR PROPANE AND IN 1967 TESTED FOR AMMONIA
EQINV	TANK VEHICLE	
QCONT		38000/LTR
SPILL		19000/KG
TEXT		LOADING PERMIT 0.53/KG/LTR AT 50/C
EQMADE		T1 STEEL
EQYEAR		1964
5. OCCUR	RELEASE	
CHEM	UN 1005	AMMONIA
STATE	LIQ. GAS PRESS. + COOL	
PRESS		175/PD/IN2
6. OCCUR	VAPORIZE	
EQINV	VAPOUR CLOUD	MUSHROOM SHAPED
7. OCCUR	BLOW AWAY	
EQINV	FRAGMENT	BOTH PARTS OF THE TANK
EQINV	TRUCK	COLLIDED WITH HEAVY OBSTACLE
8. OCCUR	EVACUATION	
HMINV	CITIZEN	IN NEIGHBOURING STREETS
HMACT		T1 STEEL PROHIBITED FOR STORAGE AND TRANSPORT OF AMMONIA
FATALS		6
TEXT		5 WORKERS AND 1 DRIVER
INJURS		15
WNDNG	TOXIC INHALATION	BURNS OF RESPIRATORY ORGANS
SCENE		TANK OF TANK VEHICLE RUPTURED

Fig. 4. Example of an accident abstract from the data base FACTS.

5.5 CAUSE CLASSIFICATION

Accidents are often analysed for the purpose of determining their cause, to try to avoid a repetition. Several coding systems for tracing the cause of an accident have been developed. The method used in FACTS will now be explained.

As has already been mentioned, in FACTS the course of an accident is translated into a chain of occurrences, which makes it possible to describe the various actions that took place during the course of the incident. An action can be considered to constitute a single isolated part of an incident. In this way the dynamic information is described. Examples of actions which may be classified during an incident are:

> natural occurrence—earthquake;
> incorrect operation—overspeed;
> abnormal condition—overheat;
> electrical failure—power breakdown;
> mechanical failure—break/burst;
> etc.

Many causes may be identified during incident analysis, or, more precisely, every single action in an incident has at least one cause. Each action, together with a number of other factors, causes the next action. These factors are the values used in FACTS.

The following flowchart indicates the cause of an indicated incident. Each subsequent action in an incident takes place as the result of the previous action. This

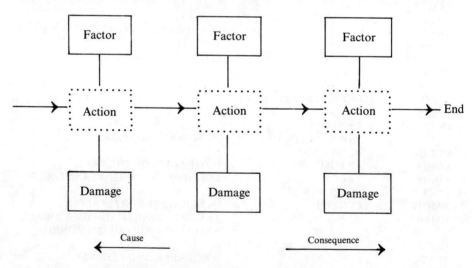

point of view makes it impossible to define one single cause of an incident without referring to certain other aspects or elements in the incident.

Definition: The cause of an incident is that cause which is related to a certain characteristic of an incident.

In accordance with the above, a 'near-miss' is an incident during which this particular characteristic did not occur but might reasonably have been expected to do so.

Example

Incident: A pipeline ruptured because incorrect assembly had caused tension.

Cause identification: If the enquiry is aimed at releases, their cause is the rupture of a pipeline (technical failure). If the enquiry is aimed at ruptured pipelines, their cause is incorrect assembly. Incorrect assembly might be considered a human failure. Schematically:

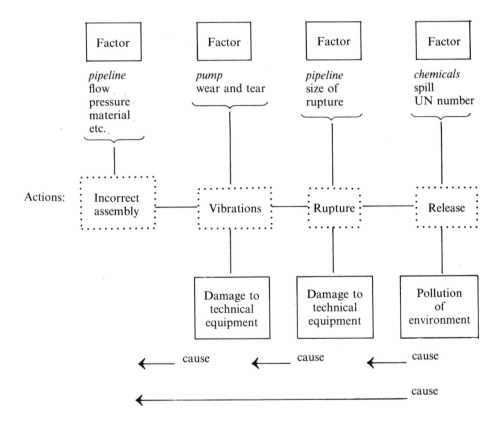

When an incident is described in this way its cause may be defined as the initial occurrence in the chain, representing the first occurrence that has come to light from the incident analysis.

To describe and classify the several actions, FACTS uses 10 different groups of occurrences, which have been subdivided into several values. Some examples are:

Slow damage
  Corrosion
  Fatigue
  Pollution
  Wear

Physical effects
  Blast wave
  BLEVE
  Blowaway
  Detonation
  Dispersion
  Dust explosion
  Explosion
  Implosion
  Fire
  Fireball
  Ignition
  Overflow
  Physical explosion
  Release
  Vaporization

Safety measures
  Traffic interruption
  System blockage
  Emergency stop
  Evacuation

Natural
  Earthquake

Erosion
Ground subsidence
Lightning

Operator errors
  Ignoring of signal
  No action
  Incorrect action
  Overspeed
  Unauthorized smoking

Incorrect equipment
  Defective working
  Not working
  Defective package
    Incorrect package
    Damaged package
    Incorrect stowage

Abnormal conditions
  Not cleaned
  Overfill/overload
  Overheating
  Underheating
  Overpressure
  Underpressure
  Incorrect composition
  Solidification/icing
  Vapour lock
  Condensation
  Runaway process

In the coding model, the occurrences can be related to several causes, such as human failure, technical failure, material cause, sabotage/vandalism, etc. It is important to realize that the way in which a particular incident story has been written and the type and amount of information that has been collected may have their particular effect on the selection of the type of cause.

5.5.1 Hierarchical Keyword List

It is of great importance that the method of coding the original incident data does not cause any loss of information. This means that specific and detailed coding is required. One must be aware that the more detail required the more keywords are needed. On the other hand, the definition of keywords must remain unique and the meaning of the different keywords must not overlap; otherwise, this could be the source of a number of different failures. A hierarchical keyword structure has been chosen to define accurately each keyword in FACTS. Some examples will explain this procedure.

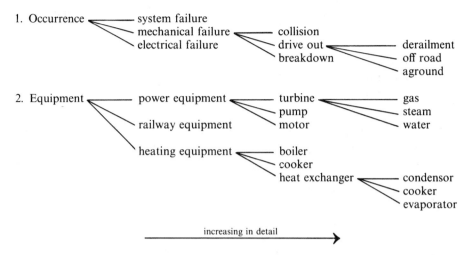

increasing in detail

Subject to how detailed the original information is, one may choose a certain level that contains these required keywords.

Another way of illustrating hierarchical structures is by using non-concentric circles. Each circle represents a certain level; a higher level indicates a more precise coding and covers a smaller area.

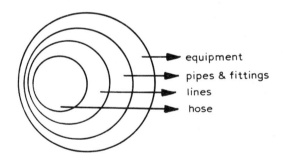

5.6 DATA BASE STRUCTURE

The data base FACTS uses an HP-3000 system. FACTS was designed with the data base management package IMAGE. The starting point is a 'network' structure, which is built up from one detailed data set and five master sets. A master contains information concerning one specific aspect (for example, accident number or value numbers). The detailed data set indicates the relationship between the variety of information from the several masters.

A short description of the data sets used follows.

The master data sets are:

FAC 1 contains all accident numbers used.

FAC 2 contains all dimensions and conversion coefficients used. With a special program all imperial dimensions used in incident reports are converted into metric dimensions.

FAC 3 contains all attribute numbers used.

FAC 4 contains all value numbers used. The relationship between attributes and values is given.

FAC 5 contains all sources used.

The detailed data set (FAC 6) gives the relationship between the various masters. In this way, a short description of the accident materializes. Each accident is described with a varying number of lines. Each line contains the following parts:

ACC	accident number;
ATTRIBUTE	attribute number;
VALUE	value number;
SRCE	information source;
TEXT	gives an explanation with regard to items and values;
DIM	stands for the dimension of a number and is also used for UN number (a UN number is characteristic for many chemicals).

5.6.1 Accessibility of Information in FACTS

To use FACTS as effectively as possible it is important to gain quick access to the information needed. In practice, it is necessary to search FACTS a number of times when a search profile is being carried out. Searching in the detailed data set requires a relatively large amount of time. Therefore an alternative solution is chosen. An inverted file structure is added to the IMAGE structure. In this way one can very quickly trace whether a certain value or attribute appears in the description of an accident. When new accidents are being added to the database the contents of the inverted file is also updated. In Fig. 5 a flowchart of the structure of FACTS and its connections is presented.

5.6.2 The Use of FACTS

To gain access to FACTS a user number and a password is required. Passwords may be divided into two groups.

Group 1: passwords giving access to all information.
Group 2: passwords giving access to the open information only.

5.6.3 Retrieval Program FAST

To search for and to prepare information from FACTS a special retrieval program (FAST) with different functions has been developed. The structure of this program is comparable to that of the HP program QUERY. The results of retrieval can be stored in a selected file. Ten 'select files' are available. Several manipulations can be executed with these select files. When FAST is used to carry out a retrieval, the program takes into account the confidentiality of the information used. FAST contains the following functions.

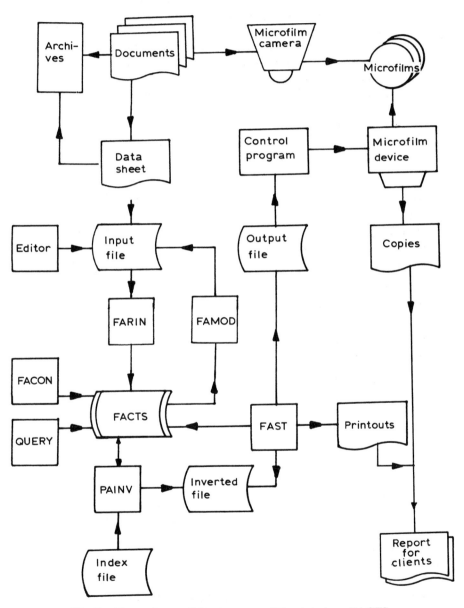

Fig. 5. Flow scheme of the structure of the data base FACTS.

5.6.3.1 Search Functions

These functions search in the detailed data set for certain attributes, values or dimension numbers. Dimension numbers are, for example, UN numbers. The following commands are possible:

GET   search the entire data base for incidents with a certain key number (attribute, value or dimension). Control and corrections are executed in the event that a key number appears more than once in one incident. This avoids double counting.

SHOW   counts how many times a key number is used in the data base.

READ   reads series numbers stored in a file. The meaning of these numbers depends on the accompanying key number, which must be defined. READ makes it possible to connect other data bases to FACTS.

5.6.3.2 Compatible Functions

These functions search in the inverted file. Simultaneously, several manipulations can be executed with the data obtained. Four different manipulations are possible.

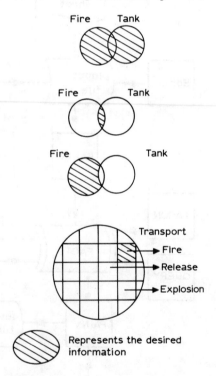

(1) SEARCH ADD fire tank
Search for those incidents containing fire and those containing tank, and combine the two series.

(2) SEARCH COMPARE fire tank
Search for only those incidents containing both fire and tank.

(3) SEARCH REST fire tank
Search for those incidents containing fire. Those incidents that also contain tank are deleted.

(4) SEARCH COUNT SEL 1 fire
Counts the number of incidents, stored in select file 1, in which fire is used. Select file 1 represents a marked part of the inverted file; for example, all incidents during transport.

5.6.3.3 Print Functions

This function records information from a select file or other file onto a printer, a monitor or file. The use of different options makes it possible to specify output in several ways. It is possible to print coded incident information (see Fig. 3) or to print the information in a table (see Fig. 6). The choice of composition of the table as well

Acc. no.	Year	Date	Cntry	Chemical(s)	Ftls	Injs	Scene
37	1978	1227	NL	Propylene			Leakage manhole tankwagon
201	1963	0304	USA	Ethylene Propylene Ethane Propane			Explosion at chemical factory
204	1974	????	USA	Ethylene Propylene Ethane Propane Propylene			Electr. power breakdown caused shutdown process
215	1970	0206	D	Propylene Benzene Light petrol Benzene	6	1	Fire and explosion of tanker 'VIG GAS 70', which ignited several tankers
228	1948	1018	USA	Propane Propylene	7	14	Ruptured lines between refinery and chemical plant
229	1972	0122	USA	Propylene Propylene		223	Derailment and explosion of several tankwagons
352	1985	1107	NL	Propylene Benzene	14	104	Explosion and fire at chemical factory

Fig. 6. Example of an accident table.

as choice of content of each column is free. Tables which are often used have standard availability.

5.6.4 Utility Programs

In addition to FAST, other programs are used, which add to, control and change the information that is stored in FACTS.

5.6.4.1 FARIN

This program introduces new incident information in FACTS, from a file containing the coded information. Key items and sources are converted into numbers. The key items used must already exist in the master data sets FAC 3 and 4. A line counter is also introduced to maintain the correct sequence of the various lines. FARIN has several control functions; for instance, it

—controls whether value and attribute numbers exist;
—controls whether the UN number is available;
—controls whether the accident number is already being used;
—converts imperial dimensions into metric units.

5.6.4.2 FACON

After a successful run of FARIN, each new series of accidents introduced into FACTS is checked by this program, which must be run to update the value of the confidential records. A periodical run of the program is necessary to check whether modifications in other records of an accident might affect the value of the confidential records.

5.6.4.3 FAMOD

FAMOD is used to modify accidents that have already been introduced. After the changes have been effected, an input file is made from the point at which the program FARIN introduces the corrected accident into the data base.

5.6.5 Handling Confidential Information

Information from certain sources, such as police, fire service and labour inspectorates, is confidential. A special routine has been developed for the handling of confidential data. This routine examines the results of each retrieval operation to confirm anonymity of the data obtained. Prints are executed only if the conditions for anonymity have been fulfilled. In this way it is possible to guarantee the anonymity of confidential information.

5.7 STORAGE OF ORIGINAL DOCUMENTS

As has already been mentioned, there are five information sources for FACTS. After the information from these sources has been introduced into FACTS, the original information is stored, and remains available. It may be very useful to have at one's disposal this information in combination with the coded information. A prerequisite is that the accessibility of this information, in combination with the coded information, should be very good. It is not a very attractive option to store the original information in the shape of documents. All original documents are recorded on microfilm. During recording, each microfilm copy is given a unique film number. When the information is being coded this film number is added to the incident information, which will be stored in FACTS. In this way there is a direct link between the microfilm archives and FACTS. The microfilm device consists of a reader unit and a printer unit which produces hard copies of the microfilm pictures.

The microfilm reader–printer has an interface, through which a link is made between FACTS and the microfilm device. The retrieval program FAST makes it possible to edit a file that contains the required film numbers. A specially developed control program reads the film numbers and activates and controls operations of the microfilm reader–printer.

5.7.1 Abstracts of Confidential Information

The confidential incident documentation is stored on microfilm, but this information is not available for external use. To obtain the benefits of this information, abstracts have been made. The relevant information is written in such a way that anonymity is guaranteed and a maximum of relevant data is represented.

In this way it is possible to augment the open information with valuable information.

5.8 APPLICATIONS AND THE USE OF FACTS

FACTS has now been in use for almost 10 years. During this time it has become clear that there is a market for the type of information FACTS supplies. The number of orders for FACTS is steadily increasing. In 1986 about 100 orders were satisfied (see Fig. 7).

Orders can be divided into two types.

(1) Requests for information about a strictly defined area; for example, information about incidents with one specific chemical, cause or piece of instrumentation.
(2) Requests of a more general type. These require a study of the topic, and usually an analysis of the information from FACTS referring to this topic.

5.8.1 Examples

Three examples of more comprehensive orders will be given.

(1) The Role of Instrumentation in Incidents
Almost any plant, whether small or large, that uses chemicals is equipped with instrumentation. Function and type may vary but instruments are essential attributes for the proper operation of a plant. Although instruments should assist in preventing incidents they do not always succeed. Special attention is given to the part instruments play in incidents. Questions such as 'how can instruments help to prevent incidents?', 'how can instruments announce changing conditions that may

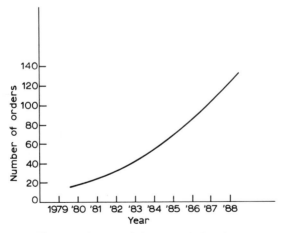

Fig. 7. The use of the FACTS data base.

lead to incidents?' and 'how can instruments help to detect temporary conditions that exclude the completion of safety procedures in case of emergency?' will be discussed. The analysis of a large number of incidents shows that similarities can be observed and that basic patterns can be recognized. From these patterns it can be concluded that appropriate instrumentation can prevent certain types of incident, in particular those cases where the error was introduced at a stage long before the incidents occurred. The data on the basis of which this analysis was carried out were supplied by FACTS.

Presence of latent errors. From data on incidents that are available in the FACTS data bank, it has been concluded that a significant number of incidents occur because of the introduction of an undetected error into the system at a stage long before the actual incident. Such errors may be called latent errors, and their presence in the system becomes manifest only at the time of the incident. In some cases, these latent errors can be identified as the initial cause, and sometimes they contribute to the course of the incident. Incidents with such characteristics are more closely examined. An aspect of particular interest is the time delay between the introduction of the error and its appearance. The question therefore is: 'Can any signal, measurement or procedure detect the presence of the error before it becomes manifest in an accident?'

Conclusions. It can be concluded from the analysis that the instrumentation of plants that use dangerous substances should be analysed for three aspects concerning unwanted and dangerous circumstances.

(1) Does the instrumentation in all circumstances represent the actual status?
(2) Have instruments been installed that announce unexpected and unwanted conditions?
(3) Tests should be carried out at intervals to verify whether existing emergency procedures can be completed in case of an emergency. Such tests may be successfully run in computer-controlled processes. Most process computers will have sufficient idle time for such simulations.

Analysis of the incidents contributed to the following statements:

(1) Operators are encouraged by their supervisor to develop versatility in plant management.
(2) Operators are aware of certain defects or peculiarities of a plant and they train themselves to cope with them.
(3) The presence of certain failures and errors in a plant can be detected; their absence can never be spotted.

(2) Classification of Incorrect Human Handling during Incidents
The aim of this study is to classify human failure during incident coding in such a way as to improve methods of analysis. The method of incident coding for FACTS does not provide for enough facilities to analyse human failure, to expose the connections between certain circumstances before the incident.

Starting points for classification are:

—The systematic classification must be based upon facts from the incident description. Making assumptions must be avoided; this means that one will not engage in psychological interpretation of human failures.
—The systematic classification must be applicable to different systems and different parts of systems.
—Loss of information through classification into categories must be avoided.

Circumstances and the observed circumstances of a situation may cause incidents. This type of information is important to arrive at a correct analysis of the human actions. It is also important to know in detail the duties of all persons concerned, whether various conflicting duties occur, how the duties are being executed and whether any deviations of these duties occur.

The following classification of incidents has been developed:

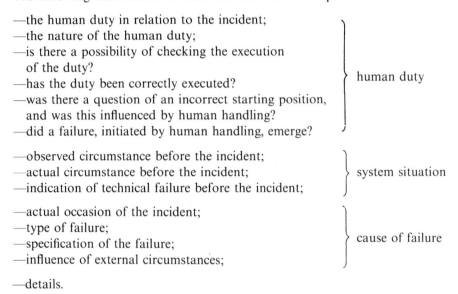

—the human duty in relation to the incident;
—the nature of the human duty;
—is there a possibility of checking the execution of the duty?
—has the duty been correctly executed?   } human duty
—was there a question of an incorrect starting position, and was this influenced by human handling?
—did a failure, initiated by human handling, emerge?

—observed circumstance before the incident;
—actual circumstance before the incident;   } system situation
—indication of technical failure before the incident;

—actual occasion of the incident;
—type of failure;
—specification of the failure;   } cause of failure
—influence of external circumstances;

—details.

(3) Reference Book to Trace Incident Causes (Causebook)
The cause analysis used to code the incident information for FACTS makes it possible to trace incident causes in a number of different parts of a plant. The book contains descriptions of actions and gives a survey of the incident causes that can occur in a large number of systems and unit operations. The structure of the book has been chosen in such a way that indices guide one to lists with several causes for different subjects. The book has been composed from incident data from FACTS. The subjects included, with their incident causes, are related to systems and operations that are both on a different hierarchical level. This means that, for example, a factory will be divided into smaller systems and units. On the lowest level, the individual compounds are given. The books will be recorded on floppy disc for greater accessibility.

5.9 NEW ADVANCES IN FACTS

When a data base such as FACTS has been intensively used for almost 10 years it goes without saying that several adjustments have been made. The structure of FACTS has been designed in such a way that this can easily be done. Adjustments or improvements planned for the near future can be divided into two directions:

(1)   to increase the accessibility of FACTS;
(2)   to increase the applications.

For both directions, an example is given below.

5.9.1 Increasing the Accessibility of FACTS by Using Expert Systems for Advanced Data Retrieval

5.9.1.1 An Application in Data Retrieval
The most successful applications of expert systems are found in the field of front-end systems for conventional software. This constitutes an important factor whenever an application of expert systems is chosen. The current expert system is a front end for FACTS. It has been developed in PROLOG.

Whenever a user of FACTS provides a search profile, an excellent query program to search the data base is available. However, the composition of the search profile is a duty only human beings perform. The key problem is the construction of a search profile that will not only answer a client's question but will also solve a client's problem. The essence lies in the difference between (see Fig. 8):

—the client's problem;
—the translation of the client's problem into a question; and
—the translation of the client's question into a search profile.

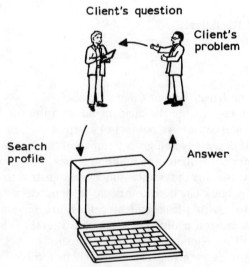

Fig. 8.   Transitions in data retrieval.

The search method. As has been stated, the solution to the problem is derived from a given search profile in three directions:

—in generalizing;
—in specifying; and
—in showing special links to the client's search profile.

Generalization of the profile is implemented to show the client attributes and values which surround the keywords in the client's profile. Thus, when an occurrence is named (e.g. the physical effect 'explosion') the system provides the user with two lists. The first list contains other 'physical effects' in connection with explosions, such as boiling liquid expanding vapour explosion (BLEVES), fires, etc. A second list contains other group names in connection with the group 'physical effects'.

Whenever a chemical is named, the system will provide four lists of chemicals: chemicals with the same type of handling prescriptions (cooled storage), or the same type of properties (boiling temperature), chemicals with the same type of application (coolant) and chemicals required to serve as catalysts in a particular process.

Whenever a specific location is reported it may be possible for the system to name (literally) surrounding locations.

Each attribute or value in the lists can be added to the search profile in a positive (AND) or a negative way (NOT). For instance, the search profile

TRANSSHIPMENT of LPG

can be specified to the profile

TRANSSHIPMENT of LPG from/to TANKLORRIES AND NOT
from/to VESSELS

Another way of improving the search profile is by means of *specifying*. The system asks questions such as: 'Could the profile be limited to a certain period of time, for example, after 1970?' The same kinds of limitation are possible for: address, location, type of company, activity, etc.

A third way of obtaining an improved search profile is the reporting of *special* 'intelligent' *links* to keywords in the original profile. For example, when the keyword UNDER-GROUND is named (as in underground storage of fuel) the system raises the question of whether a water-collecting or water-pollution area is the client's key issue.

The search method turns out to be a tool to present keywords in a logical order to the user of the data bank. At the appropriate time the system offers the user appropriate attributes as 'reminders'.

The expert system will be implemented as a front end for FACTS. However, the methods used are applicable to all hierarchical or relational data bases.

5.9.2 Increasing the Applications

By order of the national organization for commercial traffic, a data base has been developed concerned with information on transport of about 2000 hazardous chemicals. The chemicals have been divided into the internationally used classes and divisions.

For all chemicals, information is given on transportation requirements, identifying warning labels, criteria for packaging, flashpoints, etc. This data base has been included in the information system VIDEOTEX, which is an on-line service of the data base to all the parties concerned.

It is obvious that there are different points of connection between this data base and FACTS. Therefore a coupling between the two has been effected. In this way questions about, for example, information on a specific type of chemical can easily be answered.

5.10 LATEST DEVELOPMENTS

After 10 years of experience with FACTS in its present state, it is now necessary to make use of new techniques and to develop new possibilities which meet the expectations of our clients. The following developments are being realized, or will be realized at the end of 1989:

- —Production of an upgraded version of FACTS on a micro-VAX based on the relational data base management system ORACLE.
- —Production of a special version of FACTS on a personal computer (PC) (see Section 5.11).
- —Establishment of a 2-day workshop, using FACTS to investigate and analyse incident information.

A new version of FACTS on a PC (PC-FACTS) is at an advanced stage. PC-FACTS will become available to all those who regularly need historical incident information. Regular users of FACTS prefer an in-house system to the limitations of the off-line access of FACTS. With PC-FACTS, we will meet a user's requirements for better access to FACTS and for more advanced tools for the use of incident information. The 2-day workshop is being developed to instruct the users of PC-FACTS. Our methodology of incident analysis and incident coding will be explained, as well as the possibilities of using the incident information, and of adding incident information collected by the users to the FACTS data set.

5.11   PC-FACTS

The TNO Department of Industrial Safety has developed a PC version of FACTS called PC-FACTS for use as an in-house system. Besides the other services of FACTS focused on information supplying for incidental cases, PC-FACTS is specially developed for those who make regular and advanced use of historical accident data and want to have flexible and advanced tools at their disposal to handle and analyse data of industrial accidents with hazardous materials.

5.11.1 Available Accident Information

PC-FACTS contains accident abstracts (Fig. 4) which give the most important details of the accidents, described in a chronological way. More detailed information can be obtained on request from our microfilm archive.

5.11.2 Structure of PC-FACTS

PC-FACTS is a menu-driven data base. The specially developed software allows the user to handle the stored accident information in a flexible way. PC-FACTS is developed in a modular way and new functions can easily be added to the system. The following standard functions are available:

—Complex search facilities. With the help of an internal library of all the available keywords, search profiles can be made using .OR., .AND. or .EXCLUDE. combinations. The result of a search is stored in a selection file. Further detailed searches using these selection files are possible.
—Free text search. Besides the keywords, the accident abstract contains free text. String search is possible for this free text.
—Selection administration to verify existing selection files and used search profiles.
—Sort routines to sort accident records in a specific sequence.
—Edit and view functions. Accidents stored in selection files can be viewed and edited.
—Print facilities to generate lists of the selected accidents according to your own specifications or to print accident abstracts.
—On-line help instructions; each menu and sub-menu contains detailed help instructions.

Besides these basic functions, the following functions are optional:

—Adding new records; these can be annually updated records which will be supplied by TNO or your own company records of incidents.
—Accident analysis; the available accident abstracts can be used to investigate the chain of occurrences during an accident.
—Graphical presentation to generate pie charts and bar graphics.

PC-FACTS is available as a shell with the standard options. A detailed manual will help the users to gain the maximum results. Depending on the criteria of the users, data sets of accident abstracts will be selected from FACTS and installed in PC-FACTS. An annual update based on the same criteria is possible to keep PC-FACTS up to date.

5.11.3 Data Sets

Examples of data sets which can be selected from FACTS are:

(1) Accidents which occurred during one of the following main industrial activities:

	Number of accidents
Storage	1 158
Transshipment	1 010
Processing	1 855
Transport	
—road	1 090
—rail	593
—pipe	965
—inland waterways	338
—sea	418
Handling and use	1 746

(2) Accidents where one of the following chemicals were involved:

	Number of accidents
Chlorine	357
Ammonia	209
Natural gas	821
Oil, several types	>2 000
Propane	558
LPG	735
Hydrochloric acid	160

(3) Accidents where a specific piece of equipment or unit is involved:

	Number of accidents
Pipelines, lines	1 580
Tank (storage, transport, etc.)	2 100
Refinery	509

The above-mentioned examples illustrate what types of data sets are possible. In addition to these examples, it is possible to create other data sets according to the criteria of our clients.

5.11.4 Hardware Requirements

IBM-compatible PC with a hard disc of at least 20 Mbyte. The PC should be equipped with an EGA or a VGA screen.

5.11.5 Software Requirements

PC-FACTS is developed with Dbase 3+ and compiled with Clipper. This means that, except for a MS-DOS version of 3.3 or higher, no additional software is necessary.

5.11.6 Availability

PC-FACTS is available to all types of clients and organizations. The use of the data base and the installed data is strictly limited to the owner of the system. Data or software may not be sold to third parties.

BIBLIOGRAPHY

1. Wingender, H. J., *Reliability Data Collection and Use in Risk and Availability Assessment*. Springer-Verlag, Heidelberg, 1986.
2. Bockholts, P., A databank for industrial safety. Seminar Industrial Safety EuReDatA—TNO, 1981.
3. Bockholts, P., Heidebrink, I., Moss, T. R., Butler, J. A., Fiorentini, C. & Bello, G. C., A survey of industrial accident databases. TNO, TECSA, RMS, European Community, Brussels, 1985.
4. Koehorst, L. J. B. & Bockholts, P., Characteristics of incident data bases for risk assessment. Report of the EuReDatA Working Group: incident data bases. TNO, September 1988.
5. *Professional Accident Investigations, Methods and Techniques*. Institute Press, 1977.
6. *Accident Prevention Manual for Industrial Operations*, 7th edn. National Safety Council, Chicago, Illinois, 1974.
7. Koehorst, L. J. B., *An Analysis of Accidents with Casualties in the Chemical Industry Based on Historical Facts*. Springer-Verlag, Berlin, 1989.

(Appendix follows)

APPENDIX: ABBREVIATIONS USED IN ACCIDENT DESCRIPTIONS

ACTIV	Activity		HFLAM	Height of flames
ADATE	Accident date		HMACT	Human action for prevention
ANINV	Animals involved		HMCIR	Human circumstances
ARCH	Archive number in library		HMINV	Humans involved
AREA	Area specified in text		HRUP	Height of rupture
CARGO	Cargo description		HUSOIL	Humidity of soil
CAUSE	Cause		ICHEM	Non-active chemicals involved
CHEM	Chemical		INJURS	Number of injured
COATING	Coating		LENGTH	Length
CONCTR	Concentration		LOAD	Amount of contents
CONTMT	Containment		LOCTN	Location of occurrence
COST	Total costs		LPIPE	Length of pipe
DATE	Additional dates		MISSNG	Number of missing persons
DCLD	Diameter of cloud		OCCUR	Occurrence
DCONT	Diameter of containment		OPOOL	Area of pool
DEPTH	Depth		ORUP	Area of rupture
DIST	Distance		PACK	Packing
DPIPE	Diameter of pipe		PHOTO	Number of photos in documentation
DRUNG	Number of drawings in documentation		POSRUP	Position of rupture
DSTIGN	Distance ignition to point of release		PRESS	Pressure
DTIME	Timespan between occurrences		QCONT	Capacity of containment
ENCIR	Environmental circumstances		RCHEM	Chemicals formed during reaction
ENINV	Environment involved		SCENE	Short description of accident
ENVDM	Environmental damage		SOIL	Type of soil
EQACT	Construction change to avoid recurrence		SPILL	Amount of spillage
EQAPPL	Use of equipment		SURFTR	Surface treatment
EQCIR	Equipment circumstances		SURR	Surrounding of occurrence
EQDM	Equipment damage		STATE	Physical state of chemical
EQINV	Equipment involved		TEMP	Temperature of chemical
EQMADE	Equipment specification		TEXT	Extra text for readability
EQSTAT	Actual state of equipment		THSOIL	Thickness of soil
EQSTDT	Date of last maintenance		THWALL	Wall thickness
EQDATE	Date of make		TIME	Local time of the occurrence
FATALS	Number of fatalities		TMCLD	Visibility time of cloud
FATANS	Number of dead animals		TMFLAM	Time of flames
FLOW	Flow		TMREL	Time of release
HCLD	Height of cloud		TYPREL	Instantaneous or continuous release
HCONT	Height of containment		WNDANS	Number of wounded animals
HEIGHT	Height		WNDNG	Cause of death or wounds

6

Reliability Data Collection in Process Plants

H. J. Wingender

NUKEM GmbH, PO Box 1313, D-8755 Alzenau, Germany

6.1 GENERAL REMARKS

The intelligent use of quantified reliability experience, and its integration into the development, design, construction and fabrication of processes, plants, systems and components, and into the corresponding maintenance and quality ensurance strategies, have achieved availabilities of better than 90% for facilities, 99% for systems and 99·9% for components in a number of industries. However, when attempting to convince plant operators and designers of the advantages of collecting reliability data, the response will often be reluctance to agree, as it is claimed that such data are inaccurate, far too uncertain and not transferable; accurate data are too expensive; the cost–benefit relation is out of balance; and expenditure on accurate data can be astronomical.

It is a common situation—not only in reliability—that quantifiable arguments will not convince, even if they are put in economic terms. The reason for this is—in my opinion—that the real cause of hesitation is concealed by the above objections. No one likes to be told he could perform better, or to submit to an outsider investigating the plant (and making sensitive information available to the outside world), or to have to tolerate disturbances in the plant's operation. Thus, convincing is not so much a matter of understanding but of trust, i.e. of human relations, for which I dare not give a recipe.

The following paragraphs touch on the subject of data collection and data treatment (using a couple of examples) and, finally, the usefulness and uncertainty of data, together with a warning.

Before starting, I would like the reader to be aware of the valuable and useful work of the European Reliability Databank Association (EuReDatA), which is assembling unification and standardization schemes for reliability data and parameters. These continuing activities are published in reports,[1-4] to which I will refer as they define an item better than I am able.

6.2 DATA COLLECTION

6.2.1 Starting Period

An incorrect approach could soon lead to disaster. Therefore, the first thing is to become aware of what one is aiming at: it is not only data, it is success. Success will have been achieved only when reliability data collection and engineering have finally become an integrated fibre—indistinguishable at a first glance—of the plant's nervous system, contributing smoothly to its successful, reliable and safe operation.

With this in mind, the first task concerns the plant staff. They know their plant, they operate it, and they are proud of it, whatever else one may believe. It is then quite obvious that they must have introduced some form of data collection system right from the beginning, that it has worked, and that it has been successfully used. Many difficulties can be avoided by accepting that such a data collection system could be advantageously adapted with only minor alterations for the reliability data collection.

The advantages of this approach are evident: if the plant is not a new one—and most frequently it is not—it will have been subjected to some development. The existing data collection forms and analysis methods have been part of this evolution and have become well adapted to the overall behaviour of the plant and its components. To an intelligent, alert observer this information—repair forms, operator log-books, etc.—reflects and reveals many of the data in which a reliability engineer is interested.

Furthermore, because the members of staff are familiar with it, the need for training can be reduced, and the failure rate in completing the forms is kept low. It is good reliability engineering to use the positive part of human factors and to avoid the negative ones, because controlling the human factor component in reliability data collection could become a problem.

A further advantage of using the established procedures as far as possible is that it avoids disturbances, which always tend to become failure sources. Clearly, a person brought in by management to improve the performance of operation will be looked upon with suspicion, and can be a source of resentment and thus trouble. If, however, these persons accept, value and use the existing procedures, which have proved sound, this will establish confidence and create an atmosphere of co-operation, which is indispensable for the task.

It has to be emphasized here that non-co-operation is as lethal as obstruction. Not only human relations but also plant performance could be seriously affected. Therefore, co-operation has to be cultivated. This will sooner or later establish trust and identification with the objectives of reliability data collection. A guide to the degree of identification is the change in the terminology used by the staff and the reliability engineer; each will adopt the other's jargon. The degree to which this goes on varies from plant to plant and is generally imperceptible for those involved.

At this stage, both sides understand why the existing data collection had to go a particular way, why some information is included and some is rejected, why more specific factors are to be included or should have been included, and why the operators are not interested in some information that is vital to the reliability engineer. It is evident that both sides have now united, as well as the tasks and the objectives. The integration process mentioned above has succeeded and established a new identity; this is the target of reliability engineering.

Of course, this is a simplified and idealized picture of what happens in reality. Much more could be said about the starting point of reliability data collection, especially about the cases which failed and why, but that would be beyond the scope of this chapter. I have stressed the point here, because I feel it is important, and it has not been mentioned very often before.

6.2.2 Performance

In the cases described here as an example, five separate yet interlinked data files were established:

—event data file;
—component data file;
—location data file;
—ambience data file;
—time history data file.

The interlinking is provided on two levels: (1) for data bank management purposes, on the technical level by specific linking descriptors (this will not be mentioned any more in the following as it is not essential in terms of data collection); (2) on the information level. To explain this I have first to describe the types of information inventories of the files.

Event data file. This contains the data for 49 descriptors, of which some are shown in Table 1. The data are taken from the repair form described later. This is because here an event is specified as any occurrence which alerts the maintenance department for a repair order. Therefore the repair order number is an event counter. For more general specifications of the term 'event', etc., the reader is referred to Refs 1 and 3.

Component data file. The number of descriptors required depends on the class of component. Fourteen classes were established for this example, and 28 descriptors were used for the class 'pump' (see Table 2).

Location data file. This uses 23 descriptors (see Table 2) and describes class, type, task, operational mode, room, specific location of the component, the unit in which it is operating, etc.

Ambience data file (environment). This contains 13 descriptors (see Table 3) for the conditions in the various areas or rooms. Because not all components of a unit necessarily face the same environment—as a result of local separation—it is necessary to establish a relationship between these conditions at component level.

TABLE 1
Event Data File Information (Example)

Administrative data
 Repair order no. (= event no.), date, text
 Event message, date, text
 Component concerned, code, unit, location

Failure data
 Detection type, date, time
 Occurrence date, time, circumstances, type

Repair information data
 Description
 Measure (repair, exchange of component)
 Defect part, type
 Start of repair, date, time
 Duration of breaks
 End of repair, date, time
 Duration of repair, effective, total
 Number of staff involved
 Total man-hours needed
 Component restart, date, time
 Duration of outage

Exchange information data (as above plus)
 Code of new component
 New location of old component

Additional information data
 Cause(s) of failure (after analysis), description
 Other components affected, codes, dates, times, description
 Multiple components failed, codes, dates, times, description
 Affected units, codes, description
 Causing unit, component, part, repair order no.
 Costs of repair

Time history data file. This contains the data of 13 descriptors (see Table 3) and describes what happened to and with the components, locations, etc., and when, as not all changes in a facility refer to 'events'.

The information in these data files is obviously not logically exclusive, i.e. if one withdraws the five information sets for one item from the files (Pump no....) and then forms the cut sets of these five sets, the file will not be empty—or if it were empty, there would be a mistake in at least one of the files. In consequence, any cut set of any two sets of those five sets must not be empty and the information overlap can be used as a check for correct and complete information input. For instance, when a component is reinstalled after treatment in the repair shop, the data on this event will be transferred into the computer and all information on this component will be accordingly rearranged in all the files automatically, However, when the wrong location code is typed, the computer will at once detect that at this location

TABLE 2
Component and Location Data File Information (Example)

Component Data File Information
Example: Pump

Internal data	External data	
	Pump	Motor
Component code no.	Manufacturer	Manufacturer
Inventory no.	Type	Type
First start-up date	Fabrication no.	Fabrication no.
Room no.	Vintage	Vintage
Maintenance type	Curves (performance)	
Location code	Throughput	
	Power	Power
	Cycles	Cycles
	Design temperature	

Location Data File Information

Component code no.
Process unit no.
Location no.
Room no., place no.
Class of component
Type of component
Inventory no. of component
Mode of operation
Use
Redundancy for location no.
Redundant component(s) at location(s) no....
Cable no.
Medium code
Medium description
etc.

the required equipment is already at the spot and a new component cannot be installed there; correction will be required. The possibility of checks was one reason for establishing several interconnected data files. Another was that it seemed more economical to keep the never changing or slowly changing information separated from the 'quickly' or 'suddenly' changing data. The third reason was that 'as many as necessary' and 'as few as possible' data had to be collected and transferred into the data files—to reduce costs and failures. Therefore, after having collected all the 'fixed' data and established the data files, the reliability data collection has been cut down to the event data collection, although all the data in the files are basically reliability data. Events are observable changes of state; they can be counted, described and located in space and time. Some of them occur regularly or are planned; e.g. periodic maintenance actions, plant shutdown for company holidays,

TABLE 3
Ambience and Time History Data File Information (Example)

Ambience Data File Information
Room no.
Room description
Pressure zone, range
Temperature range
Humidity range
Dimensions
Atmosphere (corrosivity indicators)
Ventilation cycles
etc.

Time History Data File Information
Date
Location
Unit
Component type, old, new (if any)
Inventory no., old, new (if any)
Component code, old, new (if any)
Manufacturer, old, new (if any)
Fabrication no., old, new (if any)
Cause of change (event no. of descriptor)
Planned outages (company holidays, weekends, etc.)
etc.

with only a few units being kept in operation (cooling, venting). These events do not need collecting and are transferred into the files as a bulk by special codes, as they are indispensable for the time history and for correct data evaluation. It is the irregular or random events with which the event data collection is mainly concerned. On the other hand, irregularities can be connected with regular events in various ways: randomly (irregularities are detected by regular inspection) or as designed (failures regularly actuate redundancies).

Which data are to be collected can best be shown using an event report form. Table 4 provides the information in a condensed form. The event report consists of four sheets:

—the repair or maintenance order;
—the repair or maintenance report;
—the event consequences report;
—the information and remarks sheet.

One would expect that an event detection sheet should also exist. However, it was never used by the reliability data collection team for one simple reason: if two or more events were nearly simultaneously detected, then with high probability the messages would reach the maintenance department and the data collection team at different times. The same event would therefore be assigned different numbers at

TABLE 4
Event Report Sheets, Information Content

Sheet no. 1, Repair order no.
Date/time of order
Issued by, addressed to
Concerns event at component
                  location
                  unit
Detected by maintenance
                  control room display
                  alarms
                  others (specify)
Date/time of detection
Type of event
Cause of event
Redundancy actuated
Shutdown of other components
                  locations
                  units
Shutdown of unit(s)
Event description
Test of order
Signature

Sheet no. 2, Repair report no.
Written by
Description of measures
Type of action (exchange/repair)
Exchange
Component removed (component/location/unit)
Component installed (component/location/unit)
Defect component moved to (repair shop/waste store/others)
Repair
Component repaired (component/location/unit)
Type of repair
Parts exchanged
Start of action (date/time)
End of action (date/time)
Breaks of action (duration)
Causes of breaks
Duration of action (total/specific)
Restart (date/time)
Staff involved (number, man-hours)
Remarks
Signature

Sheet no. 3, Consequence report no.
Date of report, written by
(a) Other affected components, units, which, where, how, why
(b) Shutdown times of those components/units
(c) Description of damage detected
(d) Description in detail of event causes
(e) Remarks
Signature

(continued)

TABLE 4—*contd.*

Sheet no. 4, Information on event no.
Date of report, written by
(a) Remarks on the actions
(delayed, fast slow, unusual occurrences...)
(b) Remarks on preparedness for action
(spare parts, tools, staff at hand...)
(c) Measures to be taken
(improvement of training...)
(d) General remarks or others
Signature

---

each place. To avoid confusion, it was decided to keep the counting of events in the maintenance department. There, the relevant information is transferred to the repair order. The number of the order is the indicating label of the event. A copy of the repair order and copies of the subsequent sheets are sent to the data collection group.

Some of the information in the sheet is in code. For instance, the component code specifies a code for a class of components (pumps) of a specific type (turbine driven), for a specific or non-specific liquid (sodium or general, respectively), etc. The item is labelled with the code when it is received at the plant the first time; subsequently, the code is kept with the item wherever it is used, in repair, or even outside the plant. The code does not expire when the item finally leaves the plant, and it must never be used for any other piece of equipment. It is an identification of an identity, even when this has ceased to exist.

The location code identifies that a given location belongs to a specific unit and has to keep a component of a specific class, type, etc., for a specific purpose and operational mode (main or redundant purpose, continuous-mode or on-demand operation, for instance). The position of installation is labelled with the code.

Only the information which can be checked on existing labels by the maintenance personnel is coded on the sheets, to avoid confusion and to permit corrections on the spot.

The second part of the information is standardized but not coded; for instance, type of detection, type of event, cause of event. To prevent misunderstandings and mistakes, the reverse of the sheet shows the usual standard expressions and some unusual ones; this necessitates the adequate training of the staff.

The rest of the information is given in common language, of which, again, a part is provided in a 'computer-friendly' way: dates, times, number of man-hours, etc. All these data are entered into the computer following the instructions on the screen. Only plain texts can cause some difficulties, if they are too extensive. However, these are mainly stored for documentation and not for analysis, although this is possible and can be very valuable.

Before leaving the topic of data collection it should be mentioned that, although for all plant-related purposes the plant-specific coding system should be kept in force (to avoid confusing the staff), for programming the computer and for external data comparison a standardized code as proposed in EuReDatA reports[1-3] is preferable.

6.3 DATA TREATMENT AND EXAMPLES

It is not intended to present details of statistical data processing. Short descriptions are given in Ref. 3, and more sophisticated information can be drawn from textbooks on the subject. Most of the examples shown will be sufficiently described by three concepts:

—failure rate λ—the measure of failure frequency is the number of failures per unit time—generally per 10^6 h (it will be mentioned in the examples if the time referred to is the operational time; otherwise, it will be calendar time);

—repair rate μ—the measure of repair performed per unit time, usually per hour (but for the formula below per 10^6 h);

—availability A in the asymptotic approach: $A = \mu/(\lambda + \mu)$.

The examples will exclusively refer to pumps, and more specifically to metering and booster pumps.

An important question concerns the failure rate dependence on the choice of time of reference, i.e. calendar time or operational time. In a first approach, the results for a 5-year period of calendar time are compared with those for intermittent intervals covering, for every item, a total of 788 days, which are actually plant operation days. However, the sets of items are different in that the reference set for the plant operation intervals is a subset of the former set (Table 5). The differences in the results cannot be regarded as statistically significant. The picture essentially changes for a more detailed consideration (Table 6), e.g. investigation of the behaviour of continuously or intermittently operating components. The data show that there is a significant difference; however, its direction may depend on the type of pump. At least, the direction is not easily predictable. Therefore, it might be useful to investigate the types of failures and the failed parts of the items; an example of such an investigation is shown in Table 7. It provides some clues for the booster pumps:

TABLE 5
Failure Rates Related to Calendar Time and Operating Time

Type of pump	No. of pumps	No. of failures	$\lambda \times 10^6$ h	Remarks
Not specified	140	1 951	321 ⎫	Uniform
Metering	39	799	468 ⎬	calendar
Booster	101	1 152	263 ⎭	time
Not specified	96	643	354 ⎫	Uniform
Metering	39	376	510 ⎬	operating
Booster	57	267	248 ⎭	time

TABLE 6
Modes of Operation and Failure Rates

Mode of operation	No. of pumps	No. of failures	$\lambda \times 10^6\, h$	Type of pump
Not specified	39	799	321 ⎫	
Continuous	14	589	961 ⎬	Metering pumps
Intermittent	25	210	192 ⎭	
Not specified	54	454	191 ⎫	Rotary
Continuous	7	44	140 ⎬	booster
Intermittent	47	410	199 ⎭	pumps

the close relation of leaking with seal failure is trivial, of course; however, it is a check for data consistency. A more interesting point is that discontinuous operation has in consequence rather frequent clutch failures. However, the booster pumps do not show a dramatic dependence on the operational mode (Table 6). The metering pumps data show this dependence very clearly in Table 6, however, but do not provide information on the cause of the high continuous operation failure rate in Table 7. This is not an unusual situation. The source of trouble is identified, but the

TABLE 7
Details of Failures (Example), Given as Percentages

	Mode of operation		
	Not specified	Continuous	Intermittent
Rotary booster pumps			
Number of items and failures according to Table 6			
(1) Type of failure			
leaking	25	40	23
electrical	20	18	21
mechanical	13	15	14
(2) Failed part			
sealing	23	38	21
clutch	12	?	20
Metering pumps			
Subgroup of sample of Table 6, not specified			
(1) Type of failure			
blockage	16	9	22
air	9	5	13
leaking	4		7
mechanical	3		7
electrical	5	3	4
(2) Failed parts			
sealings	13	5	19
pump head	5		7
valve	5	4	5

TABLE 8

Failure Data for 50 Pumps; 25 Metering Pumps—Odd Numbers, 25 Booster Pumps—Even Numbers

No.	Failures	λ_{LL}	$\bar{\lambda} \times 10^6$	λ_{UL}	No.	Failures	λ_{LL}	$\bar{\lambda} \times 10^6$	λ_{UL}
1	15	192	342	565	26	10	109	228	420
2	14	175	320	536	27	30	462	685	978
3	7	64	160	329	28	7	64	160	329
4	13	158	297	508	29	13	158	297	508
5	9	94	205	390	30	8	79	183	360
6	20	279	457	705	31	12	142	274	479
7	11	126	251	449	32	20	279	457	705
8	5	37	114	266	33	12	142	274	479
9	5	37	114	266	34	8	79	183	360
10	6	50	137	298	35	24	351	548	815
11	5	37	114	266	36	8	79	183	360
12	18	244	411	649	37	7	64	160	329
13	40	652	913	1 243	38	6	50	137	298
14	8	79	183	360	39	33	519	753	1 058
15	45	749	1 027	1 374	40	7	64	160	329
16	9	94	205	390	41	8	79	183	360
17	53	901	1 210	1 577	42	27	407	616	897
18	8	79	183	360	43	34	538	776	1 084
19	32	500	731	897	44	9	94	205	390
20	11	126	251	449	45	21	297	479	733
21	34	538	776	1 084	46	16	209	365	593
22	8	79	183	360	47	6	50	137	298
23	37	595	844	1 296	48	43	710	982	1 322
24	5	37	114	266	49	9	94	205	390
25	10	109	228	420	50	37	595	845	1 190

cause of trouble remains concealed. In such cases, information and expertise from outside the data bank have to be gathered.

Indispensable for the assessment of availabilities is the knowledge of repair times or repair rates. A check through some of the pump data—samples were taken from the data bank for metering pumps and booster pumps—has shown that the mean values of the repair times are all between 1 and 3 h. The maximum repair time for a metering pump was 2 days. This was because a spare exchange pump was not available. The repair time is not the only time taken into account. What is really required is the mean outage time and its uncertainty. To arrive at a sound value for the outage time, a plant-specific access and waiting term is to be added, which also takes account of maintenance delays caused by weekends, etc.

A first clue concerning repair times, uncertainties and the consequences for availability can be provided by the following example. The basic data are:

—maximum pump failure rate in Table 8:

$$\lambda = \left(1200 \pm \frac{400}{300}\right) \bigg/ 10^6 \, h \quad (95\% \text{ confidence level});$$

—'repair' rate taken from a mean outage time of 5 h, comprising 3 h of mean repair time and an extra 2 h covering delays; the uncertainties are based on an assumption of a 100% uncertainty of the mean repair time:

$$\mu_1 = \left(0.2 \pm \begin{smallmatrix} 0.3 \\ 0.1 \end{smallmatrix}\right) \times 10^6/10^6 \, \text{h};$$

—repair rate taken from the maximum repair time of $c.$ 50 h with a 50% uncertainty assumed:

$$\mu_2 = \left(0.02 \pm \begin{smallmatrix} 0.02 \\ 0.01 \end{smallmatrix}\right) \times 10^6/10^6 \, \text{h}.$$

Using the formula for availability and a simple error propagation approach, the following results are derived:

$$A_1 = 0.992 \pm \begin{smallmatrix} 0.005 \\ 0.012 \end{smallmatrix} \quad \text{for 5 h outage}$$

and

$$A_2 = 0.943 \pm \begin{smallmatrix} 0.03 \\ 0.06 \end{smallmatrix} \quad \text{for 50 h outage.}$$

At this point I have to emphasize that the data examples shown in the tables must not be applied for engineering purposes. Data application requires that the uncertainties of the data are known. Moreover, the real source of the data—the facility they were drawn from and its characteristics—has to be taken into account. Thus, it would not have made much sense if I had provided the data together with its error bands. For those readers, however, who like playing statistics, I have prepared Table 8. It contains data for 50 pumps. The selection was not biased except for the following features:

—25 metering pumps—odd numbers;
—25 booster pumps—even numbers;
—selected from all areas of the plant;
—earlier checks have made it evident that the time behaviour of failures is in good agreement with the exponential distribution, which could be Weibull, although this is not significant;
—the 95% confidence limits for the item λ values are derived from the χ^2 distribution, under the assumption of normal distribution of λ; this has been checked in some cases.

6.4 UNCERTAINTY, APPLICABILITY AND CAUTION

If it is assumed that component X is not very reliable and that the failure rate is about as high as the repair rate, then the availability is about 0.50. Because of the high failure frequency both rates are closely known (good statistics). Component Y shows a good availability, let us say 0.99; the failure rate is low, about 1% of the repair rate. Because of the low failure frequency both rates are inexactly known (bad statistics). Nevertheless, many buyers will choose component Y and not bother about the inaccuracies of λ and μ. Of course, if one asks them to introduce reliability engineering, some of them will at once start caring about inaccuracies of λ and μ, and will complain that these data are far too uncertain. The term 'far too' is indefinite and has to be quantified.

The values of λ, μ and A have been determined:

for component X

$$\lambda = \mu \qquad A = 0.50$$

for component Y

$$\lambda = 0.01\mu \qquad A = 0.99$$

A reasonably extreme assumption for the uncertainties $\Delta\lambda$ and $\Delta\mu$ could be:

for component X

$$\Delta\lambda \approx \Delta\mu = 0.5\mu$$

for component Y

$$\Delta\mu \approx 10\mu \qquad \Delta\lambda \approx 10\lambda \approx 0.1\mu$$

Using a simple error propagation approach, the formula for the uncertainty of the availability A can be derived (see Fig. 1). Using the formula will give the results for ΔA as follows:

for component X

$$\Delta A \approx 0.20$$

for component Y

$$\Delta A \approx 0.14$$

(The reader should not worry about some serious defects in the values; for instance, an error indication such as $A = 0.99 \pm 0.14$ is of course a monstrosity, as, by definition, A cannot be greater than 1.0. Such a defect results from the simplifications in the approach used here, and does not affect the basic line of reasoning.)

Surprisingly, at a first glance, it appears that the resulting uncertainty for an item with 1000% (factor 10) uncertainty in the basic data is smaller than that for an item with 50% uncertainty in the data. This behaviour can be more clearly seen in Figs 1 and 2, derived by the same simplified method as above and suffering from the same limitations. Figure 1 shows the relative error of availability plotted against the total range of availability from 0.0 to 1.0, and Fig. 2 gives the information more specifically for availability values from 0.9 to 1.0. One of the values for X or Y is fixed (0.5) and the other is the parameter of the curves. Which refers to λ or μ is unimportant because of the equivalence provided by the symmetry of the formula.

The essential part is that the accuracy of the availability of the highly available items is but little affected by the inaccuracies of the basic data. Moreover, the

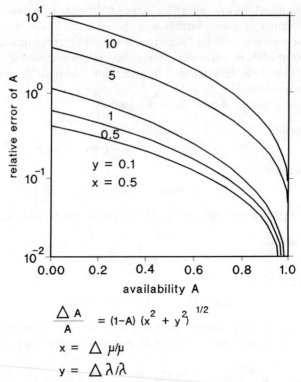

Fig. 1. Uncertainty of component availability because of basic data uncertainties (simplified approach).

accuracy of the repair rate can be fairly easily controlled by training, etc., which will result in small uncertainties of μ.

The situation described depends upon the fact that the model is based on the mutual exclusion of failed and not-failed states and that this model is sufficiently exact for most purposes. From this it becomes clear that complementary pieces of information can be derived from each of the states. This leads to the formula for availability, which indicates that for highly reliable items, i.e. $\mu \gg \lambda$, the results to all intents and purposes will not change with even considerable variations of λ. Consequently, it can be stated that the choice of the buyers mentioned above reflects a considerable feeling for reliability. The following conclusions can be drawn:

—Sound reliability engineering does not necessarily depend on highly accurate basic data but is very sensitive to a reasonable balance of these data.
—With a mathematically correct reasoning and formalism at hand it is possible to determine the basic data uncertainties maximally permissible for the achievement of the required minimum uncertainty of availability. This limit can then be used to reduce the data collection effort required and thus the cost.

It has to be emphasized that these relations have been shown here on the component

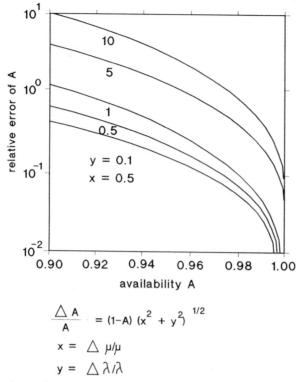

$$\frac{\triangle A}{A} = (1-A) \left(x^2 + y^2 \right)^{1/2}$$

$$x = \triangle \mu/\mu$$

$$y = \triangle \lambda/\lambda$$

Fig. 2. Uncertainty of component availability because of basic data uncertainties (simplified approach); extended availability axis.

level. They need further investigation for availability of systems which involve more than one component. Furthermore, the simplifications have to be removed and an appropriate consideration of statistics is mandatory.

However useful the tools for statistical data analysis are, reality is far richer and full of surprises, which cannot be handled by means of statistics.

Figure 3 shows an unsuccessful attempt to fit the failure data of car dashboard instruments with exponential and three-parameter Weibull distributions. The figure shows the cumulative failure probability vs the instrument lifetime ($=$ car lifetime). The fit parameters of the distributions and the χ^2 (PX) and Kolmogorov–Smirnov (PK) test results are listed below the diagram. As the applicability of three-parameter Weibull fits had been shown for other car part failures (for instance, brake linings), a search for non-stochastic patterns of the raw data was performed for a variety of parameter combinations.

The interesting search result is shown in Fig. 4. The failures per months are plotted against the calendar time for car batches, each line comprising a 1-month fabrication batch. The failure peaks at a specific calendar time form a striking pattern—the other peaks are not considered here, although they are of interest too. The non-stochastic characteristic of the raw data are the reason for the poor fit.

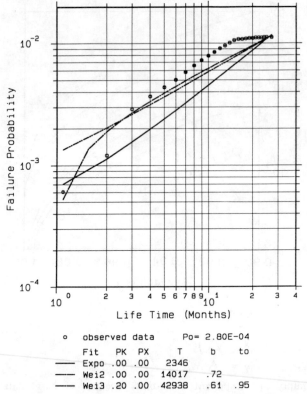

Fig. 3. Dashboard instrument failures, cumulative distribution.

Such non-stochastic behaviour must be searched for, and it is important for the reliability engineer to have the search tools. However, these means do not find the cause of the data properties, but they help in this task.

A further consideration of the data revealed that the peaks coincide with the summer holiday period. Car drivers have their cars inspected and repaired before they start their trips. Thus, it is not the real data of failure occurrence which is reported by the workshops to the data bank. The data are contaminated by the behaviour of the car owners. This holds for car instruments but not for brake linings, however. A driver concerned about the function of the brakes goes immediately to a workshop. In consequence, the data reporting is up to date and the stochastic character of failure occurrence is valid.

Nevertheless, knowledge of the patterns revealed is important for spare parts fabrication and storage.

The overall presumption in all the previous considerations and approaches is that the failure rates are not subject to major changes because of external causes. This is, however, the main feature of the problem of data transferability and applicability. The following example illustrates the importance of meticulous observation of this aspect.

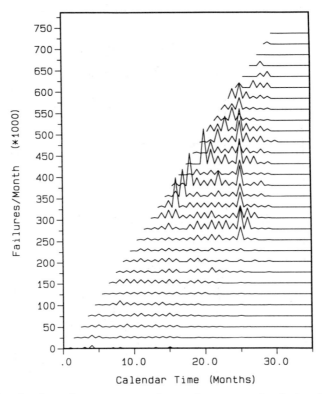

Fig. 4.   Result of raw data pattern search revealing non-stochastic data behaviour.

Figure 5 shows two approaches to remote handling. The upper design version consists of a row of cells housing nuclear chemical processes. The cells are covered with lids. The canyon contains a crane which carries the manipulator devices. The operations are carried out from a shielded cabin on the crane, and viewing is by mirror and periscope.

The second design involved the use of TV. Operation from a remotely located and shielded control room became possible. During the planning it was proposed that operation could be improved by removing the cell covers, because shielding was now thought to be superfluous. It was believed that the availability of the process could be increased, because it was no longer necessary to open the cells for crane access and close them again by the manipulator crane. The result of this approach was a considerable change in the atmosphere in the canyon: it became corrosive and contaminated, and because of this the failure frequencies of the crane, the switches, the cables, etc., increased. Repair was more frequently required. Moreover, the repair time also increased, as a result of the decontamination necessary before hands-on repair. The availability of the crane was severely reduced; this greatly diminished the availability of the process, which urgently needed the handling device. All this went hand in hand with an increasing radiation exposure of the staff,

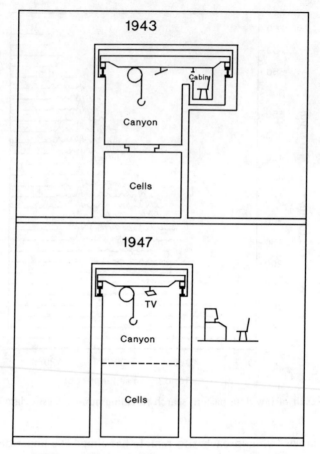

Fig. 5. Remote handling concepts (example).

as a result of more frequent and more extended repair tasks on more contaminated equipment.

The establishment of TV viewing from a shielded, remote control place should have been an improvement but the second step—the removal of the cell cover—so affected the availability of the vital piece of equipment and of the whole process that it completely negated the advantages thus gained.

REFERENCES

1. Luisi, T. (co-ordinator), Reference classification concerning components reliability. EuReDatA Project Rep. 1, S.A./I.05.01.83.02. Commission of European Communities, Joint Research Centre, Ispra, 1983.
2. Garnier, N. (co-ordinator), Proposal for a minimum set of parameters in order to exchange reliability data on electronic components. EuReDatA Project Rep. 2, S.P./I.05.E3.85.25. Commission of the European Communities, Joint Research Centre, Ispra, 1985.

3. Stevens, B. (ed.), Guide to reliability data collection and management. EuReDatA Project Rep. 3, S.P./I.05.E3.86.20. Commission of the European Communities, Joint Research Centre, Ispra, 1986.
4. Gabelli, G. & Smith, A. L. (co-ordinators), Materials reliability. EuReDatA Project Rep. 4, S.P./I.05.E3.85.38. Commission of the European Communities, Joint Research Centre, Ispra, 1985.

7

The Centralized Reliability Data Organization (CREDO); an Advanced Nuclear Reactor Reliability, Availability, and Maintainability Data Bank and Data Analysis Center

H. E. Knee

The Centralized Reliability Data Organization, Reliability and Human Factors Group, Engineering Physics and Mathematics Division, The Oak Ridge National Laboratory, Oak Ridge, Tennessee 37831, USA

7.1 THE BASIS FOR CREDO

The Centralized Reliability Data Organization (CREDO) is a data bank and data analysis center, which since 1985 has been jointly sponsored by the US Department of Energy's (US DOE's) Office of Technology Support Programs and Japan's Power Reactor and Nuclear Fuel Development Corporation (PNC). It focuses on reliability, availability and maintainability (RAM) data for components (e.g. valves, pumps, etc.) operating in advanced nuclear reactor facilities. As originally intended, the purpose of the CREDO system was to provide a centralized source of accurate, up-to-date data and information for use in RAM analyses necessary for meeting DOE's data needs in the areas of advanced reactor safety assessments, design and licensing. In particular, creation of the CREDO system was considered an essential element needed to fulfill the DOE Breeder Reactor Safety Program's commitment of 'identifying and exploiting areas in which probabilistic methods can be developed and used in making reactor safety Research and Development (R&D) choices and optimizing designs of safety systems'.[1]

The initial development of the CREDO system tended to be relatively conservative. Efforts within the program focused on obtaining specific data and information that, within a short period of time, made the system a unique and valuable asset to the US DOE's liquid metal reactor (LMR) program. In particular, it was felt as early as 1982 that the CREDO system represented the world's largest compilation of liquid metal component data from operating facilities. It was during this stage of the development of the system that Japan's PNC expressed interest in the CREDO system. Following discussions between the US DOE and Japan's PNC, the two organizations agreed to co-sponsor CREDO efforts from 1985 to 1988. It was agreed that (a) PNC and DOE would jointly fund the developmental costs of the CREDO system; (b) PNC would collect and transmit to ORNL CREDO-type input data from Japan's JOYO LMR and four liquid metal test facilities; (c) DOE would establish for PNC in Japan a parallel CREDO system, entitled FREEDOM; and (d) DOE would transmit to PNC CREDO-type data from the Fast Flux Test Facility (FFTF), the Experimental Breeder Reactor-II (EBR-II), as well as data from four organizations operating US DOE-sponsored liquid metal test facilities. The agreement between the US DOE and Japan's PNC has shown itself to be beneficial to both organizations. For PNC, the agreement meant rapidly establishing and utilizing an existing quality-assured data source in support of the probabilistic risk assessments of their newest LMR design, MONJU. For the US DOE, the agreement provided for enhancement of the statistical meaningfulness of its existing data base population. It also meant a period of shared costs that allowed continued support of the system. In 1988 a second phase of the cooperative agreement between the US DOE and Japan's PNC was put into place, which continues the initial agreement to September 1992 and involves several new initiatives, including translation of the data system to a more commercially available data base management system (DB2) and data collection at an additional advanced reactor test loop in Japan.

Effectively, the development of the CREDO system since the late 1970s has generally been carried out at a level of approximately 5 person-years per year, including data collection efforts at the data sites, and has been done with the objective of establishing a viable RAM system for future needs. During the years of development, however, CREDO efforts have provided data, information and analysis support for a number of research efforts carried out in the advanced concepts area. Although these efforts initially tended to be rather sparse, they demonstrated CREDO's ability to satisfy user needs. Furthermore, the CREDO staff has completed a number of internally motivated analyses that have been, or will be, presented at various conferences.[2-8] Section 9 of this chapter lists various studies performed by the CREDO staff and illustrates the wide diversity of applications of CREDO data.

Most recently, interest in the CREDO system and its data has come from designers working with advanced liquid metal concepts. Specifically, this interest is from the PRISM (Power Reactor Inherently Safe Module)[9] and earlier from the SAFR (Sodium Advanced Fast Reactor)[9,10] concepts (described in Ref. 9). Furthermore, DOE has recently required probabilistic risk assessment (PRA) studies to be carried out for FFTF, EBR-II and PRISM. The CREDO system will function as one of the primary sources of data and information for these efforts. These advanced LMR systems will use, as their primary data source, the wealth of operational experience available in the CREDO system. Emphasis is being placed on the use of CREDO data for the design phases of whichever design is chosen by the US DOE. The fusion energy program has also expressed interest in the CREDO system—primarily in the format, architecture and structure of CREDO's data base management system (DBMS). Their data base for performance analysis of fusion systems is entitled FUSEDATA (Fusion Systems' Data Base),[11] and utilizes the basic

CREDO format and structure for collecting data relevant to fusion system performance. Lastly, CREDO data and information have been used to support design efforts associated with a US liquid metal cooled space reactor.

The CREDO system represents the world's largest collection of advanced reactor component data from operating facilities. Its goal in the short term is to provide an archive for data from currently operating liquid metal facilities to meet the data and information needs of the advanced reactor community. Its longer-term goal is to be a center for liquid metal RAM research.

7.2 CREDO—AN HISTORICAL PERSPECTIVE

In autumn 1975 a meeting was held at the US Energy Research and Development Administration (ERDA) headquarters, with participants representing the ERDA, the US Nuclear Regulatory Commission (US NRC), national laboratories, universities and other members of the nuclear community. The purpose was to discuss the general requirements for a National Advanced Reactor Reliability Data System (NARRDS). Subsequent to the meeting, ORNL was asked by the ERDA to formulate a program that would put into operation the general specifications identified at the NARRDS meeting. ORNL's program plan included (a) a feasibility study to identify data sources, users and types of data to be collected; (b) the development of data collection formats and data evaluation procedures; (c) the initiation of data collection activities at relevant US DOE-sponsored advanced reactor facilities; and (d) the establishment of an effective data base management system (DBMS).

The first major task was a comprehensive feasibility study that examined the status of existing RAM efforts and helped to identify RAM data needs of the advanced reactor community. The study included an extensive literature review, an examination of previous and existing reliability data bases, site visits to organizations managing current data base efforts, and discussions with a number of personnel from reactor facilities, test sites, analytical groups, etc., who were potential users, and some of whom were also potential suppliers of RAM data. In addition to identifying specific types of data that a comprehensive and centralized reliability data organization should address, the study also identified seven characteristics that were felt to be important for the development of a successful reliability data center. These were:

(1) The system must be 'user-oriented'; that is, care should be taken throughout all phases of planning and implementation to ensure responsiveness to the differing needs of its diverse community of users.

(2) Data collection methods must ensure continued, complete accumulation of data on a timely basis, in a concise manner, and with minimum impact on the reporting facility.

(3) A well-defined, consistent procedure for evaluation of data (ensuring its validity, precision and applicability) should be established.

(4)   The data collected should be broad in scope; that is, quantitative failure data associated with safety systems should be of primary concern. However, other types of data must also be collected to gain the broad perspective necessary to be useful to a large number of diverse users. In particular:

   (i)   Qualitative data including qualitative component failure information, engineering data, human interaction data, etc., must be collected because they are essential for common-cause analyses and for incorporating risk assessment into safety design.

   (ii) Data for the balance of plant (BOP), as well as the nuclear island, must be included. The primary reason for this is that many of the assumed initiators for potential reactor accident sequences are events which occur in the BOP (e.g. loss of electrical power, turbine trip, steam-line rupture).

   (iii) Maintenance data must be collected because they are essential for a complete and thorough reliability assessment. In particular, assessment of the availability of safety-related components and systems requires analysis of both reliability and maintainability. In addition, availability studies and assistance in improving plant availability is a key concern of operating facilities and should be a primary means of providing feedback to these reporting facilities.

(5)   The feedback of useful data, information services and analysis services to reporting facilities was believed to be vital to the successful operation of the data organization. Strong cooperation by reporting organizations was seen as absolutely necessary, and the most effective factor is provision of services that directly benefit the facility.

(6)   Support and assistance from a broad range of experienced personnel in the RAM, risk assessment, safety, statistics, plant engineering, etc., fields can and should be encouraged. A means for formal and informal input by representatives of the many types of government, industry and private organizations concerned with these areas must be provided.

(7)   CREDO should serve as a focal point for the international exchange of reliability data and information. Regular exchange of information and cooperation with operating data systems in other countries will benefit all involved organizations.

From 1978 (the initiation of the CREDO system development at ORNL) to 1980 three major accomplishments were achieved: (1) the design of the input/output structures for the CREDO system, (2) the initiation of data collection activities at the EBR-II and the FFTF, and (3) the putting into operation of CREDO's DBMS. Although each of these accomplishments will be discussed in greater detail later in this chapter, they are introduced in the following paragraphs.

During 1978, the general input, output and DBMS requirements were defined. Information from the feasibility study, and an intensive review of the existing reliability and statistical analysis literature and methods, led to the identification of potential data types for inclusion in the CREDO system. Simultaneously, efforts were focused on the identification of an appropriate DBMS that would provide flexible and efficient handling of the various data types. Specific results of these initial efforts included:

(1) Identification of 44 generic components (e.g. valves, mechanical pumps, cold traps, etc.; a 45th component, a liquid rheostat, was added to the list several years later). A list of CREDO components is given in Table 1.
(2) Identification of the three basic data types for collection by the CREDO system (engineering data, event data and operating data).
(3) Identification of various standardized qualitative output (e.g. component engineering inventories and summaries) and quantitative RAM measures to be calculated by CREDO's DBMS (e.g. failure-rate-per-failure-mode based on an exponential distribution, mean-time-to-repair-per-failure-mode, etc.).
(4) Identification of the various data sites that would contribute data to the CREDO system.
(5) An assessment of the existing DBMS technology, and decision to use existing DBMS technology at ORNL.

During 1979, the CREDO data formats associated with the three data types were developed. The formats tended to be more detailed than the data structures of other data systems. In particular, most of the data forms include a number of narrative

TABLE 1
CREDO Generic Component List

Annunciator modules	Logic gates
Batteries	Mechanical control devices
Circuit breakers and interrupters	Mechanical pumps
Cold traps and vapor traps	Motors
Contactors and starters	Non-nuclear sensors
Control rod drive mechanisms	Nuclear detectors
Demineralizers	Penetrations
Electrical buses	Pipe and fittings
Electrical conductors	Plugging meters
Electrical and electronic connectors	Pressure vessels and tanks
Electric heaters	Reactor control rods
Electromagnetic pumps	Recombiners
Filters/strainers	Recorders
Fuses	Relays
Gas dryers	Rupture devices
Gas movers	Signal modifiers
Generators	Signal transmitters
Heat exchangers	Support and shock devices
Indicators	Switches
Instrument controllers	Transformers
Instrument power supplies	Turbines
Internal combustion engines	Valves
Liquid rheostat	

CREDO BASE ENGINEERING DATA FORM
(Use for All Components)

---

1. REPORT IDENTIFICATION

(a) Report I.D. No. _____ (b) Site*† _____ (c) Unit*† _____
             (CREDO Use Only)

(d) Report Date* __/__/__
          Mo. Da. Yr.

(e) Report Status:* _____New _____Change _____Delete
     If not "New," Date of Previous Report __/__/__
                    Mo. Da. Yr.

---

2. COMPONENT IDENTIFICATION

                                                  Yes No

(a) Name*† _____ (b) Site I.D. No.* _____ (c) PPS __ __

(d) C.I.D. No. _____ (e) Model No. _____
        (CREDO Use Only)

(f) Manufacturer _____ Code _____

(g) Spec./Standard No. _____ (h) Safety/Quality Class(es) _____

(i) Drawing No(s). _____ ____Site ____Mfg.

(j) Date Installed* __/__/__   Date Removed __/__/__
       Mo. Da. Yr.   Mo. Da. Yr.

____Failed   ____Censored   ____Extension: ____Design ____Usage

---

3. COMPONENT USE AND GENERAL DESIGN INFORMATION

(a) System*† _____ (b) Subsystem*† _____

(c) Design Function _____

(d) Application _____

(e) Design Life _____(Hours) _____(Cycles)

---

4. OPERATING FACTORS†   (a) Unit Status*   (b) Operating Factor (%)*

                               1. _____   _____

                               2. _____   _____

                               3. _____   _____

---

5. DUTY FACTORS†   (a) Unit Status   (b) Cycling Rate (per hour)*

                               1. _____   _____

                               2. _____   _____

                               3. _____   _____

---

6. MAINTENANCE AND INSPECTION/TEST DATA

(a) Maintenance Interval and Type _____

(b) Inspection/Test Interval and Type _____

_____

_____

---

*These items must be completed for a legitimate submission.

†These items must be completed with coded words.

CREDO Base Engineering Data Form   **page 2**

---

7. RADIATION EXPOSURE

  (a) Neutron Flux Level _____ neutrons/cm²sec

---

8. REDUNDANT REPLICATE COMPONENTS

  (a) Number of RRCs _____
     RRC site I.D. No(s). _____, _____, _____,
     _____, _____, _____, _____,

---

9. REMARKS, SPECIAL INFORMATION

  _____
  _____
  _____
  _____
  _____
  _____
  _____

---

10. SIGNATURES

	(a) Report	(b) CREDO
Last Name, Initials	_____	_____
Signature	_____	_____
Site Phone No.	_____	_____
FTS No., if any	_____	_____

---

11. DESCRIPTIVE FIELDS, KEYWORDS AND DESIGN PARAMETERS (CREDO USE ONLY)

  (a) Field No./Keyword

  _____/_____   _____/_____
  _____/_____   _____/_____
  _____/_____   _____/_____
  _____/_____   _____/_____
  _____/_____   _____/_____
  _____/_____   _____/_____

  (b) Design Parameters

No.	Value	Units	No.	Value	Units
___	_____	_____	___	_____	_____
___	_____	_____	___	_____	_____
___	_____	_____	___	_____	_____
___	_____	_____	___	_____	_____
___	_____	_____	___	_____	_____

Please verify that an engineering data supplement has been attached if required.

Use the reverse side of this form to add any additional engineering data or descriptive information desired.

Fig. 1. CREDO Base Engineering Data Form (used for all components).

fields that allow for the elaboration of topics that are relevant to the component and its operating history. It was felt that, to enhance the richness of the information to be provided to CREDO users, i.e. to provide a wide spectrum of data and information to CREDO's diverse audience of users, the system had to contain enough data so that analysts could make intelligent decisions related to the applicability of information to their analyses.

The current formats have changed considerably from their initial states. These changes were implemented at a time when data collection activities were being initiated. In general, major changes to the data structure usually cannot be carried out efficiently once a large amount of data has been collected. Originally, the engineering data for any of CREDO's generic components were collected on a single

COMPONENT DESCRIPTORS

1. Type	2. Functional Application	3. Functional Characteristic
__Ball	__Bypass	__Angle
__Blade	__Flow Control	__Conventional
__Multiblade	__Isolation/Stop	__Cryogenic
__Opposed Blade	__Level Control	__Five Way Selection
__Butterfly	__Multipurpose	__Four Way Selection
__Check	__Pilot	__Multivarying
__Cylinder	__Pressure Control	__Rotating Disk
__Diaphragm	__Pressure Relief	__Six Way Selection
__Gate	__Temp. Control	__Spring Check
__Globe	__Time Cycled	__Swing Check
__Louver	__Vacuum Relief	__Three Way Selection
__Multiventuri	__Other	__Wye
__Needle		__Other
__Nozzle		
__Plug/Piston	Keyword _ _ _ _ _ _ _ _	Keyword _ _ _ _ _ _ _ _
__Poppet		
__Other		

Keyword _ _ _ _ _ _ _ _

4. Medium Processed	5. Primary Seal	6. Operator Type
__Air	__Bellows	__Electric Motor
__Chemical Solutions	__Bellows & Freeze	__Electric Solenoid
__Inert Gas	__Bellows & Packing	__Explosive Device
__Liquid Gas	__Freeze	__Float
__Petrofuels	__Gas Injection	__Hydraulic
__Petroleum Oils	__Metal	__Manual
__Radioactive Gas	__O-Ring	__Mech/Spring
__Radioactive Waste	__Packing	__Pneumatic
__Silicones	__Plastic	__Self Operated
__Sodium	__Rubbers	__Other
__Sodium/Potassium	__Other	
__Steam		
__Vacuum	Keyword _ _ _ _ _ _ _ _	Keyword _ _ _ _ _ _ _ _
__Water		
__Other		

Keyword _ _ _ _ _ _ _ _

Fig. 2.   CREDO Engineering Data Supplement; component descriptors and design data for valves (valve).

form. When it became apparent that additional data that were specific to the component were necessary for a more complete and concise description, a proper engineering data submission was defined as completion of a CREDO Base Engineering Data Form (see Fig. 1), and an Engineering Data Supplement (see Fig. 2 for an engineering data supplement for a valve). The base form is used to gather data that can relate to *any* of the generic components, e.g. location, installation date, suggested preventive maintenance schedule, etc. The supplement form is used to gather data that pertain specifically to a type of component, e.g. data for a valve include its actuator type, the medium it processes, its inlet/outlet diameters, etc.

The CREDO Event Form (see Fig. 3) has also changed over the years. To provide information that might be more useful for common-cause/common-mode (CC/CM) failure analyses, several additions were made to the form. In general, data banks tend to address inadequately the types of data and information that many CC/CM analysts find useful. Thus, the CREDO staff modified the event form to include information such as a description of the last test/calibration experienced by the component before the event that is currently being reported on, and a narrative section which allows for the reporting of effects on other components or systems, including outage time. It should also be noted that the CREDO base engineering form was also modified to allow for a greater emphasis on CC/CM information. A

7. Valve to Pipe/Equipment Connection

__Buttweld
__Dissolving
__Flange and Weld
__Flat Flange
__Gravity Seal
__National Pipe Thread
__Pressure/Squeeze Tubing
__Raised Flange
__Socket Weld
__Special Thread
__Thread and Weld
__Tubing and Flange
__Tubing and Thread
__Tubing and Weld
__Other

Keyword _ _ _ _ _ _ _

12. Valve Operator Controller

__Discrete Mode
__Variable Mode

Keyword _ _ _ _ _ _ _

8. Seal Material

Keyword _ _ _ _ _ _ _

9. Body Material

Keyword _ _ _ _ _ _ _

10. Pipe Material

Keyword _ _ _ _ _ _ _

11. Seat Material

Keyword _ _ _ _ _ _ _

Refer to CREDO materials list (Table 6, Appendix A of the CREDO Guide for Completing Data Input Form and insert a coded word for material).

Fig. 2—*contd.*

Design Parameters	Value	Units
1. Design Pressure	_____	PSIG
2. Design Temperature	_____	DEGF
3. Nominal Operating Pressure	_____	PSIG
4. Nominal Operating Temperature	_____	DEGF
5. Nominal Pipe Size(Largest Dimension)	_____	IN
6. Nominal Valve Size	_____	IN
7. Nominal Valve Stroke	_____	IN
8. Operator Actuation Force	_____	LB
9. Operator Actuation Time	_____	SEC
10. Operator Actuation Torque	_____	FTLB
11. Operator Motor Rating	_____	HP
12. Operator Motor Voltage*	_____	
13. Pneumatic/Hydraulic Pressure to Operator	_____	PSIG
14. Valve Operator Signal Converter Input*	_____	
15. Valve Operator Signal Converter Output*	_____	

----

*Refer to CREDO component descriptors unit abbreviations for proper units (Table 7, Appendix A of the CREDO Guide for Completing Data Input Forms).

Fig. 2—*contd.*

field was added which asks for the number of replicate, redundant components in the same system, and their location. To complete these rather detailed forms, a *Guide for Completing Data Input Forms* was written (the original version was published locally at ORNL, with a selected and limited distribution; the most recent revision is cited as Ref. 12).

The changes to the data forms, as well as other major changes to the CREDO system over the years, have been accomplished with the consent and advice of a CREDO Steering Committee (CSC). Formed initially in 1979, it was composed of nationally recognized experts involved with various aspects of LMR design/safety/ RAM, data base management, statistics, etc. Its function was to provide general guidance to the CREDO staff and the US DOE in the development and operation of the CREDO system. The CSC operated through its three working groups, which addressed issues that were specifically related to and included (1) the gathering of data, priorities for component and system data collection, its data format and relationships with the reporting sites; (2) the evaluation of data, including the screening of data from the sites, cataloging, computer entry, data request processing, statistical analyses, etc.; and (3) the types of output, interactions with requesting users, the setting of priorities concerning data requests, data security, etc.

During 1979, progress was also made in the formulation of CREDO's DBMS. The structure of the DBMS was defined in terms of various search routines and subroutines from ORCHIS (Oak Ridge Computerized Hierarchical Information System)[13] and a FORTRAN driving program that would operate under a data base management system developed from the JOSHUA system.[14] ORCHIS contains many convenient routines for the management of scientific data files, but does not provide a general means for relating diverse data maintained in separate files which have different structures. This relational need was satisfied by the JOSHUA software through a general flexible framework for maintaining and relating data files. The combination of the JOSHUA and ORCHIS systems provided the CREDO system with the versatility, flexibility and efficiency required for a large RAM data center.

Data collection activities were also initiated for the first time at the EBR-II and FFTF. These initial efforts were accomplished by the CREDO staff at ORNL, who communicated via telephone/letters with reactor site personnel, when needed. Eventually, the data collection responsibilities were shifted to site personnel at the EBR-II in 1980, and at the FFTF in 1981.

CREDO's DBMS was implemented late in 1980. The ability to control the management of collected data through the use of an IBM computer (initially the IBM-360/91, now the IBM-3033) was a significant milestone for the CREDO system. It meant that the emphasis that had been focused on the definition and putting into operation of the CREDO system could be focused on enhancing CREDO's data store and, as possible, its user services. During 1980, the CREDO staff developed *CREDO's statistics* package, CREST. This software provided a number of statistical analysis capabilities, including the capability of assuming five different failure probability distributions on which to base a calculated failure rate. It also provides a coefficient of determination and a Kolmogorov–Smirnov statistic for each distribution chosen. A more in-depth discussion of CREST will be provided later in this chapter.

Achievements within the CREDO system beyond 1980 focus primarily on progress associated with data collection. During 1981, data collection activities were initiated with four US DOE-sponsored organizations operating liquid sodium test facilities. These organizations were (1) the Energy Technology Engineering Center (ETEC), (2) the Westinghouse Advanced Energy Systems Division (WAESD), (3) General Electric's Advanced Energy Systems Department (GE/AESD) and (4) Hanford Engineering Development Laboratory (HEDL). Data collection from these much smaller liquid metal facilities was necessitated by the limited number of liquid metal data sources in the USA. The collection of data at the WAESD test loops was completed in 1984 and the collection of data at ETEC continues.

Currently, interest in the CREDO system is relatively widespread. With the current emphasis on development of the PRISM design and PRAs for LMRs, DOE

CREDO EVENT DATA REPORTING FORM

---

1. REPORT IDENTIFICATION

(a) Report I.D. No. _____ (b) Site*ᵗ _____ (c) Unit*ᵗ _____
       (CREDO Use Only)

(d) Report Date* __/__/__ (e) Occurrence Title _____
       Mo. Da. Yr. _____

(f) Report Status:* ____New ____Change   (g) Previous Report Date __/__/__
                                             Mo. Da. Yr.

(h) Related Reports: UOR_____ Other_____

(i) Event Date* __/__/__   Event Time _____hours
       Mo. Da. Yr.

---

2. EVENT NARRATIVE

_____
_____
_____
_____

(Attach additional narrative on separate sheet if necessary)

_____

---

3. EVENT DETECTION/IMMEDIATE ACTION

(a) Detection Date* __/__/__ Time _____ (b) Method of Detection*ᵗ_____
(a) Detection Date Mo. Da. Yr.
(c) Time/Detection to Initial Action*ᵗ _____ (d) Operating Status: Unit*ᵗ _____
                                           Subsystemᵗ _____
(e) Initial (Immediate) Action_____

---

4. COMPONENT FAILURE DATA

(a) Component Name*ᵗ _____ (b) CREDO I.D. No.*ᵗ _____
(c) Site I.D. No.*ᵗ _____ (d) System*ᵗ _____ (e) Subsystem*ᵗ _____
(f) Component Description _____

(g) Event Type*ᵗ _____ (h) Event Mode*ᵗ _____
(i) Event Cause*ᵗ _____ (j) Event Severity*ᵗ _____
(k) Primary* _____ Secondary* _____
(l) Event Cause Narrative _____
_____
_____

(Attach additional narrative on separate sheet if necessary)

(m) Event Effects: Subsystem _____ Hours Lost _____
                 Unit _____ Hours Lost _____
                 Other Items Affected _____
(n) Critical Parts _____

*These items must be completed for a legitimate submission.
ᵗThese items must be completed with coded words.

Fig. 3. CREDO Event Data Reporting Form.

CREDO Event Data Reporting Form   **page 2**

5. CORRECTIVE ACTION

(a) Maintenance Action[†] _____ (b) Administrative Action[†] _____
(c) Interim _____

(d) Final _____

6. HUMAN INTERACTION DATA

(a) Human Initiator? Yes □ No □   If Yes, Explain _____

(b) Human Interaction/Engineering Potential _____

7. MAINTENANCE DATA

(a) Restoration Time (Hours/Manhours):* (i) Total __/__
    (ii) Administrative __/__   (iv) Indirect Repair __/__   (vi) Checkout/Retest __/__
    (iii) Logistics __/__   (v) Direct Repair __/__   (vii) Restart __/__
(b) Time Since Last (i) Maintenance _____ (ii) Testing _____
(c) Maintenance Narrative _____

8. REMARKS

9. SIGNATURES

	(a) Report	(b) CREDO
Last Name, Initials	_____	_____
Signature	_____	_____
Site Phone No.	_____	_____
FTS No., if any	_____	_____

*These items must be completed for a legitimate submission.

[†]These items must be completed with coded words.

contractors are realizing the wealth of data available, and are using the system more frequently. In addition, the European liquid metal community has informally expressed some interest in the possible establishment of a cooperative data exchange agreement that would support European liquid metal designs.

As the CREDO system continues to mature, greater emphasis is being placed on user services and the generation of CREDO-based analyses. In addition, as interest in the CREDO system increases, emphasis will be placed on the further inclusion of non-US data sources. In the long term, one of the goals of the CREDO system is to be an international center for liquid metal analyses and quality-assured data.

7.3 DATA INITIALLY IDENTIFIED FOR INCLUSION

At the onset of CREDO data collection activities in the late 1970s, there were a relatively limited number of existing liquid metal component data sources. Only one LMR, the EBR-II, was operating in the USA. A second unit, the FFTF, was still a few years away from start-up, and a third unit, the Clinch River Breeder Reactor (CRBR), was still in the design stage. These three units formed the basis for CREDO data sources and represented a significant technical population that was viewed as potential future users of the CREDO system. Spread across the USA there were also several liquid metal test and experimental facilities. These sites generally contained portions or mock-ups of the proposed FFTF, CRBR, and other advanced system and component designs. After recommendation from the CSC and endorsement by the US DOE, it was agreed that test facility data, i.e. data on the components that make up the facility, should be incorporated into the data base. Incorporation of data which focused on items being tested in the test facility was considered to be of lesser importance. The primary reason was that data for 'item-under-test' components tended to be compiled in existing sources that could be addressed when resources allowed. Not only would the incorporation of test facility data enhance the significance of the population of CREDO data from the primary data sites but it would also provide data and information about components that tend to be operated in typically more severe environments (providing meaningful data for analysts interested in off-normal and emergency operability). This decision led eventually to the collection of data from liquid metal systems at the following sites: Los Alamos National Laboratory (LANL), the HEDL, Argonne National Laboratory (ANL), GE/ARSD, Mine Safety Appliance Research (MSAR), ORNL, Rockwell International Energy Systems, ETEC and WAESD. The CREDO staff also identified the availability of component data for major components from several previously operated LMRs, e.g. FERMI, HALLAM, SRE (Sodium Reactor Experiment), EBR-I and the LANL MPRE (Molten Plutonium Reactor Experiment). Data for pumps, steam generators, heat exchangers and large valves were collected at these units.

Originally, the scope of the CREDO system focused on the collection of data and information on all components contained in an operating unit, regardless of a component's location or importance to achieving facility goals. This scope was identified at the 1975 NARRDS meeting when the resources to be dedicated to CREDO data collection efforts were forecast to be much larger than those that were actually received. As FFTF has approximately 50 000 components, and CRBR would have contained an even larger number, priorities had to be developed for effective use of limited resources. Specifically, a list of priority components and systems for which data would be collected was developed by the CSC and approved by the US DOE. Generally, the components of initial interest to CREDO are:

(a) those components whose failure could have adverse impact upon the unit's operation, e.g. technical specifications or safety class components;
(b) those components which are exposed to or are associated directly with a liquid metal environment;
(c) those components which are liquid metal specific;
(d) those components operating in environments not tracked by other nuclear data bases.

This list of priorities, in conjunction with a desire on the part of the US DOE to concentrate initially on mechanical components in liquid metal systems, served as the basis for all CREDO data collection efforts to date. One exception to this order of priorities was a decision to exclude *routine* electrical or electronic component data. This was done because these data are generally more available in other data bases, and because the rapidly developing technology in electronic components would make data from the test loops, EBR-II and, to some extent, FFTF and CRBR less pertinent for future reactor designs. Tables 2 and 3 present listings of the components initially given top priority. These lists have been used to provide general guidance for all data collection to date. As most of these data have been collected, efforts have been initiated to re-evaluate CREDO's component priority lists, to ensure that the CREDO system can supply the data needs of PRISM, MONJU, and the PRAs associated with FFTF and EBR-II.

7.4 CREDO COMPONENT DESCRIPTION AND CLASSIFICATION

The CREDO system is a data bank that addresses information that is primarily at the component level, i.e. most of the data compiled by the CREDO system focus on any of the 45 generic items as identified in Table 1. The use of a generic component taxonomy for data collection helps make explicit a categorization of components and provides for 'standardization' of input. Definition of an appropriate component level is to some degree dependent upon the types of analyses to be performed and the analyst. CREDO's generic component taxonomy was chosen at a level that was felt to be most practical and most interesting to most analysts for most analyses. Some limited information is collected at a higher level (reactor system/subsystem level) and at a lower level (component parts). It was felt that systems-level data of the kind collected for CREDO generic components would be of much greater interest as the number of systems (comparable systems) became large enough for comparisons to be made. With a limited number of data sites, this was judged to be relatively far into

TABLE 2
Top Priority Mechanical Type Components

Component/subsystem	Type
Control rod system components	Roller mechanism
Heat exchangers	Sodium (Na) to Na intermediate heat exchangers, and Na to water steam generators
Centrifugal pumps	Na flow—large volume
Piping and associated components	Na or sodium/potassium (NaK) environments
Valves	Na or NaK environments
Electromagnetic pumps	Na or NaK environments
Vessels	Reactor vessels, or vessels in Na or irradiation environments
Core restraint and support systems	Na or irradiation environments

the future. The information on liquid metal systems currently addressed by the CREDO system does not form a comprehensive and statistically complete source of RAM information at a system level. It does, however, provide a high-level, case history-like summary of actual system operating experience related to nearly unique systems. CREDO's generic system definitions allow for a qualitative insight into the operation of such systems and allow for the tracking of system effects.

CREDO components comprise a set of mechanical, electrical and electronic devices which were designed to function in liquid metal and liquid metal support systems. Data reported to the CREDO system are in three categories, as follows.

7.4.1 Engineering Data

An engineering data record (see Figs 1 and 2) provides a unique description of a particular component. This record consists of design and operating characteristics of the component for its particular application in its unit or system. Engineering data are usually reported once per component, preferably before its initial operation, and the data are updated as necessary. When a fault occurs, the engineering data are uniquely linked to the event report record to allow for

TABLE 3
Top Priority Electrical Type Components

Component/subsystem	Type
Flux sensors	Neutron detectors (fission, compensated ion chambers)
Na to air leak detectors	Aerosol or continuity types
Leak detectors (water to liquid sodium)	Oxygen or hydrogen meters, helium (He) sparger
Na level sensors	Inductive probe
Pressure transducers	NaK capillary type
Ultrasonic flowmeters	Na or irradiation environments

significant flexibility in describing the population of interest to the analyst. Engineering data can be updated to account for (1) significant changes in environmental or physical conditions, (2) different applications of the component throughout its lifetime, or (3) changing system operating philosophies/control strategies (e.g. operation of a system at a higher than normal temperature, pressure, flow rate, etc.).

7.4.2 Event Data

The event data file contains detailed data of reportable occurrences for components being tracked by the CREDO system. These data (see Fig. 3) include a narrative description of the event, the method of detection, failure mode, failure cause, corrective action taken, the effects of the event on related systems, the degree to which human interaction propagated or mitigated the event, the most recent maintenance experienced by the component before the occurrence of the event, etc. A liberal number of narrative sections have been placed in the Event Data Reporting Form to provide CREDO users with additional insight related to the circumstances surrounding a particular event. The combination of unit operating times with individual component operating factors, for each reactor mode, permits a reasonably precise estimate of component operating hours (certainly more precise than merely assuming that the operating time is identical to the total time that the component is installed).

7.4.3 Operating Data

The operating data consist of a set of chronologically sequential operating records which provide a profile of the accumulated operating history of the overall reporting unit. Each operating data record (see Fig. 4) specifies the hours of unit operation in up to five specified modes (e.g. power operation, hot standby, cold standby, etc.) that are characteristic of the operation of the unit during a particular report period.

The CREDO system requires that each component be identified as an element within only one generic reactor system and subsystem. The generic system and subsystem listings were patterned after their respective designations at the FFTF, and reflect their functional nature. They are not presented here because of space limitations, but may be found in Ref. 9. Generic systems and subsystems allow for consistent reporting from the various data sites even when the nomenclature between sites is not consistent. The generic system/subsystem taxonomies used in the CREDO system provide a common structure through which data analysts may communicate. Once familiar with CREDO's system/subsystem taxonomies, a user may seek data from a number of different sources without having to become familiar with each one's system taxonomy.

The 'philosophy' for designating generic CREDO system boundaries is conceptually straightforward: systems are defined on the basis of the *function* that a group of components perform (as opposed to being defined by the location of the

CREDO OPERATING DATA REPORTING FORM

1. **REPORT IDENTIFICATION**

   (a) Report I.D. No. _____   (b) Site* _____   (c) Unit* _____
                          (CREDO Use Only)
   (d) Report Date __/__/__
                   Mo. Da. Yr.
   (e) Report Period Dates: (f) Start __/__/__   (g) End __/__/__
                                             Mo. Da. Yr.   Mo. Da. Yr.

2. **OPERATING TIMES**

   MODE-1*_____   _____Hours
   MODE-2*_____   _____Hours
   MODE-3*_____   _____Hours
   MODE-4*_____   _____Hours
   MODE-5*_____   _____Hours

3. **NUMBER OF CREDO EVENT REPORTS THIS REPORTING PERIOD FOR THIS UNIT:__**

4. **FACILITY AVAILABILITY DATA**

   (a) Design Output**_____   (b) Authorized Output This Report Period**_____
   (c) Report Period Total Output**_____
   (d) Outages:
                                    Number   Hours Expended
                      Scheduled   _____   _____
                      Unscheduled   _____   _____
   (e) Comments/Discussion_____
       _____
       _____
       _____

   (f) Transients or Cycles (for Test Facilities)
       Number of Transients or Cycles This Period_____
       Total Number of Hours at Transient or Cyclic Conditions_____

5. **SIGNATURES**

                                    (a) Report   (b) CREDO
   Last Name, Initials   _____   _____
   Signature   _____   _____
   Site Phone No.   _____   _____
   FTS No., if any   _____   _____

   *These items must be completed with coded words.

   **Output units depend on type of facility and are specified by mutual agreement of CREDO and
   site staffs.

Fig. 4. CREDO Operating Data Reporting Form.

components). For example, all components whose primary function is to provide sodium fire protection are grouped in the Sodium Fire Protection System, even though they may be located among components in other systems.

Although conceptually simple, the application of the CREDO system boundary philosophy can, in reality, be somewhat difficult, especially at sites where components hold membership in more than one system (e.g. the Plant Protection System (PPS)). In addition, defining the system membership of components located at the interface of two or more systems may be difficult. Numerous examples of multi-system membership problems have arisen in connection with the PPS. Most of the components within the PPS have dual functions. Items such as nuclear instrumentation or flow instrumentation are designated as part of the PPS as well as part of the Instrumentation System. Cases have been encountered in which a majority of the components in a site-designated PPS system hold dual memberships. As a specific example, we consider neutron flux detectors used to provide power level indications to the reactor operator. The site may consider these detectors to be part of the PPS (because they supply input to the shutdown logic circuitry), but they are also considered to be part of the Nuclear Instrumentation System.

In CREDO, the problem of the duality of system membership for many of the components in the PPS has been circumvented by not designating the PPS as a generic system. Other dual-natured systems, e.g. the Engineered Safety System (ESS), are treated similarly. In effect, the CREDO system uses generic system and subsystem taxonomies that are respectively mutually exclusive of one another. However, because for safety and risk assessments it is important to know which components are related to the PPS, a check box is included on the CREDO Base Engineering Data Form (see Fig. 1) so that the component can be flagged as being part of the PPS. In the case of the neutron flux detectors cited above, the CREDO system considers them to be part of the Flux Monitoring System, but they are also flagged as being part of the PPS. Those few components that are uniquely assigned to the PPS by a particular data site are assigned to some other system in CREDO. For example, scram rods uniquely assigned to the PPS at their sites are assigned to the Reactor Shutdown System in CREDO. Thus, all components of the PPS are accounted for in other systems but can be called by searching for an entry in the check box which designates the component as being part of the PPS.

7.5 DESIGN OF DATA INPUT

7.5.1 The CREDO Base Engineering Data Form

The CREDO Base Engineering Data Form (see Fig. 1) is a two-page report which must be completed for every component to be tracked by the CREDO system. The form consists of 11 blocks of information that include:

- the reporting site and report status;
- the generic component type and its use;
- the component's operating and duty factors;

- the component's scheduled maintenance/inspection data;
- the component's average radiation exposure;
- the number and location of all replicate, redundant components;
- special remarks.

It should be noted that some of the most important entries on this form are the operating factors and the duty factors (i.e. cycling rates). An operating factor is a well-founded engineering estimate of the percentage of time that a component is operating when the unit (reactor or test facility) is in a particular operating mode. The duty factor is a similar estimate of the average number of state changes that a component undergoes per unit time when the unit is in a particular operating mode. Because the estimations of operating factors and cycling rates depend on the definitions of 'operating' and 'cycling' for each component, the CREDO staff has given operating and cycling definitions for each of its generic components.[12]

7.5.2 The CREDO Engineering Data Supplement Form

For every component tracked by the CREDO system, a CREDO Base Engineering Form supplies general information about the component's operation and a CREDO Engineering Data Supplement Form presents specific component data. As a result, a separate Engineering Data Supplement Form exists for each of the 45 generic CREDO components (see Fig. 2 for the Engineering Data Supplement Form for valves).

The Engineering Data Supplement Forms are designed to provide CREDO with three types of information on the component: (1) a description of the component in terms of its engineering parameters, (2) materials data for critical parts of the component, and (3) design and operating parameters for the component. It provides the user with a list of items from which to choose, to define the component population of interest for his analyses. All items, including qualitative and quantitative entries, may be used in data searches.

7.5.3 The CREDO Event Data Reporting Form

The CREDO Event Data File contains detailed information about any non-normal occurrence to a component that is tracked by the CREDO system. In particular, events for which a submission to the Event Date File should be made are described as follows:

- an unscheduled maintenance or unscheduled repair is performed on a component (e.g. a failed or malfunctioning component);
- a subsystem, system or the unit itself undergoes an unanticipated change from normal operation (e.g. an unscheduled scram or spurious operation occurs, a safety system is activated, etc.), and the change can be attributed to a component malfunction or failure (e.g. a component malfunction that affects other items);

- a repair or replacement of a component occurs during a scheduled maintenance inspection that was to include 'a repair or replacement only *when necessary*' (e.g. inspection reveals that a component has deteriorated to the point of replacement);
- during a maintenance inspection, a component is found to exhibit abnormal characteristics (e.g. out of tolerance limit switches);
- a component fails to perform its function for any reason not covered by the previous items.

It should be noted that these guidelines for the identification of CREDO reportable events tend to overlap and are provided to ensure that all events of interest to CREDO are addressed.

The CREDO Event Data Reporting Form (see Fig. 3) is a two-page report containing nine blocks of information that include:

- identification of the reporting site, the title of the event and the date of the event;
- a narrative description of the event;
- the method of detection of the event and what immediate actions were taken;
- the corrective actions taken;
- the extent to which human actions were involved in propagating or mitigating the event;
- details related to the last maintenance, test or calibration before the event;
- special remarks.

7.5.4 CREDO Operating Data Reporting Form

Knowledge of the operating history of a reporting unit is essential for the generation of various component and system RAM parameters. This is the primary function of a fourth data reporting form, the CREDO Operating Data Reporting Form (see Fig. 4). The form requests that the operating history of the unit (reactor or test facility) for the reporting period be given in terms of the number of hours that the unit has operated in each of its specified operating modes, and in terms of its availability. The form consists of five blocks of information that include:

- identification of the reporting site and the start and end dates of the report period;
- a listing of the hours that the facility spent in each of its operating modes;
- the number of CREDO event reports submitted from the facility for the current report period;
- facility availability data, including design output, authorized output, total output, and the number of outages and transients.

It is important that the operating modes listed on the Operating Data Reporting Form be identical to those listed on the CREDO Base Engineering Data Forms for a given facility during a given time period. This is required because the component operating factors given on the Engineering Data Forms are combined with the facility's operating hours to determine the operating lifetimes of the components of interest to the data analyst.

Together, the various CREDO data files permit very detailed description of components, and accounting of their life histories. The efficiency and flexibility in the management of this data by CREDO's DBMS permits users to access and manipulate data at any level required for the particular RAM analysis of interest.

7.6 CREDO's DATA BASE MANAGEMENT SYSTEM

The DBMS structure within the CREDO system uses the essential DBMS elements from a system named JOSHUA, which was developed at Savannah River Laboratories (Aiken, SC, USA). This system has many features, such as an efficient hierarchical data manager with record-level security, a terminal monitor for time-sharing applications, and a precompiler for FORTRAN applications.

The JOSHUA data manager supports a hierarchical tree structure which allows each data record to have a unique descriptive name. This name is composed of up to 16 qualifiers separated from one another by periods. Each qualifier specifies a level in the hierarchical framework of the data base and allows a particular attribute of the data record to be named. To illustrate its application, an example from our CREDO data bank is presented. The level structure of record names for CREDO engineering data is

FILE.VERSION.SITE.UNIT.SYSTEM.COMPONENT.CREDO ID

Each of these levels, or segments, is a general classification of an attribute which a data record possesses. A 'FILE' segment of the record name specifies one of the three broad classes of data with its own level structure, i.e. ENGR (for engineering data), OPER (for operating data) or EVENT (for event data). The 'VERSION' is included to permit continued tracking of a particular component as it experiences major changes such as physical relocation to another part of the plant. The 'extension' of a component's lifetime allows the DBMS to reflect major changes that affect component operability and, subsequently, its RAM. The 'extension' requires additionally stored data in the form of subsequent versions of the original engineering form. The levels beyond 'VERSION' are SITE, UNIT, SYSTEM and COMPONENT (a generic type, e.g. valve), designations that are self-explanatory.

The CREDO ID (CID) is a unique eight-character code assigned by the CREDO staff to each component tracked by the CREDO system. It uniquely identifies, for a specified period of time, a component that is operating in a particular SITE and UNIT. This number stays assigned to a component throughout its lifetime and is never reused, even if the component fails in a catastrophic manner.

All records in the data base are cataloged in a general binary tree by using 16-byte nodes of the following form:

Qualifer name	
Next sibling	First child

The 'qualifier name' is one of the 8-byte alphanumeric qualifiers used in a record name. The 4-byte 'next sibling' field is a link to the next node at the same level in the tree structure. The 4-byte 'first child' field is a pointer to the first node that is its subordinate in the next level (see Fig. 5 for an example diagram of the pointers). In this diagram, all of the horizontal arrows represent the 'sibling' links and the vertical arrows represent the 'child' links. The only exception to this is that for the last level of the tree structure the 'child' field will point to the proper data record. Within this field there is a one-bit flag which indicates whether the link is to another tree level or a data record, as in the last row. To find a given record, for example A1.B2.D2.J3 in the above tree, level 1 is searched first via the list of 'sibling' links until the first qualifier 'A1' is found. The 'child' pointer for this node gives the location of the first node (of the linked list) to be searched for the second qualifier, i.e. 'B2'; and so on. Thus, the nodes visited in the search for the record name are A1, B1, B2, D1, D2, J1, J2 and J3. This sequence of records is termed the 'path' traveled to find the record. In the JOSHUA system, several methods are used to minimize the number of disk 'reads' necessary to locate a given record. First, the tree nodes are physically stored separately from the actual data records. For a given block size, a greater number of tree nodes can be moved into the main memory (per disk read) than if data were to accompany them. This results in a higher probability that the same block will contain the next needed tree node. Second, several of these 'pages' or blocks of tree nodes are retained in main memory at any one time. Before a 'read' for another group of nodes is made, all in-core pages are checked to see if the needed node is contained within them. Lastly, several node 'paths', like the one illustrated above, are kept in main memory. These are very useful when the order of record retrieval is approximately sequential. In short, the search algorithm for a record name does the following: (1) traces in-core paths as far as possible; (2) checks all tree node blocks in main memory for the presence of the next node; (3) if it is not found there, the correct page is read from disk into the least most recently used page in memory; (4) updates the path for this node; and (5) repeats all steps until all of the qualifiers have been found. The actual data records are read and written to disk by FORTRAN direct access I/O statements, with the proper record number being found by the data manager. The use of FORTRAN I/O facilities requires that all programs which read and write to the data base know the exact I/O list structures. The data manager is accessed from various software programs via subroutine calls, under control of JOS (the JOSHUA Operating System). JOS, which is the backbone of the JOSHUA system, is run as a continuous job under the IBM-3033 OS/MVS. It consists of a re-entrant control program, a terminal and a batch monitor; various other re-entrant and serially reusable resident modules (such as the data manager); and several

ORNL—DWG 80—9284

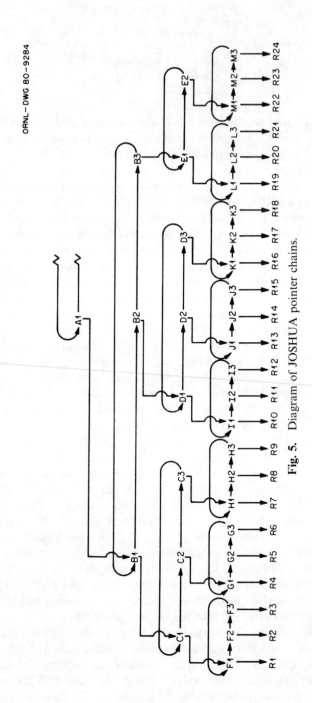

Fig. 5. Diagram of JOSHUA pointer chains.

control blocks for maintaining system integrity. The terminal monitor was developed for hard-wired IBM-3270 series terminals which are full-page, buffered devices. An abundant selection of terminal commands provide all necessary functions for data maintenance, manipulation, editing, batch job submission and module execution. The batch monitor allows for execution of modules which require a longer turnaround time than is generally desired for a terminal.

One of the most useful services of the JOSHUA system for the applications programmer is a precompiler for FORTRAN. In most other cases where software is accessed through FORTRAN, the access is with CALL statements. A package, such as the JOSHUA system, which provides a wide range of useful options, sometimes tends to have very long, cumbersome parameter lists. For this reason, a pre-processor was written that would transform a 'JOSHUA FORTRAN' statement into 'standard FORTRAN calls' with the proper arguments. For instance, if the programmer wanted to read the 'ENGR version 0' record from the data base for

HEDL.FFTF.INERTGAS.VALVE.VA00001A

the following could be used:

READ('ENGR'.'0'.'HEDL'.'FFTF'.'INERTGAS'.'VALVE'.'VA00001A')X

where X equals a, b, c, ... and a, b, c, ... are the names given to the values stored in the record. This statement would be 'commented-out' by the precompiler and replaced by the FORTRAN calls that were needed to perform the desired function. Thus, all the programmer needs to read this record is the record name and the I/O list structure.

Updating of CREDO records can be accomplished by simply writing the new corrected record using the exact name of the record containing the old data. The new record overwrites the old one and any space adjustments are handled automatically by the data manager. If it is necessary to save the older information it can be renamed before the overwriting.

The information in CREDO may be selectively retrieved by search requests using CREDO data-processing modules. The current CREDO data-processing modules can be classified into three basic groups: those which perform calculations with the data, those which display the data either in full-form structure or an abbreviated inventory listing, and those which merely copy CREDO data records from one device to another. Before discussing the user requirements for accessing each module group, some basic input and logical unit requirements for all the modules will be presented.

CREDO data may be from either the Engineering (ENGR), Operating (OPER) or Event (EVENT) files. All three types of data are required by each of the modules which perform calculations, whereas only certain files or combinations of files are needed by the other modules.

A listing of the available modules, their functions and the corresponding required CREDO data files (with associated file type [J = JOSHUA and S = sequential] in parentheses) are presented in Table 4.

The binary logical operations 'and' and 'or', which permit the selection and

TABLE 4
CREDO Data-Processing Modules

Job type	Module	Task	Search logic	Files required
Copying	ENCOPYSS	Copies CREDO data	NO	ENGR(S) → ENGR(S)
	ENCOPYSJ	from a sequential	NO	ENGR(S) → ENGR(J)
	EVCOPYSS	file into another	NO	EVENT(S) → EVENT(S)
	OPCOPYSS	sequential file or	NO	OPER(S) → OPER(S)
	OPCOPYSJ	into JOSHUA[a]	NO	OPER(S) → OPER(J)
Data display	ENINV	(INV) lists a brief	YES	ENGR(J)
	ENINV1	inventory of a specified	YES	ENGR(J)
	ENFORM	group of forms (records)	YES	ENGR(J)
	EVINV	in a given data set;	YES	EVENT(S)
	EVINV1	(INV1) sorts the data	YES	EVENT(S)
	EVFORM	generated in a search;[b]	YES	EVENT(S)
	OPINV	(FORM) displays a	YES	OPER(J)
	OPFORM	specified group of	YES	OPER(J)
	COINV	records as CREDO forms;	YES	EVENT(S) & ENGR(J)
	COINV1	(EVSUM) displays an	YES	EVENT(S) & ENGR(J)
	EVSUM	EVENT data summary	YES	EVENT(S) & ENGR(J)
Data analysis	FAILRATE	Calculates the failure rate of each of the specified components	YES	EVENT(S), ENGR(J), OPER(J) & Scratch(J)
	LIFETIME	Calculates the total lifetime of each of the specified components	YES	EVENT(S), ENGR(J) & OPER(J)
	FAILTIME	Calculates the failure rate and the lifetime of each of the specified components	YES	EVENT(S), ENGR(J), OPER(J) & Scratch(J)
	REGURG	Combines the two output files from a lifetime calculation (AUXINFO & LIFETIME) and produces an input file for the CREST statistical analysis code	NO	AUXINFO (unit 87) & LIFETIME (unit 88)
Multiple analysis	PATHLT	Executes the LIFETIME module followed by the REGURG module	YES	EVENT(S), ENGR(J), OPER(J), Scratch(J), AUXINO & LIFETIME
	PATHFT	Executes the FAILTIME module followed by the REGURG module	YES	are all used in multiple analysis jobs
	QAP	Executes the QAP (QA preprocessor) module	YES	EVENT(S), ENGR(J) OPER(J), writes records in a JOB level data set(J)
Data checking	QA	Executes the QA module	YES	EVENT(S), ENGR(J), OPER(J), JOB level data set for scratch records(J), and JOB level data set written by QAP(J), MFGID data sets(S)

[a] Except for special cases, EVENT data are always stored on a sequential file.
[b] Sorted by Site, Unit, System, Component and CREDO ID except ENINV1, which is sorted by Site, Unit, System, Component, Site ID and CREDO ID.

grouping of data record subsets from a main body of records, are the basis for search specifications. These connective words correspond, in set theory, to the operations 'intersect' and 'union', respectively. Furthermore, an algebraic system can be constructed which satisfies all of the axioms of Boolean algebra. Such a system includes the prefix 'not', which designates the complement of the set to which it is attached.

In the structure of input data for search specifications, all data are free-form, i.e. blanks are ignored and there are no restrictions on card columns (except for the continuation character and asterisk, which must appear in column 1). If the user wishes not to specify any search restrictions, the entry 'NODATA' is made, and all records will then be accepted in the search.

The syntax for a Boolean search consists of a set of one or more 'and' strings of commands called specifications. If search restrictions are to be applied then these specifications are entered as follows:

```
DATA
        SEARCH MOS
            (Specification 1)
        SEND
        SEARCH MOS
            (Specification 2)
        SEND
           :
        SEARCH MOS
            (Specification N)   (N .LE. 10)
        SEND
DEND
```

The variable 'MOS' denotes the sense of the specification and is optional. If a negation, i.e. complement, of a specification is desired, 'MOS' should be entered as 'NOT'. 'MOS' has a positive default assigned. The 'SEND' (search-end) command concludes the data for each search specification. It is important to note the effect of multiple search specifications (i.e. more than one SEND card). In general, record sets resulting from each search specification will be processed separately. The system, however, tries to use effectively information that is generated from previous search specifications. 'DEND' (data-end) denotes the conclusion of all search data.

Each specification takes the following form:

OS COMMAND11 'and' COMMAND12 'and' COMMAND13 'and'...'and' COMMAND1N(1)
OS COMMAND21 'and' COMMAND22 'and' COMMAND23 'and'...'and' COMMAND2N(2)
OS COMMAND31 'and' COMMAND32 'and' COMMAND33 'and'...'and' COMMAND3N(3)
        :   :   :
OS COMMANDM1 'and' COMMANDM2 'and' COMMANDM3 'and'...'and' COMMANDMN(M)

The variable 'OS' denotes the sense of each 'and' string, and is optional. If a negation, i.e. complement, of an 'and' string is desired, 'OS' should be entered as 'NOT' or 'N'. 'OS' is positive by default.

Each of the commands which make up the specification states a particular condition which must be met by the admitted class of records. Combinations of such commands, by linking horizontally with 'and' and vertically with 'or', further narrow or broaden respectively the records which will satisfy the specification. The 'and' and 'or' connectives are applied according to this structure, i.e. horizontally for a string of 'ands' and vertically for a string of 'ors'.

Commands are used to set the qualification standards for the screening of records by relating the fieldname to a particular data value. Commands relate either test or numeric fields with data values. Their syntax varies as follows:

Commands for text fields: OS ⟨FIELDNAME⟩VALUE1,VALUE2,...,VALUEN;
                           OS ⟨FIELDNAME(I)⟩VALUE;
                           OS ⟨FIELDNAME⟩ = VALUE1,VALUE2,...,VALUEN;
                           OS ⟨FIELDNAME(I)⟩ = VALUE;

The variable 'OS' denotes the sense of the command (optional) and is entered as was shown above. 'FIELDNAME' is required to be a valid text fieldname (or an alias) in the file(s) of interest. The subscript 'I' restricts the search to the Ith position of a field which may have multiple data values. The fieldname subscript may be omitted, which necessarily means that every double word in the field will be checked to match the word contained in 'VALUE'.

The '=' (equal sign) is acceptable for clarity in the data but is ignored by the program. 'VALUE' should contain an eight-character alphanumeric string (normally upper-case) which may optionally be enclosed in single quotes for clarity. A sequence of eight-character strings separated by commas, i.e. VALUE1, VALUE2, VALUE3,..., VALUEN, may be entered, for example, when an entire field is examined (i.e. the omission of a subscript). This admits a record if 'VALUE1' and 'VALUE2' and 'VALUE3' and ... and 'VALUEN' are all found within the field. 'VALUE', or any of the eight-character strings from a 'VALUE' sequence, may be preceded by an 'N:', as follows:

                    OS ⟨FIELDNAME⟩N:VALUE;
                    OS ⟨FIELDNAME⟩N:VALUE1, N:VALUE2,..., N:VALUEN;

where some (not necessarily all) of the eight-character strings in the sequence are prefixed with 'N:'. The prefix 'N:' denotes the complement of the preceded value and can be interpreted as meaning 'all values except...'. The last character of each command should be a semicolon.

Commands for numeric fields: OS ⟨FIELDNAME(I)⟩.EQ.VALUE;
                              OS ⟨FIELDNAME(I)⟩.LT.VALUE;
                              OS ⟨FIELDNAME(I)⟩.LE.VALUE;
                              OS ⟨FIELDNAME(I)⟩.GT.VALUE;
                              OS ⟨FIELDNAME(I)⟩.GE.VALUE;
                              OS ⟨FIELDNAME(I)⟩.NE.VALUE;

'FIELDNAME' should be a valid numeric fieldname (or an alias) in the file(s) of interest. The subscript 'I' restricts the search to the Ith position of a field which may have multiple data values. The fieldname subscript may be omitted, in which case the first number ($I = 1$ position) in the field will be compared with the number contained in 'VALUE'.

'VALUE' should contain a valid integer number (for an integer numeric field) or a valid real number (for a real numeric field). The negation of the numeric command can also be achieved by entering the complement of the conditional, e.g. '.GE.' for '.LT.', '.LE.' for '.GT.' and '.NE.' for '.EQ.', etc. 'VALUE' may optionally be entered within single quotes for clarity. The last character of each command should be a semicolon.

The following example of a search specification is presented to illustrate the CREDO search logic. It is not necessarily typical of a CREDO system data search:

```
SEARCH
    ⟨SITE⟩ANL;⟨UNIT⟩EBR-II;⟨SYSTEM⟩PRIMRXHT;⟨COMP⟩PIPE;
SEND
```

The effect of this example request is that the records of all primary reactor heat transport system pipes at the ANL EBR-II facility are accepted.

7.6.1 Automated Data Checking

One of the most time-consuming aspects of developing a comprehensive data system such as CREDO is the process of collecting and entering field data into the computerized DBMS. The process involves many hours of searching through records, talking with maintenance personnel, etc. The data gathered must provide a consistent picture of the operation of components and systems being addressed. Although, at times, individual pieces of data may seem to be appropriate, taken in conjunction with other pieces of data, they do not form a consistent scenario. The data collector at the sites thus has the task of translating operating or failure experiences into manageable pieces of information via CREDO's data collection formats. The process, however, does not end here.

Data from the reporting sites are shipped to the CREDO offices at ORNL, either on magnetic tape or in hardcopy format. The latter requires additional work on the part of the CREDO staff. Specifically, hardcopy data must be entered into the computer system, and a check for errors in transcription must follow. This step is avoided if the data are transmitted on tape.

The data screener has three primary goals. First, a check must be made to see if the form is at least minimally complete. Although the data collectors at the sites strive to complete each form to the greatest degree possible, some data may not exist or may not be in a form that is economically feasible to process. Some of the data on CREDO's data forms, however, *cannot* be omitted if the form is to be accepted as a valid CREDO data record.

It is the first task of the data screener to ensure that the necessary entries are present and that any additional supporting information that is provided in the narrative fits within the required data structure. The screener's second goal is to check the correctness of entries that have been provided. This involves checking of the spelling of keywords, ensuring that proper units have been associated with entered design and operating parameters, checking to see that quantitative entries fall within operational limits, and, in general, ensuring that the data that have been supplied make sense.

The third goal is that of consistency, and involves making sure that the data that have been received logically mesh with previous data received. As this involves previously submitted data, it sometimes requires the data screener to search for related data in the data system and to verify its logical consistency with the new data received.

For example, if the data being screened are an event record, several checks must be made. First, an engineering form for the component experiencing the event must be in the data system, which in effect acknowledges the existence of the component. If the engineering record exists, then the date of the event should be within the lifetime of the component as recorded on the engineering form. If the data being screened are an engineering record, a check must be made to ensure that no other component with the same CREDO ID number exists (i.e. it must be a unique record). The data screener must ensure that if the record indicates that the component has been removed from service, and that it was removed because of failure, then a corresponding event record exists.

The data screener must read all narrative data to see if the information provided 'fits' the particular circumstances. The CREDO data screener is effectively a situation analyst, i.e. the screener must have a thorough familiarity with previously collected data and a knowledge of systems and components, and must determine through engineering judgement whether the data are of high quality and are consistent. Data screening is task intensive and requires dedicated personnel for processing. Because of these factors, effort was focused toward the development of a computerized data-checking program. Its primary purposes were (1) to remove some of the more mundane checking tasks from the requirements of the data screener and (2) to minimize the searching that had to be done by the screener to check data consistency.

Although the total elimination of manual screening has not been achieved, and is probably not altogether desirable, it has been estimated that CREDO's consistency checking program has allowed the data screener to process twice as many data forms as was possible without the automated checking feature. At the same time, it has reduced even further the already low rate of screener error.

The consistency checking program is a combination of two separate programs. The first, QAP (quality assurance program), is a preprocessing program. Its purpose is to write selected fields of data onto scratch files for later comparison with data that are being entered into the system. For example, if the data to be entered consist of a number of different components from the FFTF, the QAP will search all engineering, event and operating records and identify all FFTF data. The QAP will then write all entered data that will be used during consistency checking onto scratch files. After these scratch files have been prepared by QAP, the QA program is ready to compare any newly entered data with the existing data base data, via the QAP scratch files.

Although data collection activities stress the completeness of the various CREDO data forms, often it is not possible to complete a form in its entirety. Because of this, the CREDO staff has prepared a list of data fields that must be completed, or that it is highly desirable to have completed. The consistency checking program compares the required data fields and flags any missing or incorrect data, e.g. improper descriptors or keywords present.

In effect, CREDO's consistency program requires the data screener to focus on only those items that do not conform to the standard rules that are necessarily associated with the data. There is, of course, some trade-off associated with automating this screening process; namely, it tends to reduce the data screener's active involvement with data. However, the CREDO staff views it as a means of relieving the data screener of more mundane tasks to permit more time for more 'interesting' work such as data analyses. In fact, as the emphasis in the CREDO system shifts from data collection to RAM analyses, the data screeners will be performing many more data analyses, and familiarity with the data and with the reactor plant/systems will be even greater than it currently is. Some level of manual screening probably will be necessary/desirable for the foreseeable future, especially for the screening of the narrative portion of all three different data format types. Much of the rich supportive information concerning the description of a component and its history of operation is contained in these narratives. Although a significant amount of the screening efforts have been 'computerized' away, the 'heart' of the information still requires the attention of a specialist employing good engineering judgement.

One of the more recent software developments completed by the CREDO staff involved the development of a PC-based data entry program entitled CIDER (CREDO Interactive Data Entry Routines). Before the development of CIDER, engineering, event and operating data were received in the form of computer output, photocopied pages from the user's guide (either handwritten or typed) or files sent via computer links between the two installations. The processing of the data after receipt was as follows: (1) the data were screened/quality assured by the CREDO staff and (2) the data were input/retyped into data files for management by CREDO's DBMS. Such a manually oriented system did not promote standardization among sites submitting data to CREDO, was susceptible to the introduction of errors and tended to be relatively labor intensive. Through the use of CIDER, the field engineer collecting CREDO data has control of the destiny of the forms that are generated. Furthermore, the files created by CIDER can be input directly into the DBMS without requirements for transcription.

The CIDER software runs on an IBM-PC to facilitate use of the code by the field engineer. It was written and compiled using Microsoft's FORTRAN Optimizing Compiler version 4.01 for a DOS operating system, and adheres to the ANSI 77 FORTRAN standards.

7.7 STATISTICAL DATA ANALYSIS AND PROCESSING

The basic goal of the CREDO system is to collect information describing liquid metal system component operation, and to categorize the information into an interactive storage/retrieval mechanism which can, upon demand, produce organized output of statistical significance. The output includes basic RAM measures of performance (metrics), and a variety of enhanced statistical analyses.

The CREDO system's standard statistical output is composed of two separate analyses. The first is the quantitative failure data summary (QFDS), which is displayed in Fig. 6. The primary metric generated is a simple exponentially based failure rate. It is calculated by taking the ratio of the total number of failures to the total number of operating hours. It should be emphasized that the population of interest is specified by the user of the system, and the specific numerical estimates made (e.g. failure rates) are highly dependent on the characteristics of the population. Another item of interest in the QFDS is a section listing the separate failure modes, the number of components that failed, the percentage of failures by mode, a 5% and 95% confidence interval around the failure rate mean, and the failure rate per mode. In addition to failure data, a section on repair data is also provided. The primary items of interest in the repair section are the calculated values for mean-time-to-restore (based on a log-normal distribution), both overall and by each failure mode. As shown in Fig. 6, the results from the QFDS are presented in an organized tabular manner for easy reading by the user.

The second analysis of the standard output of CREDO is the *CREDO's statistical* package entitled CREST. CREST is a FORTRAN-IV code composed of one program and 13 subprograms. It can be used with commercial plotting systems such as 'DISSPLA' to generate graphical representations of failure distributions.

Graphical techniques are used extensively by data analysts because they offer an easy, convenient means of identifying and examining overall trends and characteristics of sizeable data sets. For example, they are used to identify relevant probability distribution functions (PDFs), their parameters and associated failure rate estimates. CREST incorporates several graphic techniques in a single module and automates much of the tedious manual work usually associated with plotting techniques.

Four main sections of CREST are available: (1) total-time-on-test, (2) hazard function, (3) maximum likelihood, and (4) trends analysis. Section 1, the total-time-on-test section, is based on work by Barlow and Campo,[15] and allows the analyst to examine the relationship between the number of failures within a data set and the times at which they occurred. In effect, this section estimates the failure rate tendencies of the data set of interest. More specifically, CREST determines if a data set exhibits increasing failure rate, decreasing failure rate or exponential failure rate tendencies. Section 1 output includes the following:

(1) a table of failure fractions;
(2) a table of total-time-on-test fractions;
(3) determination of increasing, decreasing or exponential failure rate tendency;
(4) a significance level dependent on the number of failures;
(5) a plot of failure fractions vs total-time-on-test fractions.

Section 2 of CREST, the hazard function section, is based on work by Nelson.[16] It allows the user to choose among five failure PDFs for modeling the failure behavior of a population of components. For each distribution chosen, this section of CREST determines the corresponding distribution parameters through applicable hazard function transformations and regression analyses. The PDFs available for the choice of the user are exponential, Weibull, normal, log-normal and extreme value (Gumbel). Linearized forms of cumulative hazard functions are used in conjunction

Component: TRAP
Type: WMESH

Site: ALL
Unit: ALL
System: ALL

Period: 01/01/78–12/31/82

Population: 118
Operating hours: 4·548E+06
Demands: 2 312
Failures: 47
Failure rate (per h): 1·034E−05
No. of failure modes: 5

Failure data, constant hazard assumed (exponential failure model)

Failure mode	No. failed	%	5% CI	95% CI	Rate (per h)	5% CI	95% CI
OTHER	2	4·26	3·4E+00	7·1E+00	4·40E−07	5·33E−08	1·59E−06
ABNORMOP	1	2·13	2·3E+00	3·5E+00	2·20E−07	5·57E−09	1·23E−06
PLUGGED	36	76·60	0·0	0·0	7·92E−06	5·55E−06	1·10E−05
BLANK	7	14·89			1·54E−06	6·19E−07	3·17E−06
NOENER	1	2·13			2·20E−07	5·57E−09	1·23E−06
OVERALL	47	100·00	2·4E+00	3·6E+00	1·03E−05	7·59E−06	1·37E−05

Repair data (log-normal distribution)

Failure mode	Contributors	μ	5% CI	95% CI	σ	5% CI	95% CI	MTTR
OTHER	2	5·2E+00	3·4E+00	7·1E+00	1·5E−01	9·2E−02	6·6E+00	1·9E+02
PLUGGED	22	2·9E+00	2·3E+00	3·5E+00	1·2E+00	9·7E−01	1·8E+00	3·9E+01
NOENER	1	1·4E+00	0·0	0·0	0·0	0·0	0·0	4·0E+00
OVERALL	25	3·0E+00	2·4E+00	3·6E+00	1·4E+00	1·1E+00	1·9E+00	5·2E+00

Fig. 6. CREDO component quantitative failure data summary

with linear least-squares methods to calculate the associated distribution parameters. A special user option has been programmed into this section which allows the choice of regular or robust linear least-squares methods. Robust linear least-squares methods employ a weighted, iterative scheme to identify potential data outliers, and provide regression results that down-weight the outlier data. Any or all five PDFs may be processed by regular or robust methods during any run of the code. The output of Section 2 includes:

(1) a table of failure lifetimes;
(2) a table of the cumulative hazard value at each failure;
(3) the values of the calculated distribution parameters for each distribution chosen;
(4) a coefficient of determination for each distribution chosen;
(5) a Kolmogorov–Smirnov statistic for each distribution chosen;
(6) a calculated failure rate for each distribution chosen;
(7) a graphical display of the linearized cumulative hazard function for each distribution chosen.

Section 3 of CREST, the maximum likelihood estimation section, allows the user to choose among three failure PDFs for modeling the failure behavior of a population of components. Using standard maximum likelihood estimation methods, this section determines distribution parameters for each distribution chosen. The PDFs offered in this section are exponential, Weibull and extreme value.

Equations derived from the maximization of appropriate likelihood functions are solved to calculate various distribution parameters. The output of Section 3 includes:

(1) the values of the calculated distribution parameters for each distribution chosen;
(2) for the exponential distribution parameter, a 95% confidence interval;
(3) the Kolmogorov–Smirnov statistic for each distribution chosen;
(4) a calculated failure rate for each distribution chosen.

Section 4 of CREST, the trends analysis section, provides a graphical display in the form of histographs of the various failure modes and failure causes experienced by a particular set of components. Failure modes and/or failure causes may be displayed. Output of Section 4 includes:

(1) a histograph in terms of per cent of the various failure modes;
(2) a histograph in terms of per cent of the various failure causes;
(3) a tabular list of the failure modes and causes, and their respective percentages.

CREST provides the CREDO user with a means of easily generating RAM metrics from advanced statistical techniques. It allows users to go beyond the typical assumption of exponentiality in doing RAM analyses and to explore the possibility of applying other distributions to their analyses. Figures 7–14 display the various types of CREST graphical output for a single data set.

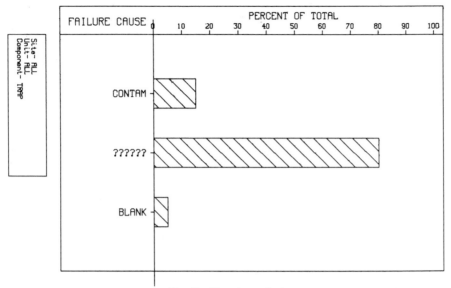

Fig. 7. Trends analysis.

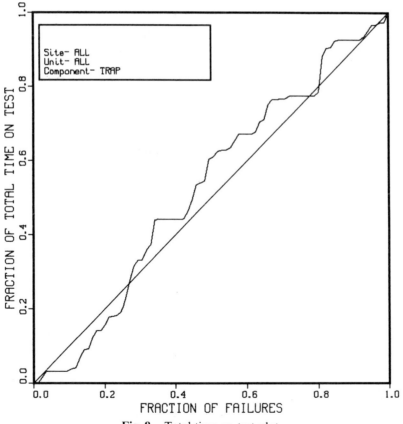

Fig. 8. Total-time-on-test plot.

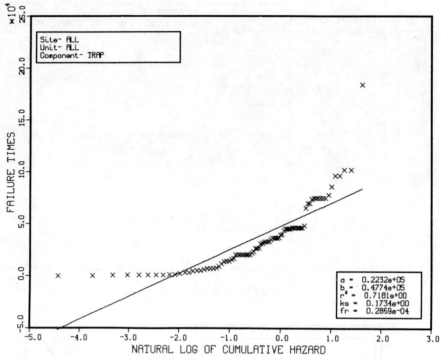

Fig. 9. Extreme value hazard plots.

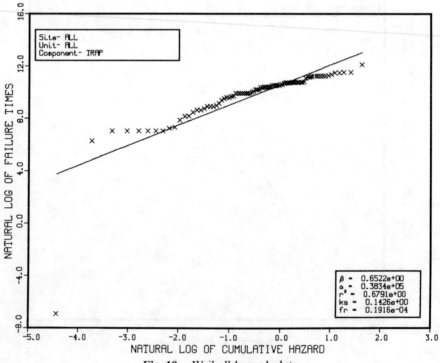

Fig. 10. Weibull hazard plots.

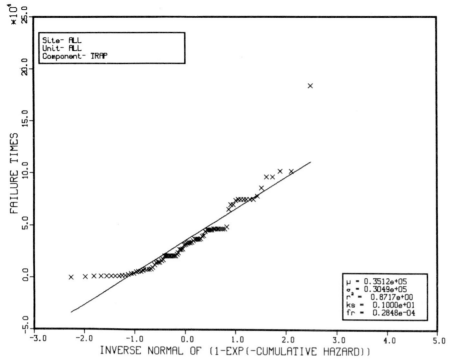

Fig. 11. Normal hazard plots.

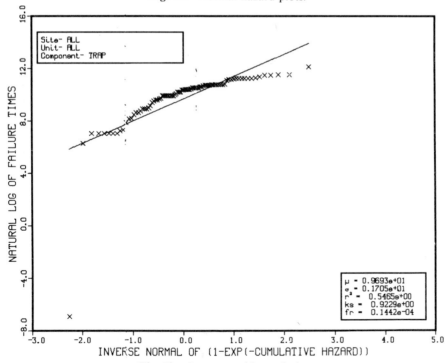

Fig. 12. Log-normal hazard plots.

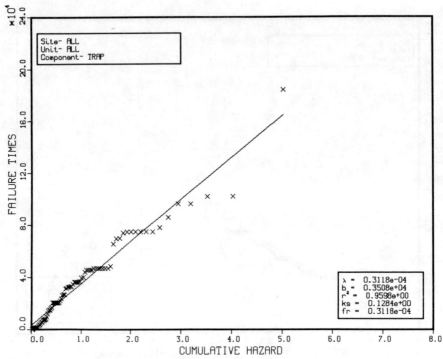

Fig. 13. Exponential hazard plots.

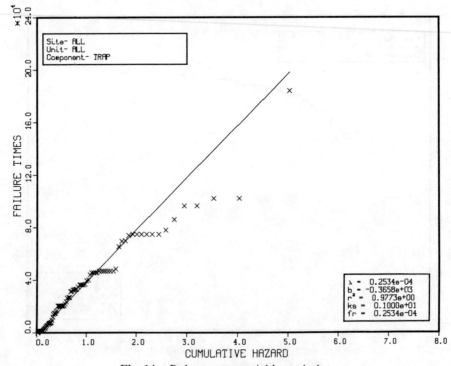

Fig. 14. Robust exponential hazard plots.

Figure 7 illustrates the trends analysis histograph for the failure cause. This relatively simple plot provides the user with a visual portrayal of the distribution of failure causes. A similar plot for failure modes is also available but not shown.

Figure 8 illustrates CREST's total-time-on-test (TTOT) plot. For each failure in a data set composed of ordered failure data, a failure fraction and TTOT fraction are calculated. The former is simply the ratio of the rank of each failure in the ordering to the total number of failures. The TTOT fraction for a particular failure is the ratio of the sum of all lifetimes with ranks up to and including the rank of the failure of interest to the sum of all lifetimes in the data set. As can be seen, the last failure will have values of 1·0 for both fractions and will lie on the 45° line that bisects the graphical display. By definition, the plot assumes that the origin is also a member of the set of plotted points. By sequentially connecting all of the points, a pattern of data can be viewed in relation to the 45° line. If the pattern crosses the 45° line at other than the two extreme points, the failure rate is exhibiting an exponential tendency with respect to time. If all non-extreme points lie either entirely above or below the 45° line, an increasing or decreasing failure tendency, respectively, is indicated. This information is useful to analysts who acknowledge a change of the failure rate with time, and require information on how it may change.

Figures 9–13 illustrate hazard plots for each of the five distributions offered in the hazard function section of CREST. The abscissa and ordinate variables are characteristic of functions of the cumulative hazard, and functions of time which effectively linearize a chosen distribution of interest. For example, the hazard function for the Weibull distribution can be linearized if logarithms of both the cumulative hazard and time are assumed. Each plot displays the respective calculated distribution parameters (the first two entries in the box in the lower right-hand side of the figure) and provides an associated regression coefficient that indicates the percentage of variation in the data explained by the line that has been fitted to the data. Although this measure gives an indication of how well the regression line fits the data, it cannot be used solely to compare fits from various distributions. To make such a comparison, CREST calculates a Kolmogorov–Smirnov (KS) statistic.[17] This statistic compares the maximum deviation between the PDF formed by the data and a theoretical PDF. Typically, distributions with small KS statistics (near zero) tend to give the better fit to a particular data set. Lastly, a failure rate based on both the distribution chosen and the calculated distribution parameters is provided.

Figure 14 illustrates a similar plot to those provided in Figs 9–13, with the exception that the plot is for the robust version of the data. A comparison of the plots provided in Fig. 13 (exponential hazard plots) and Fig. 14 (robust exponential hazard plots) will reveal the same data but with two different regression lines. It can be seen that for the last three to four data points the robust technique has minimized their influence on the calculation of the best-fit line. Thus, if the last three to four points are indeed outliers, the robust estimate of the failure rate may be more representative of the population. Robust versions of all five distributions are available in CREST.

The CREST package provides the CREDO user with a statistics tool that allows significant flexibility in analyzing failure data. Future efforts planned for CREST are the inclusion of other PDFs.

7.8 CREDO DEVELOPMENT EXPERIENCE

There are a number of approaches that may be used in creating new data bases. One such approach is the collection of information only on those components which have been failed. Another approach is the continuous collection of data on a whole population of components (both failed and unfailed) of interest. For the former approach, the number of components on which data are collected goes to completeness over a period of time, because eventually every component type is of interest. This approach has the advantage of requiring fewer resources initially, as data are collected only once on specific items of interest (items which have a history of failure). Historical data are acquired at whatever time a decision is made to examine a specific type of equipment. Typically, at that time, teams of specialists descend on a facility to collect and record data. These data are based on facility operating files. Subsequent operation of the component is usually not followed. A disadvantage of this approach is that a good perspective and accounting of a population of data is usually not achieved early in the data collection effort. Much tends to be known about the failed portion of the population, and relatively little is known about the non-failed portion.

The development of the CREDO system focuses on the latter approach, mentioned above. Each component is pedigreed at the time it is decided that the operational characteristics of the components in a system or facility are to be tracked (preferably before initial operation). Whereas typically more resources are required at the time of data base formation, to tabulate all of the engineering and operating records of the component, this approach has the advantage of containing the operational characteristics of a wide variety of component types. Component, system and facility performance characteristics are then followed throughout the facility lifetime.

The architecture, or structure, of the CREDO system was developed to allow for a high degree of flexibility during search efforts. Event, engineering or operating information can be ordered, or ranked, according to any input keyword. In addition, searches can be conducted based on constraints imposed by multiple keywords (12–15 can be handled with ease). Flexibility in search capabilities provides the user with a powerful tool with which to examine and investigate the data base contents.

The development of the CREDO system emphasized the ability to generate quantifiable criteria from the data base contents. Numerical measures related to a component's reliability, availability or maintainability can aid in identifying those components whose poor performance has the most adverse impact on the successful achievement of system mission. For example, the performance of one type of component (e.g. valves) can be compared against another (e.g. monitors), and these can be compared against the entire system. That is, critical items lists can be developed. One of the specialized software programs that has been developed for

CREDO analyses is a computer program entitled 'CRITTER'. It provides a list of critical items from specified searches of the entire data base. In general, overall trends and characteristics of a variety of equipment types can be more easily deduced using this program. Analyses of system performance are therefore possible when data are recorded for the whole equipment population. This approach has been proven successful and will not change in subsequent CREDO data collection activities.

The development of quantitative methods for data analyses came about rather naturally within CREDO. Once data management capabilities were identified, efforts focused on the development of output that were basic to RAM analyses, i.e. exponentially based failure rates, mean-time-to-repair based on a log-normal distribution, etc. After a short while, the sophistication of information that was requested increased. This led to the development of CREST and its alternatives to the exponentially based failure rates. The development of the 'CRITTER' program indicates the latest analysis tool developed by CREDO. Experience has shown that, in general, a high degree of methodological sophistication is not necessary during early development efforts. Rather, such sophistication will result from a conscientious effort on the part of the development staff to meet the data request needs of the users of the data base.

The scope, bounds and interfaces of the CREDO data collection efforts were carefully defined once it was decided to collect data on the whole component population. These definitions emerged from the relatively detailed front-end analysis that was carried out before the actual development of the CREDO system. Some of the general areas where a feasibility study such as this could be highly beneficial are the identification of (a) potential users of the system, (b) their data/information needs, (c) potential data sources, (d) the types of relevant analyses that are of interest, and (e) associated research areas.

The experience gained through the involvement of a number of experts from areas that overlap with, or are tangential to a data base effort, was highly beneficial to CREDO. Information and suggestions provided by the CSC allowed the CREDO system to develop with a sensitivity toward user needs. In addition, the CSC provided informal promotion of the CREDO system to users, via 'word of mouth'.

Lastly, the moral support and belief of a strong program champion is one of the primary reasons for the longevity and scope of the current system.

7.9 ACHIEVEMENTS AND FUTURE DIRECTIONS OF CREDO

The CREDO system is currently the world's largest source of liquid metal component RAM data from operating facilities. Its successful compilation of both US and Japanese data points toward a potentially much broader system that can function as an international center for the management of advanced reactor system and component data from all over the world. CREDO's generic structure, and its generic component and system/subsystem taxonomies, allows it to be a potentially effective source of information for non-liquid metal analyses and a potentially effective management system for nuclear as well as non-nuclear component data.

During the course of CREDO development, the requests for CREDO data, information and analyses have gradually increased in both number and complexity. Early requests were limited by a relatively small and volatile data population. As a result, few data requests could be processed, and most that were processed provided qualitative input to the requesting users. As the data population of components became more complete, quantitative estimates of RAM metrics were also requested and provided. The following are typical studies of the current data base which have resulted from formal user requests: assessments of flow and control systems; failures which have resulted in sodium fires; evaluations of the root cause of leakages in pumps and valves; the causes of motor failures; the effect on mechanical components of exposure to liquid sodium; evaluations of the performance of sensors for leaks, levels, pressure, temperature and neutron flux; and the evaluation of the performance of heat exchangers and decay heat removal systems. Data have been provided for such diverse applications as strategic petroleum reserves storage in salt mines, conventional coal-fired electricity generating stations, nuclear fusion reactor design, space nuclear reactors and advanced terrestrial nuclear reactor systems. To date, over 40 major (but informal, i.e. not generally published in the open literature) CREDO system assessments have been conducted. Numerous responses have been made to smaller, specific requests. It should be noted that these requests for data, information and analyses have been received without formal publicity. It is expected that the number and complexity of the data requests will increase greatly once such 'advertising' is initiated.

As historical data collection activities come to a close (during 1988), a new aim of applying the system to more specific analyses is being pursued. Specifically, this evolving activity of CREDO consists of analyses of the data already on hand to improve the design of subsequent liquid metal systems, e.g. inherently safe nuclear reactor designs, reactors in space, etc. RAM assessments of plant operation data are performed for this purpose. These assessments are systematic evaluations of facility performance and, in effect, accelerate the learning process so that lessons learned from operations of present systems can be incorporated more rapidly into follow-on designs. Studies have been completed on the physics of valve failure,[2] a comparison of valve reliabilities in sodium vs water environments,[4] plant maintainability critical items,[5] plant reliability critical items,[6] and plant availability critical items.[7,8] Extensive RAM evaluations of CREDO data have effectively been initiated and, with continued support, will increase.

After approximately 10 years of operation (12 years from inception), the CREDO system has become a valuable source of liquid metal component operating experience for both the USA and Japan. Its primary short-term applications will be in the areas of support for US advanced nuclear reactor concept designs and PRAs, and Japanese probabilistic risk assessment of the MONJU liquid metal breeder reactor. There is also interest in the advancement of RAM methodologies through basic research and the broadening of the scope of CREDO to encompass a 'systems perspective', i.e. a perspective that includes the human as a dynamic system element.

The CREDO system has experienced a significant longevity (in terms of data base lifetimes) because of the large number of dedicated individuals who have been associated with the program over the years. Their efforts have resulted in a valuable asset for both the USA and Japan.

For further information, please contact:

M. S. Smith, Manager,
The Centralized Reliability Data Organization,
The Oak Ridge National Laboratory,
PO Box 2008,
Oak Ridge, TN 37831-6360,
USA

Telephone: (615)-574-5488, (FTS)-624-5488
Telefax: (615)-576-6169

ACKNOWLEDGEMENTS

This work was sponsored by the US Department of Energy, Office of Technology Support Programs, and Japan's Power Reactor and Nuclear Fuel Development Corporation, and was prepared by the Oak Ridge National Laboratory, Oak Ridge, TN 37831, operated by Martin Marietta Energy Systems, Inc., for the US Department of Energy under Contract DEAC05-840R21400.

REFERENCES

1. Gavigan, F. X. & Griffith, J. D., The application of probabilistic methods to safety R&D and design choices. In *Nuclear Systems Reliability Engineering and Risk Assessment*. Society for Industrial and Applied Mathematics, Philadelphia, PA, 1977, pp. 22–41.
2. Bott, T. F. & Haas, P. M., Initial data collection efforts of CREDO: sodium valve failures, 5th Symp. on Reliability Technol., April 1978, University of Bradford, Bradford, UK, NCSR-R20, 1978.
3. Bott, T. F., Haas, P. M. & Manning, J. J., Sodium component reliability data collection at CREDO. *Trans. Am. Nucl. Soc. 25th Annual Meeting*, 3–7 June 1979, Atlanta, GA, Vol. 32, TANSAO 32 1-832, 1979.
4. Painter, S. L., Knee, H. E. & Humphrys, B. L., CREDO data analysis: a comparison of liquid metal and water valve reliabilities. *Proc. Int. Conf. Nuclear Power Plant Aging, Availability Factor and Reliability Analysis*, San Diego, CA, 8–12 July 1985.
5. Haire, M. J., Knee, H. E., Manning, J. J., Manneschmidt, J. F. & Setoguchi, K., An examination of maintenance activities in LMR facilities: an analysis by the Centralized Reliability Data Organization (CREDO). To be presented and published in *Proc. Reliability '87 Conf.*, Vol. 2, Birmingham, UK, 14–16 April 1987, pp. SC/1/1–10.
6. Humphrys, B. L., Haire, M. J., Manning, J. J., Manneschmidt, J. F. & Setoguchi, K., CREDO data analysis: an examination of reliability critical items. *Int. Conf. Fast Breeder Systems*, Vol. 1, Pasco, WA, 13–17 September 1987, pp. 3.6–11.
7. Koger, K. H., Haire, M. J., Humphrys, B. L., Manneschmidt, J. F., Setoguchi, K. & Nakai, R., Assessment of critical component unavailability in liquid metal reactors. *Proc. Am. Nucl. Soc. Summer Meeting*, 12–16 June 1988, San Diego, CA.

8. Koger, K. H., Haire, M. J., Humphrys, B. L., Manneschmidt, J. F., Setoguchi, K. & Nakai, R., The Centralized Reliability Data Organization (CREDO) assessment of critical component unavailability in liquid metal reactors. *Nucl. Technol.*, **85** (1989) 251.

9. Trauger, D. B. & White, J. D., Safety-related topics from the Nuclear Power Options Viability Study. *Nucl. Safety J.*, **27**(4) (1986) 467–75.

10. Catron, J., New interest in passive reactor designs. *EPRI J.*, **14**(3) (1989).

11. Musicki, Z. & Maynard, C. W., The organization and collection of systems data in fusion. In *Proc. 5th EuReDatA Conf.*, Heidelberg, 9–11 April 1986, *Reliability Data Collection and Use in Risk and Availability Assessments*, ed. H. J. Wingender. Springer-Verlag, Berlin, 1986, pp. 90–9.

12. Manning, J. J., Knee, H. E., Seagle, P. F., Allen, M. L., Anderson, M. L., Humphrys, B. L. & Painter, S. L., *CREDO Guide for Completing Input Forms*. ORNL/TM-9892, 1986.

13. Brooks, A. A., Oak Ridge Hierarchical Information System (ORCHIS) status report—July 1973. ORNL-4929, 1974.

14. Honeck, H. C., *The JOSHUA System*. E. I. DuPont de Nemoirs & Co., Savannah River Laboratory, DP-1380, 1975.

15. Barlow, R. E. & Campo, R., Total time on test processes and applications to failure data analysis. In *Reliability and Fault Tree Analysis—Theoretical and Applied Aspects of System Reliability and Safety Assessment*, ed. R. E. Barlow, J. B. Fussell & N. D. Singpurwalla. Society for Industrial and Applied Mathematics, Philadelphia, PA, 1975, pp. 451–81.

16. Nelson, W., Hazard plotting for incomplete failure data. *J. Quality Technol.*, **1**(1) (1969) 27–52.

17. Phillips, D. T., Applied goodness of fit testing. Publ. 1 in Monograph Ser. AIIE-OR-72-1. Operations Research Division, American Institute of Industrial Engineers, Norcross, GA, 1972.

8

The Fabrication Reliability Data Analysis System DANTE-QC1

Hiroshi Mizuta

National Space Development Agency of Japan,
2-4-1, Hamamatu-cho, Minato-ku, Tokyo 105, Japan

&

K. Takahasi, K. Kamimura, T. Yamaguchi, S. Masuda

Plutonium Fuel Division, Tokai Works,
Power Reactor and Nuclear Fuel Development Corporation,
Tokai-mura, Ibariki-ken 319-11, Japan

8.1 INTRODUCTION

The quality control method in use at present is to inspect the interim product to determine the standard of the product, and if an inferior product is found the process is corrected or the product is batch-rejected. The cause of the inferior product is then sought. However, with this method action is taken after finding the inferior product, so both the cost of correction and the loss of the batch increase the overall cost.

A more sophisticated quality control system is required to cut costs of production and improve quality of mixed oxide fuels. This new system extends the quality control from the characteristics of product to the process conditions at the time of fabrication to find the abnormal condition of the process. To establish this system, the abnormal real time, both of the interim product and of the process, must be shown in graphical form to the operator by the data base, thus permitting the optimum quality control to be achieved.

The Power Reactor and Nuclear Fuel Development Corporation (PNC) has produced several types of mixed oxide (MOX) fuels which have been used for the Advanced Thermal Reactor, 'FUGEN', and the Experimental Fast Breeder Reactor, 'JOYO', in the PNC Plutonium Fabrication Facility (PPFF). As of December 1986, the accumulated production of MOX fuel is about 58 000 fuel pins. The PPFF production technique is so reliable that no failure of fuel pins has been found in FUGEN and JOYO. This is based on adequate process and quality control.

This fabrication knowledge must be integrated in the data base for higher-level quality control. This is the reason for the development of DANTE. DANTE (Data ANalysing Technology for Engineers) -QC1 is a data analysis system for nuclear fuels with a relational data base management system. The development of the system started on the PRIME550 in 1981 and was converted to FACOM M380R, with analysis and graphics functions, in 1984. The system was installed in the quality control process during 1984 and 1986.

This paper was arranged from the original Japanese DANTE-QC1.[1]

8.2 CONCEPT OF THE DANTE CODE SYSTEM

DANTE has three functional features: (1) full relational data base management system, (2) numerical calculation capability, and (3) advanced output graphics function.

The DANTE code system is divided into four subsystems and data bases, as shown in Fig. 1. The first is a data base management subsystem, the second is a graphics processing subsystem, the third is an analysis code management subsystem, and the fourth is a quality control subsystem.

The data base management subsystem consists of five modules: (1) the command processor, (2) the data dictionary, (3) the path finder, (4) the relational access manager, and (5) the file system and transaction manager, as shown in Fig. 2. A brief description of these modules follows.

8.2.1 The Command Processor

All commands to the DANTE code system are input using the DANTE query language, which is similar to the IBM SQL. The command processor interprets the received DANTE query language and changes the user's command to an internal command. A user of the DANTE code system can use two methods. One is to input

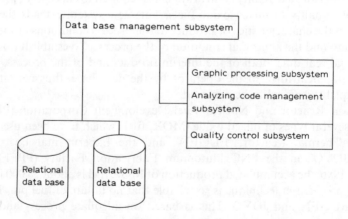

Fig. 1. Structure of the DANTE-QC1 code.

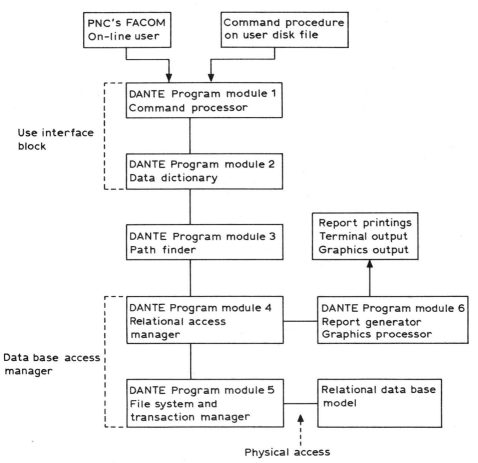

Fig. 2. Structure of the DANTE data base system.

the DANTE language directly from a terminal, and the other is to input from a previously written command file using the DANTE language.

8.2.2 The Data Dictionary

The data dictionary is a component which functions with the command processor. In the data dictionary, all tables, data fields, functions and access paths to the data base are described. The user is able to treat the data base by name and obtain information—data attributes, data headings and so on. The data dictionary is automatically maintained by the DANTE code system. Its information can be retrieved and modified using easy commands.

8.2.3 The Path Finder

The path finder is a component between the command processor and the relational access manager, which receives the user's requirements from the command processor and decides on an optimum access path in the DANTE system for accomplishing it.

8.2.4 The Relational Access Manager

The relational access manager is a component which actually reads records from the data base, relates them to other records and passes the results to the graphics processing subsystem. The relational access manager functions with the file system.

8.2.5 The File System

The file system is a component that interfaces with the data stored on the disk drives.

The graphics processing subsystem presents the results of a search and analysis as two-dimensional tables, or two-dimensional graphs, or scatter diagrams, or histograms on a colour graphics display.

The analysis code management subsystem creates input data from analysis codes, executes the analysis and stores the results on the data base.

The quality control subsystem loads inspection and process data from a process minicomputer, checks the status of the fabrication line using the control chart method and draws control charts.

8.3 DATA BASE CONFIGURATION

8.3.1 DANTE-QC1 Configuration Overview

DANTE-QC1 (called DANTE hereafter) is a program system which analyses the process conditions based on input questions, collects object data during a data base search based on these questions, performs the designated routine and displays the output in the selected format on the required terminal. This processed data is generally expressed in two-dimensional table format as this is the form most easily understood by the user.

A number of interrelated items must sometimes be processed simultaneously when data are used in table form. The system selects the necessary items from the various tables and processes them simultaneously. A system which offers this type of processing is generally called a relational data base management system.

DANTE performs the following internal processing:

(1) it analyses the meaning of the input sentence;
(2) it searches the data base;
(3) it performs computational processing according to the data obtained;
(4) it outputs the results to the selected device in the required format.

The user can obtain the following outputs from DANTE, as shown in Fig. 3.

(1) characters and numerical values can be printed out on a line printer in a designated format;

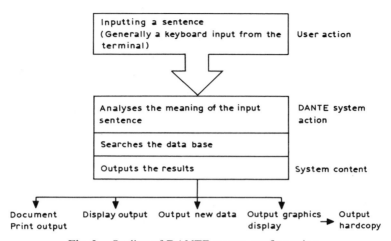

Fig. 3. Outline of DANTE system configuration.

(2) characters and numerical values can be printed out on a terminal in selected formats;

(3) input data items from other sources can be converted to disk files in selected formats;

(4) graphics output can be sent to a graphics display.

Several important terms are defined below before an overview of DANTE is given.

Table: A table is an elementary unit of the data base controlled by DANTE, and data are presented to the user in table format. DANTE controls a number of tables. The user can perform various operations, including addition, subtraction, multiplication and division on any data items in these tables.

Field: A field signifies an item contained in the table. Each field contains one or more items of data. The user supplies the name for each field and it is controlled by the designated field name.

Record: A record is a string of adjacent data items containing the actual data for one table. As a subordinate record is called a field, the number of data items in a record corresponds to the number of fields.

DANTE classifies the data into tables, fields and records as described above. A table refers to a two-dimensional table in which the fields are represented in units along the horizontal axis, and the records are represented in units along the vertical axis. This relationship is shown in Fig. 4.

Fields and records are both contained in one table, as shown in Fig. 4. The user sets the necessary search conditions for this table.

The relationships between tables, fields and records are shown below:

Field   Table

Record   Table

{Data | (Field Record) Table}

	Field A	Field B	Field C	Field D	Field E	Field F
Record	1	A	5·0	A X	100	1·5
	2	B	4·9	B X	164	−0·6
	3	C	3·2	A X	523	3·2
Record 4	4	D	3·8	C Y	365	−3·5
	5	E	6·2	D Y	12	6·4
	6	A	7·3	C Y	6	−0·1
	7	B	4·4	E Y	3625	−3·9
	8	E	2·1	B X	15	120·3
	9	D	0·5	C Y	3	4096·0

Fig. 4. Table outline.

In summary, each data item in a table is identified by a record and a field (3·8 is record 4 in field C in Fig. 4). It is very important to understand the concept of records and fields when using DANTE. The structure of DANTE is shown in Fig. 5.

DANTE is a data base management system that operates in the format of tables as shown above. The user must have the following information to operate the system:

(1) What is the format of the desired table? The name of the field or the format of the stored table must be known.
(2) The table must be registered in the system using the DANTE CREATE command.
(3) The data must be registered in the table using the DANTE LOAD command.
(4) The table must be processed using the DANTE LIST and PILOT commands.

8.3.2 General Concept of a Relational Data Base

Section 8.3.1 shows DANTE to be a table-operated system. The fields and records in these tables are searched after the necessary conditions are applied. Relational data bases are explained in detail as they relate to DANTE.

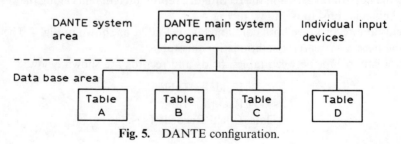

Fig. 5. DANTE configuration.

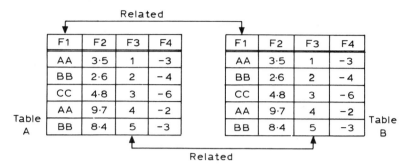

F1	F2	F3	F4
AA	3·5	1	−3
BB	2·6	2	−4
CC	4·8	3	−6
AA	9·7	4	−2
BB	8·4	5	−3

Fig. 6. Concept of relational fields.

Definition of a relational data base: A relational data base is a system for making arbitrary selections between individual fields and records of data stored in an arbitrary table format and computing the results. The results can immediately be obtained in a numerical table or graphical form.

The relation between two or more tables is indicated by the same field name where the data are fundamentally the same (see Fig. 6). Such fields are called relational fields, and the user can employ a relational field to connect two or more tables containing the same data into one table. Thus, a relational field connects two or more tables. The relationship described above is shown in Fig. 7.

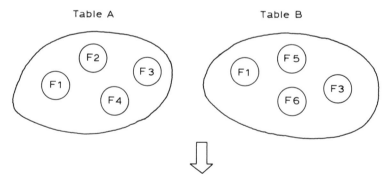

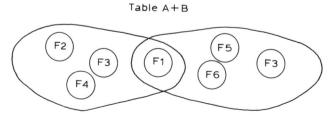

Fig. 7. Relational operation.

Table A+B

F1	F2	F3	F4	F5	F6
AA	3·5	1	-3	-2·5	1
BB	2·6	2	-4	6·4	3
CC	4·8	3	-6	3·8	-5
AA	9·7	4	-2	-4·6	6
BB	8·4	5	-3	-3·0	7

Fig. 8. Example concept of relational fields combining Tables A and B with relation F1.

A relational operation connects two or more tables, which can then be used as one table, as shown in Fig. 7. The result of combining Tables A and B with relational operation F1 is shown in Fig. 8.

Explanation of the relational operation shown above: To obtain a single table such as that shown in Fig. 8 with the process shown in Fig. 7 in DANTE, it is only necessary to designate the field that is common between the tables. This field is called the common field. Moreover, a more complex relationship can be designated with DANTE as shown below, so that connections which are stronger than simple table-to-table connections are possible:

(1) the equation connecting a field can be used in addition to the name of the field when designating a field;
(2) the space between the top and bottom of the spacing between selected records can be designated to connect tables;
(3) the fields of other tables can be used as conditions for connecting tables.

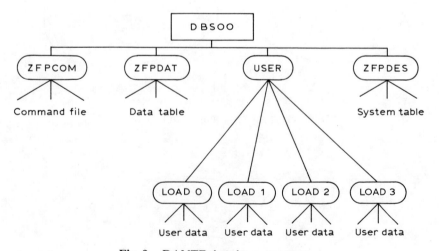

Fig. 9. DANTE data base structure.

8.3.3 Data Base Structure

Data set attributes of the DANTE M380R OSIV/MSP E20 system are shown here. The data base tree structure of DANTE is shown in Fig. 9. Data base DBS00 is used as an example. DBS00, ZFPCOM, ZFPDAT, USER, ZFPDES, LOAD0,... are system files called directories. The data base is managed in a tree structure under these system files. These files are defined as a data set under OSIV/MSP, and some rules apply to this data set.

The following format for the data set name is a necessary part of the data set command rules:

$$DSN = USER\ ID.PATH\ NAME$$

This path name is a combination of individual directory names along the tree structure path and the object data set name shown in Fig. 9. For example, if the user called LOAD0 wants to copy the data from MT, etc., to DANTE as his object data set, it is necessary to name the data set as follows:

$$DSN = USER\ ID.DBS00.USER.LOAD0.DATA\ SET\ NAME$$
$$(FIXED)$$

DANTE controls all the data in these structures, as described above.

8.3.3.1 Necessary System Data Set
DANTE requires the following data sets at the time of execution.

(1) Root directory file. This is the centre of the directory of the data base.

Example: DSN = P2515.DBS00

(2) Global command file directory. This is a directory file for storing the common data base command file (command procedure).

Example: DSN = P2515.DBS00.ZFPCOM

(3) Data table file. This is a directory table file to control the data set registered as the relational data table.

Example: DSN = P2515.DBS00.ZFPDAT

(4) User directory management file. This is a directory file that controls the directory files of the user.

Example: DSN = P2515.DSB00.USER

(5) User directory. This is the user ID (identification) used by DANTE to store and manage the user fixed commands and data.

Example: DSN = P2515.DBS00.USER.LOAD0

This example shows a user directory called LOAD0.

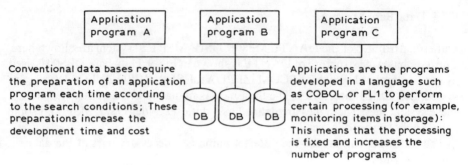

Fig. 10.   Format of conventional data base.

(6) System table. This is the directory file which stores and manages the data used by DANTE.

Example: DSN = P2515.DBS00.ZFPDES

The data sets described above are the basic data sets necessary for the execution of DANTE. DANTE can function after these data sets are defined, and creates or deletes such data sets.

8.3.4 Differences between Conventional Data Bases and DANTE

These differences are as follows:

(1)   an application program is not necessary;
(2)   development time is short (to configure the data base);
(3)   search conditions can be freely designated.

The format of a conventional data base is as shown in Fig. 10.

8.4 PROCESSING FUNCTION

8.4.1 Input Sentence Presentation

The grammar of the language for communication with DANTE will now be explained. The definitions of terms such as verbs and nouns used here are slightly different from those used in normal language theory.

8.4.1.1 Language Theory and Basic Grammar
The input sentences used to communicate with DANTE are composed of the following types of words:

(1)   verb: commands to DANTE (commands and auxiliary verbs);
(2)   noun: the object of commands to DANTE;
(3)   keyword/parameter: these relate and modify verbs and nouns.

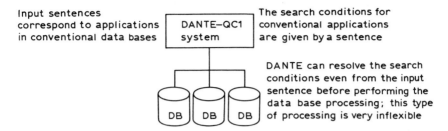

Input sentences correspond to applications in conventional data bases | DANTE–QC1 system | The search conditions for conventional applications are given by a sentence

DANTE can resolve the search conditions even from the input sentence before performing the data base processing; this type of processing is very inflexible

Fig. 11.   Format of DANTE.

The conversation with DANTE uses descriptions in sentence form that combine the verbs, nouns and keyword parameters described below. Verbs and nouns are treated by DANTE, as shown in Fig. 11. Nearly all the nouns used in the DANTE conversational language are the names of tables and fields defined by the user, as shown in Fig. 12.

The sentences in DANTE conversational language have the structure shown in Fig. 13, in which the words have the following functions:

command verb: displays the processing for DANTE;
object case clause: clause that presents the search data;
condition clause: clause regulating the search conditions.

Those words used in conversing with DANTE that correspond to individual items in Fig. 13 are cited below.

Command verb
(1)   LIST: indicates the search results on a numerical output
         display.   ⟨verb⟩
(2)   PLOT: indicates the search results on a graphics output display.   ⟨verb⟩
(3)   CREATE: creates a new table.   ⟨verb⟩
(4)   LOAD: loads basic data to a table.   ⟨verb⟩
(5)   Other.

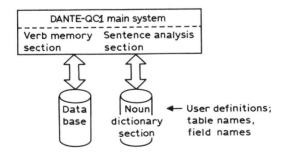

Fig. 12.   Treatment of nouns and verbs by DANTE.

Fig. 13.   Input sentence structure of DANTE.

Object case clause
(1)   Table name.   ⟨noun⟩
(2)   FIELDS: designates the field that is the object of the search. ⟨keyword⟩
(3)   X: designates the field that contains the *X*-axis value.   ⟨keyword⟩
(4)   Y: designates the field that contains the *Y*-axis value.   ⟨keyword⟩

Conditional clause
(1)   FROM: designates the first search object record.   ⟨keyword⟩
(2)   TO: designates the last search object record.   ⟨keyword⟩
(3)   FOR: designates the logical description for the search.   ⟨keyword⟩
(4)   JOIN: designates the treatment which combines data by lines. ⟨keyword⟩
(5)   Others.

The conversation with DANTE (input sentence) is composed of commands, object case clauses and conditional clauses as described above. Each word that is a structure element is classified as a verb, noun, keyword or parameter.

The fundamental grammar of DANTE conversational language is summarized below.

(1)   Command sentences all begin with a verb command.
(2)   Command sentence must include an object case clause.
(3)   Conditional clauses may be added as necessary.

Accordingly, the simplest commands have the form indicated in Fig. 14.

8.4.1.2 Command Expression
Before the user can make an enquiry of DANTE regarding a problem that is under consideration, the problem must first be put into DANTE conversational language. This is the single most important element in DANTE. To clarify the command expression, an example showing the correspondence between the problem description in natural language and the description in DANTE conversational language is given below with an explanation.

(1)   Problem description in natural language
The search takes fields FM2¥LP, FM2¥BET and FM2LPD from table FM2SO, and sums FM2¥PU02 and FM2¥GAS from table FM2¥BU. This search is performed on records 10–40.

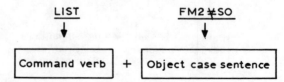

Fig. 14.   Simplest example of DANTE input command.

(2) Phrase analysis
>   The search fields are (FM2¥PU02 + FM2¥LP) in table FM2¥BU and
>   FM2LP, FM2¥SSS, FM2¥LPD in table FM2¥SO. The conditions require
>   that 31 items from records 10 to 40 be processed.

From (2) above it can be seen that the problem sentence has two meanings
(signals). One is the field definition as the search object ((fields FM2¥LP,
FM2¥BET, FM2¥LPD, (FM2¥PU02 + FM2¥GAS) are defined as the search
object)) and the other is the record definition as a search condition (the search is
from record number 10 to record number 40). This sentence takes the form of two
definitions in DANTE, as follows:

Field definition: FM2¥LP, FM2¥SSS, FM2¥LPD,
                (FM2¥PU02 + FM2¥GAS)
Record definition: FROM 10 TO 40

The above problem becomes a search of the two tables FM2¥SO and FM2¥BU.
DANTE distinguishes between them by modifying the corresponding table name
with a period '.' immediately after the field name. Therefore, when the above natural
language description corresponds to DANTE conversational language, the field
name to be created as the search object becomes the following:

Fields FM2¥LP, FM2¥BET, FM2¥LPD in table FM2¥SO and
the sum of fields FM2¥PU02, FM2¥GAS in table FM2¥BU

⇒ FM2¥SO.FM2¥LP, FM2¥SO.FM2¥BET, FM2¥SO.FM2¥LPD,
  (FM2¥BU.FM2¥PU02 + FM2¥BU.FM2¥GAS)

By describing the above object field name as a parameter corresponding to the field
keyword, the object case clause (FIELDS clause) to DANTE can be completed as
follows:

FIELDS FM2¥SO.FM2¥LP, FM2¥SO.FM2¥BET, FM2¥SO.FM2¥LPD,
  (FM2¥BU.FM2¥PU02 + FM2¥BU.FM2¥GAS)

Moreover, a description of this problem can be easily created as a conditional clause
in DANTE conversational language:

Search required from record 10 to record 40

⇒ FROM 10 TO 40—condition clause to be created
              (record number condition)

8.4.1.3 DANTE Input Sentence
The above description of the problem in natural language can be replaced in
DANTE as follows:

Command verb
  LIST

Table A

	F1	F2	F3
1			
2			
3			
4			
5			
6			
7			
8			
9			

Table B

	F4	F5
1		
2		
3		
4		
5		
6		
7		
8		
9		
10		
11		
12		
13		
14		
15		

Fig. 15. Tables with different record conditions.

Object case clause
FIELDS FM2¥SO.FM2¥LP, FU2¥SO.FM2¥BET, FM2¥LPD,
(FM2¥BU.FM2¥PU02 + FN2¥BU.FM2¥GAS)

Condition clause
FROM 10 TO 40

By examining the input condition above, it can be seen that the input sentence described in natural language indirectly makes the assumption that tables FM2¥SO, FM2¥BU have a one-to-one correspondence to the records. If FM2¥SO and FM2¥BO include records of different items, natural word descriptions such as 'field of FM2¥SO' and 'field of FM2FM2¥BU' cannot be used. This state is shown in Fig. 15.

8.4.2 Search

Searching is the main function of DANTE. The user can use all of the functions listed below with the search function of DANTE.

(1) Parameter survey search. Data from among those that have been collected and registered that match special criteria are assembled and displayed in graphical or list format.

(2) Analysis processing. Statistical values such as maximum, minimum and standard deviation are obtained for the collected data and an estimation is performed on the mother group.

(3) Data making process. Data from among those that have been collected and registered that match special criteria are collected and displayed in graphical

LIST	Keyword

Fig. 16. LIST command format.

or list format and an input file is made with other codes. Inverse processing can also be performed.

The search commands for DANTE are used for the above purposes. The processing commands used for search are LIST and PLOT. LIST outputs the process data in character format and PLOT displays them graphically.

8.4.2.1 Search Command
The search command is used to analyse the search processing function.

(1) LIST command. The format of the LIST command is shown in Fig. 16. The individual keywords are used as follows:

(1) TO: designates the last record displayed.
(2) BY: designates an incremental increase in the search record.
(3) FIELDS: designates the field to be displayed.
(4) FORMAT: designates the format when displaying a record.
(5) NO HEADING: designates no display table.
(6) FOR: designates the search conditions.
(7) GROUP: designates the grouping key of the record.
(8) LENGTH: designates the maximum output length.
(9) ORDER: designates sort key for display record.
(10) LINES: designates maximum line.

Procedures for the list command are accomplished by using the above keywords.

(2) PLOT command. The format of the PLOT command is shown in Fig. 17.

8.4.3 Basic Manipulation

The basic manipulations of DANTE are described in general below:

(1) table monitoring;
(2) field monitoring;
(3) select field monitoring;
(4) select field monitoring with conditions;
(5) computational processing for field data;

PLOT	Keyword

Fig. 17. PLOT command format.

(6)   format conversion for field data;
(7)   relational processing for field data (field relational);
(8)   relational processing of field data (line relational);
(9)   print output editing (includes screen output);
(10) field data graphics processing;
(11) general data set creation (other code interfaces);
(12) general data set load (other code interfaces).

8.5 APPLICATION OF DANTE FOR PIE DATA ANALYSIS

In this section the application of DANTE is described. A large amount of post-irradiation examination (PIE) data are obtained with JOYO fuel. Among these data, fission gas release data are studied using DANTE. We examine the relationship between fission gas release rate and fabrication characteristics such as plutonium homogeneity and grain size. Figure 18 shows fission gas release rate as a function of linear heat rate, with burn-up as a variable. The data of fission gas release rate were

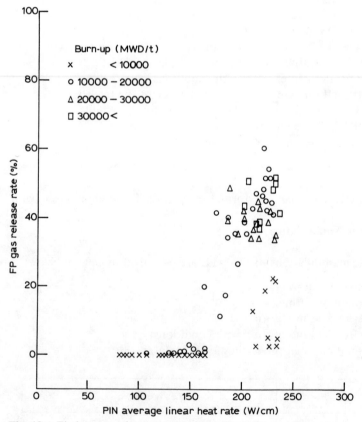

Fig. 18.   Fission gas release rate as a function of linear heat rate.

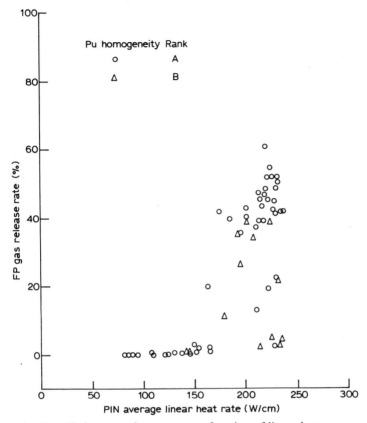

Fig. 19.   Fission gas release rate as a function of linear heat rate.

obtained by pin puncture test after irradiation in JOYO. It seems that fission gas
release has a threshold of linear heat rate at about 170 W/cm, and fission gas release
becomes noticeable for the pellet with burn-up of over 10 000 MWD/t. As shown in
Fig. 17, the data of fission gas release rate with burn-up over 10 000 MWD/t are
scattered over a wide range. To clarify the cause of this wide scatter, we investigated
the influence of plutonium homogeneity and grain size on fission gas release rate
using DANTE.

Figure 19 shows fission gas release rate as a function of linear heat rate, with
plutonium homogeneity as a variable. A plutonium homogeneity is defined as three
ranks (A, B and C) from alpha-autoradiographs. Rank A, B and C fuel pellets have a
U-spot of 0–50, 50–200 and >200 μm in diameter, respectively (a U-spot is a
uranium-rich region in fuel pellets). As shown in Fig. 19, no significant difference
between ranks A and B is observed. To reject the effect of burn-up on fission gas
release, fission gas release rate with burn-up range from 10 000 to 20 000 MWD/t is
plotted vs linear heat rate, and is shown in Fig. 20. It is seen that the plutonium
homogeneity has no significant influence on fission gas release rate within the region
of rank A and B U-spot size.

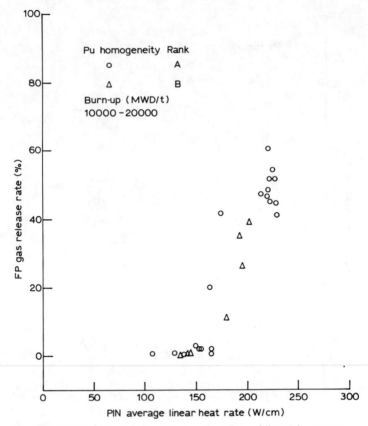

Fig. 20.   Fission gas release rate as a function of linear heat rate.

Influence of the grain size of the fuel matrix on the fission gas release is also investigated. Figures 21 and 22 show fission gas release behaviour as a function of grain size (which is determined from metallography). In Fig. 21 all data available are plotted and in Fig. 22 the data limited to burn-up of 20 000–30 000 MWD/t are plotted. In both figures, no significant difference is observed.

Recently, Kamimura *et al.*[2] reported that the fission gas release rate of the MOX fuel for the PNC thermal reactor is similar to that of UO_2 fuels, and the fission gas release rate of co-converted fuels is smaller than that of the mechanically blended fuels, as shown in Fig. 23. These results were obtained from the IFA-529 irradiation test data for a thermal reactor to examine a difference in fission gas release behaviour. The IFA-529 experiment was carried out as a part of joint research program between PNC and Japan Atomic Energy Research Institute (JAERI) with the participation of the OECD Halden Reactor Project.

An important point is that the irradiation temperatures of thermal reactor fuels are considerably lower than those of FBR fuels. We think that in this region of thermal reactor fuel temperature fission gas release rate is sensitive to the plutonium homogeneity of MOX fuels. We will analyse the IFA-529 quality control data in

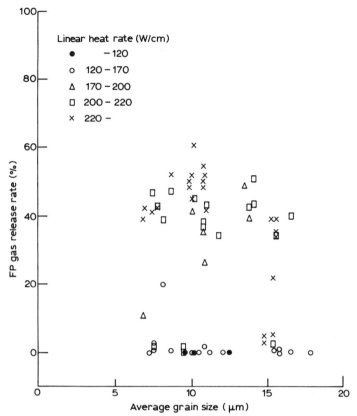

Fig. 21. Fission gas release rate as a function of fuel grain size.

more detail. The use of DANTE for analysis of a great amount of data is expected to be a very powerful tool.

8.6 FUTURE DIRECTIONS

8.6.1 Registered Data Completion

At present, fuel inspection data, production processing data and a portion of the post-irradiation examination (PIE) data of JOYO MK-II are registered in DANTE. Fuel material data, production processing data and inspection data for FUGEN, from first charge fuel production to fuel now in production, will be registered in DANTE.

8.6.2 Expanding the Analysis Function

(1)   The dispersive analysis function will be expanded to analyse experimental production data based on the experimental planning method.

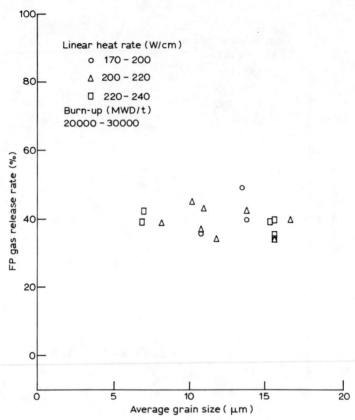

Fig. 22. Fission gas release rate as a function of grain size.

(2) Three-dimensional graphics output will be provided for the analysed results, using correlation analysis between three variables.

(3) Data exchange with other systems. Provisions will be made for data exchange (data file transmission) with other systems (DANTE-II,[3] data collection systems, JOYO Fuel DBS, etc.). In addition, an attempt will be made to port the access, search and output of analysed results from F9450-II to DANTE- QC1.

(4) Use of Japanese. Effort will be expended to make use of Japanese characters.

(5) Process monitoring system development. A process monitoring system using DANTE is under development as the advanced quality control system called QUEEN4,5. The QUEEN (QUality Evaluation and ENhancement aided sys-system is a quality control and data management system which is used for the MOX fuel fabrication line. It is based on the relational data base in DANTE. A user can obtain information on the production process using QUEEN. Figure 24 shows a summary view of QUEEN, where VSAM is a Virtual Sequential Access Method compatible with IBM VSAM system, and RJE is a Remote Job Entry system from the Plutonium Fuel Fabrication Facility to the computer centre. The inspection and process data are gathered by minicomputer. The

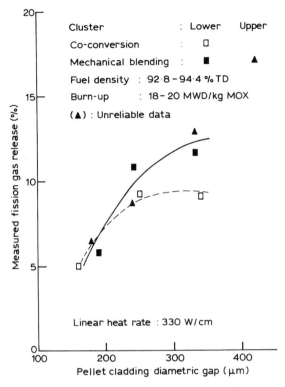

Fig. 23. Fission gas release as a function of pellet to cladding diametric gap (μm).

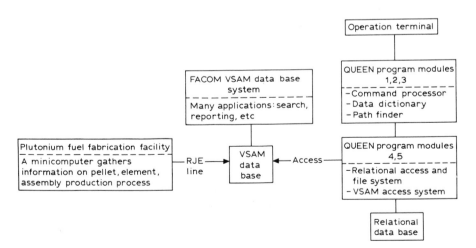

Fig. 24. Structure of the QUEEN system.

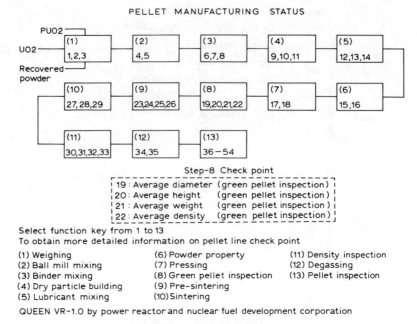

Fig. 25.   A sample output of pellet fabrication line status.

data consist of three groups corresponding to pellet, fuel element and fuel assembly. These data are then transmitted to the FACOM computer, which is compatible with the IBM 309X. QUEEN accesses the data from the VSAM data base and stores the data as proper relational data base tables. QUEEN has three functional features for checking the status of fabrication line, including the capability to monitor the control state of each process, data query and

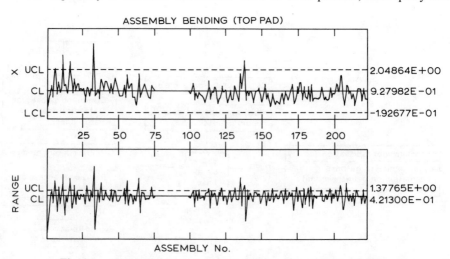

Fig. 26.   A sample output of control chart of assembly process.

analysis capability, and graphics output capability. The data query and graphics output capabilities are exactly the same as those of the DANTE system. A sample output for pellet fabrication line status is shown in Fig. 25, and a sample output of the control chart for an assembly process is shown in Fig. 26.

REFERENCES

1. Takahashi, K., Yamaguchi, T., Asahara, S. & Masuda, S., DANTE-QC1. PNC-SN8430-86-12, 1986, p. 3.
2. Kamimura, K., Kaneda, K. & Yokouchi, Y., The fission gas release rate of the MOX fuel for thermal reactor of PNC. *Nucl. Engng*, **33** (1987) 7.
3. Kamimura, K., Asahara, S. *et al.*, Fuel data analysis system DANTE-II. PNC-SN841-83-63, 1983, p. 3.
4. PNC Internal Report, Quality control data analysis system (development report), 1985, p. 6.
5. PNC Internal Report, Quality control data analysis system (outline of manipulation), 1985, p. 12.

9

Reliability Data Banks at Electricité de France (EDF)

H. Procaccia

Direction des Etudes et Recherches, 25 Allée Privée—Carrefour Pleyel, 93206 Saint-Denis, Cedex 1, France.

9.1 THE ORIGINS

At the beginning of the 1970s, when Electricité de France (EDF) opted for a policy of rapid development of its PWR nuclear power plant programme, the demonstration of the anticipated benefit with respect to the required safety was the major objective of engineers. At that time only foreign experience was available, and the collection and recording of this experience in a computerized data bank was decided upon for use in prospective studies, while waiting for the creation of specific French data banks as from 1978. All the collected data are recorded in the EDF Research and Development Directorate central computer (IBM) located at Clamart (near Paris), either directly for the foreign data bank or by the plant local computer (CII), with subsequent transfer onto the central IBM, for the French data banks. These data banks are particularly concerned with reliability and availability of plants, or of their components. Only the component reliability data bank will be described here in detail.

9.2 HISTORY AND OBJECTIVES OF THE EDF DATA BANKS

First let us look at the history of the data banks in France.

9.2.1 The First Step

In 1970 French experience in the nuclear field came mainly from the first generation of gas-cooled reactors. In these plants, as in the conventional fossil units, records of general operation results, or of main component incidents, were established periodically by either daily telex, monthly or annual reports, or, when an incident occurred, by plant or component failure forms and incident or accident reports.

For the most part the records were collected in manual data bases, which have been used in particular for planning studies of the new generation of PWR nuclear power plants (expected availability) and for estimating the design parameters of the critical components from the anticipated number of transients thus expected during the plant life.

In 1974, when the US Nuclear Regulatory Commission published (in the Grey Books) the monthly records of US plant operation and incidents,[1] EDF took the opportunity to use these more appropriate data for their own studies and initially decided to create a computerized data bank based on the US experience for units with power output of more than 400 MW.

The information collected from the Grey Books was implemented using the analysis of the *Atomic Energy Clearing House*[2] and the *Nuclear Power Experience* publications,[3] and through direct access to the Westinghouse domestic data bank, OMAR (Operating and Maintenance Analysis Reports), in the framework of a specific agreement between EDF and Westinghouse.

The EDF data bank is named in France Fichier d'Incidents (INC) and in the USA FOMAR (French OMAR). This bank has been further extended to include data from German and Japanese plants (since 1974), and then from Swedish, Belgian and Swiss plants (data published every year by the International Atomic Energy Agency (IAEA)),[4] and from 1978 data coming directly from the French units.

The quality of the data collected is excellent when the information originates from EDF, good when extracted from the Grey Books (controlled by other sources) and relatively poor from IAEA (these data are exhaustive only for significant events).

Until now the data bank has been mainly used to put figures on the expected plant availability factors vs age (planning), to obtain realistic fuel loading campaigns, to determine reliability parameters of components which are not followed by the EDF reliability data bank (SRDF; see below), to estimate the ageing effect on a plant's reliability and availability, for research on the critical components (on plant availability or plant shutdown), and principally to make international comparisons, which will allow us to distinguish initiator incidents which will probably occur in France, or plant sectors (systems or materials) where studies are necessary to improve availability, reliability or safety.

9.2.2 The Second Step

The second step concerns the first preliminary safety analyses of EDF's PWR nuclear plants.

The absence of specific experience in the area of PWR plants led EDF to use data from gas-cooled reactors and thermal fossil units, then data extrapolated from the literature (and mainly from the Rasmussen study), with a final verification using data from real EDF experience. For this reason, at the end of 1973, a working group of specialists belonging to the French Safety Authority and to EDF was created with the objective of defining which data should be collected and how they should be collected and analysed. By the end of 1976, the working group concluded with the creation of a reliability data bank called Système de Recueil de Données de Fiabilité

(SRDF), and a pilot exercise was set up on the first six French PWR units: two units at Fessenheim and four units at Bugey.

In the beginning, the SRDF was very ambitious: 8000 elementary components per pair of units were to be monitored in the data bank; very quickly, however, a drastic reduction to 800 components was made. The main reasons for this reduction were the following:

- For the determination of failure rate—in operation or on demand—one needs to know not only the failures associated with the components but also the operating time or the number of demands up to the time the failure occurs; for this the necessary number of specific counters to be installed was judged unrealistic.
- The second reason was more human: at the end of 1976, Fessenheim unit 1 was commissioning (coupling in April 1977), and the most urgent priority was to operate this start with minimum interference.

In fact, this voluntary limitation of the components monitored in the SRDF has been beneficial to the quality of the data bank.

In 1983 the experience of the pilot exercise led to extension of the SRDF monitoring to 1100 components per pair of units, and this was implemented for every EDF PWR unit and for the fast breeder reactor of Creys Malville. By the end of 1986 more than 10 000 failure forms had been collected, and for the following years about 5000 failure forms/yr are expected (more than 40 units are in operation). The reliability parameters obtained until now were used first for the verification of the PWR units' safety studies. At present, they are more frequently used for operating procedure determinations and component test and maintenance frequencies optimizations. The main reliability parameters are published in a book entitled *Recueil Périodique de Données de Fiabilité* (RPDF).

9.2.3 The Third Step

At the beginning of the 1980s, because of the rapid development of the French PWR nuclear programme, and in consequence of the amount of information to be stored, for the EDF technical or operating services, the constructors, the safety authorities, the ministries, and for the national and local authorities, it was decided:

—to computerize the national operating statistic data bank, and
—to create, on the model of the FOMAR data bank, a French event data bank called EVT (Fichier Evénement).

The mixing of these two banks gives a new availability and reliability data bank: le Recueil de Données de Fonctionnement des Centrales REP (RDE), which produces a record of the operating results and plant incidents for each EDF nuclear unit, published every month.

At this time (end of 1986), about 20 000 events have been collected in the EVT data bank. This information is mainly used by working groups of specialists who analyse plant safety, plant operational problems and component reliability, and who decide on specific studies or modifications.

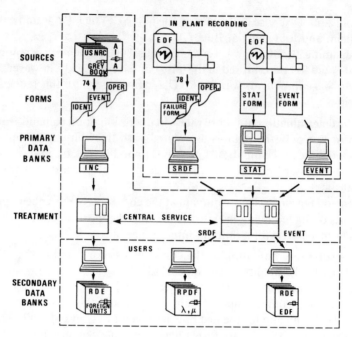

Fig. 1. Organization of data bank at EDF.

Figure 1 shows a general presentation of the EDF data collecting system, Fig. 2 gives the typical form of the RDE handbook, and Fig. 3 represents the computation of reliability parameters for the turbine inlet regulating valve in the RPDF book.

9.2.4 The Fourth Step

After several years of plant operation and statistical analysis of the main component incidents collected in the above national data bases, it became necessary to explain the origin and causes of these incidents, to follow their evolution, and to adapt the operating procedures, and in-service inspection and maintenance, to limit and control the evolution of these incidents. This led to the creation, from 1986, of new specific data bases:

—relative to the material of the components—mechanical and chemical characteristics, origin, tests, control, etc.;
—relative to the on-line collection of transients affecting some sensitive components or structures;
—relative to the modifications adopted for the components or the operating procedures;
—relative to the in-service inspection (reactor vessel and primary pipe weldings, reactor internals, steam generator tubes, control rods, guide tube pins, etc.);
—relative to human error; and
—relative to the maintenance history of the components.

BLAYAIS 4 MONTHLY REPORT - OPERATION RESULTS

			FEBRUARY 1985		
1 PUISSANCE CONTINUE NETTE	910 MWe		DU MOIS	Depuis le 1ᵉʳ janvier	Depuis le 1ᵉʳ couplage
2 NOMBRE D'HEURES CALENDAIRES	(h)		672	1 416	
3 TEMPS DE CRITICITÉ DU RÉACTEUR	(h)		668	1 412	13 323
4 TEMPS D'ARRÊT EN DISPONIBILITÉ DU RÉACTEUR	(h)		4	4	767
5 TEMPS DE MARCHE ALTERNATEUR COUPLÉ	(h)		666	1 410	12 604
6 TEMPS D'ARRÊT EN DISPONIBILITÉ DE LA TRANCHE	(h)		0	0	0
7 ÉNERGIE THERMIQUE BRUTE PRODUITE	(GWh)		1 693	3 710	32 543
8 ÉNERGIE ÉLECTRIQUE BRUTE PRODUITE	(GWh)		571	1 263	11 092
9 ÉNERGIE ÉLECTRIQUE NETTE PRODUITE	(GWh)		545	1 209	10 565
10 FACTEUR D'UTILISATION EN TEMPS DU RÉACTEUR	(%)		99,4	99,7	82,8
11 FACTEUR D'UTILISATION EN TEMPS DE LA TRANCHE	(%)		99,1	99,6	80,2
12 COEFFICIENT DE PRODUCTION DE LA TRANCHE	(%)		89,2	93,8	73,9
13 COEFFICIENT DE DISPONIBILITÉ DE LA TRANCHE	(%)		94,1	97,2	74,9

DATE	PERTE (H)	PUISS INDIS (MW)	C T	SYST	MAT	DESCRIPTION	BLAYAIS 4 FEVRIER 85
ARRET DE TRANCHE / REDUCTION DE CHARGE							
05.02.85	5	910	3	RGL		ARRET D'URGENCE A 3H21 PAR D PHI/DT SUITE A UN LACHER DE GRAPPES EN RAISON DE LA DEFAILLANCE D'UN COMPOSANT RGL. RECOUPLAGE A 8H45. DOC 221 NO/02.85 ET DOC 223 NO 23.	
10.02.85	14	145	7	CRF	PO	ARRET DE LA POMPE DE CIRCULATION CRF 02 PO EN RAISON D'UN BRUIT IMPORTANT DU MULTIPLICATEUR.	
14.02.85	100	270	7	CRF		BAISSE DE CHARGE A 70% DE LA PCN POUR PROTECTION DU CONDENSEUR LORS DU FONCTIONNEMENT AVEC UNE SEULE POMPE DE CIRCULATION.	
INCIDENTS N'AYANT DONNE LIEU NI A ARRET DE TRANCHE, NI A REDUCTION DE CHARGE							
25.02.85	11	0	9	TEG	VY	INETANCHEITE DU CLAPET TEG 006 VY. NETTOYAGE DE CELUI-CI PAR GONFLAGE A CONTRE-COURANT DE TEU 001 BA.	

CONSÉQUENCE SUR LA TRANCHE (CT)

0 - SANS CONSÉQUENCE
1 - DÉCLENCHEMENT TRANCHE
2 - DÉCLENCHEMENT TURBINE
3 - A.U. RÉACTEUR
4 - A.U. + I.S.
5 - MISE EN SERVICE EAS
6 - ILOTAGE
7 - BAISSE DE CHARGE
8 - MISE EN ANTENNE
9 - INDISP.té PARTIE FONCTIONNELLE

Fig. 2. RDE typical monthly form.

Some of these data are collected directly from the manufacturer, but the main part will be retrieved on-line from each plant computer, with seven specific technical software programs tested, at present (1989), on two EDF sites: Gravelines (six units) and Cattenom (two units). These software are:

P1 = maintenance, which includes a components data base, the management of anomalies, and preventive and corrective maintenance;

P2 = human resources, including in particular the maintenance man-hours;

P3 = component resources, including spare parts;

P4 = operation, which includes statistics, events and transient data banks, fuel history, waste, safety and radiation protection;

P5 = historical, including the SRDF data bank;

P6 = documentation, including the test and repair procedures;

P7 = costs.

MATERIEL : *Soupape de réglage* *admission HP* BLOC RPDF: 0 306	FONCTIONNEMENT CUMULE : *CUMULATIVE OPERATING HOURS* 2,36 . 10^6 heures				SOLLICITATIONS CUMULEES : *NUMBER OF* *DEMAND* 8,48 . 10^3 soll.			ECHANTILLON : 192 *SAMPLE* MATERIAL x AN : 618 *EQUIPMENT* *x YEAR*	
TYPE DE DEFAILLANCE *FAILURE RATE*	Nb. DE DEFAILLANCES *FAILURE NUMBER*			TAUX DE DEFAILLANCE *FAILURE RATE*				DUREE *DURATION*	
	EN SERVICE N	EN TEST T	EN ENTRETIEN E	EN FONCTIONNEMENT *IN OPERATION* $x 10^{-6}$ /h			A LA SOLLICITATION *ON DEMAND* $x 10^{-3}$ /h	heures DE REPARATION *REPAIR*	hours DE DEFAILLANCE *UNAVAILABILITY*
				MOY.	INF. SUP.	σ	MOY. | INF.SUP. | σ		
COMPLETE *CRITICAL*					0,6		0,2	32	
EN FONCTIONNEMENT *IN OPERATION*	2	1		0,7			0,35		
A LA SOLLICITATION *ON DEMAND*	3				2,7		0,7		
A L'ARRET *DURING STAND BY*									
TOUTES DEFAILLANCES *ALL FAILURES*								33	560
EN FONCTIONNEMENT *IN OPERATION*	32	1	3	15,2	11,3 20.1		0,23		
A LA SOLLICITATION *ON DEMAND*	5	1					0,6 | 1,26		
A L'ARRET *DURING STAND BY*			52						

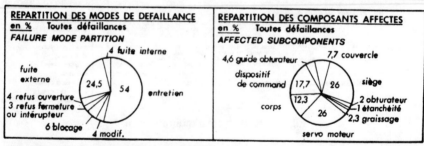

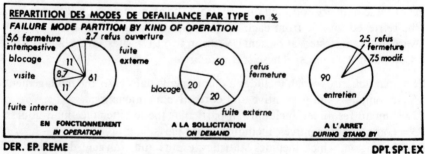

DER. EP. REME   DPT. SPT. EX

Fig. 3.   Computation of reliability parameters for a turbine inlet regulating valve (RPDF) in
the RPDF book.

9.3 SRDF

The SRDF is a typical components reliability data bank; it allows the computation of:

- The component failure rates: in operation, in stand-by or on-demand; their development with time, if any; and the upper and lower bounds for certain confidence levels.
- The corresponding unavailability and the mean time to repair.
- The modes and causes of failure.
- The affected subcomponents.
- The consequences of the failure on the plant.

To achieve this objective, SRDF is composed of three subfiles:

- The descriptive or identification file, which gives the characteristics (mainly its limits) of every component monitored by the data bank; this file is established once and is modified only when a component is replaced or added.
- The operating file, activated only once a year, which collects the operating time and the number of demands recorded for every component.
- The failure file, which collects all the necessary information to calculate the reliability parameters of the components.

9.3.1 Equipment Coverage

The components monitored in SRDF were selected according to their importance, in relation to either the safety or the availability impact of the equipment on the plant. At present, about 1100 pieces of equipment per pair of units are monitored; automation or control components are excluded because of the difficulty of obtaining the number of demands, and also because of the development of a specific data bank called SRDFA. Because of the difficulty of obtaining data, manual valves are also excluded. The selection of the components was driven by the following rules:

(1) Functional choice:
   For safety reasons, it was decided to monitor

   - reactor cooling systems,
   - safeguard systems,
   - service systems powering the operation of the above systems.

   For availability reasons, complementary systems were selected:

   - main steam system,
   - feedwater system,
   - high-power electric system (6·6 kV).

(2) Component choice:

   - Fluid system; when possible, the following components are selected:

      main tank,
      pumps,

pressurized check valves,
electric or pneumatic valves (stop valves, regulating valve, etc.),
heat exchangers.

For these components, the temperature scale starts from ambient to 345°C, and the pressure scale is from 1 to 170 bar:

- Electric system:

batteries,
rectifiers,
electric panels with switchgear,
transformers,
generators,
diesel generators.

The voltage scale starts from 12 V DC to 6600 V AC and the power scale is from some kilowatts to 15 MW (the main generator—900 or 1300 MW—is not included in SRDF).

These rules lead to the selection of the following components:

(1) Mechanical equipment (excluding valves): total = 187 for a pair of 900-MW units:

tanks	35	
compressors	8	
heat exchangers	30	(including three steam generators)
diesel generators	4	
pumps	92	
turbines	6	
filters	12	

(2) Valves: total = 509, made up of 108 check valves, 60 safety valves, 192 pneumatic valves and 149 electric valves.

(3) Electrical equipment: total 372:

generators	8
motors	102
switches	152
rectifiers	28
transformers	26
electric panels	30
batteries	26

9.3.2 Information Gathering

As stated above, the SRDF subfiles are fed from three types of forms: the descriptive (or identification), the operating and the failure forms.

9.3.2.1 The Identification Form

Each component has one identification form, which defines exactly the composition of the component, its limits, the operating conditions and the main characteristics: fluid, size, pressure, temperature, etc. The identification form is divided into two parts: the first part, identical for all components, gives general information, and the second is specific for each kind of component: valve, pump, electric motor, switches, etc. As an example, an identification form for a chemical and volumetric control pump is given here.

The common part. On the display screen of the site computer the main coded characters are the following:

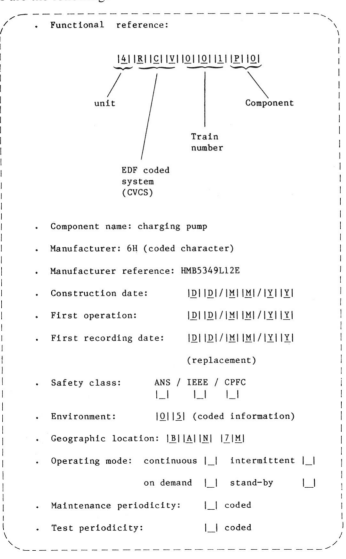

```
    •  Functional  reference:


           |4| |R| |C| |V| |0| |0| |1| |P| |0|
             \__/  _____/ \____/  \____/
              /         |          |        \
           unit         |          |      Component
                        |          |
                        |        Train
                        |        number
                        |
                  EDF coded
                  system
                  (CVCS)


    •  Component name: charging pump

    •  Manufacturer: 6H (coded character)

    •  Manufacturer reference: HMB5349L12E

    •  Construction date:    |D| |D|/|M| |M|/|Y| |Y|

    •  First operation:      |D| |D|/|M| |M|/|Y| |Y|

    •  First recording date: |D| |D|/|M| |M|/|Y| |Y|

                             (replacement)

    •  Safety class:     ANS / IEEE / CPFC
                         |_|    |_|    |_|

    •  Environment:      |0| |5| (coded information)

    •  Geographic location: |B| |A| |N|  |7| |M|

    •  Operating mode:  continuous |_|   intermittent |_|

                        on demand  |_|   stand-by       |_|

    •  Maintenance periodicity:    |_| coded

    •  Test periodicity:           |_| coded
```

The specific part. Specific information is collected onto a display screen, as follows:

```
  . The type of pump |_|

  . Its geometry       |_|

  . The fluid nature (17 possible choices)
    |0|1| to |1|7|

  . The coupling system (5 cases) |0|1| to |0|5|

  . The mode of flowrate variation (7 possibilities)
    |0|1| to |0|7|

  . The transmission system (6 cases)
    |0|1| to |0|6|

  . The type of gland (7 cases): |0|1| to |0|7|

  . Rotations per minute:  |_||_||_||_||_|

  . Nominal power:         |_||_||_||_|

  . Nominal flowrate:      |_||_||_||_||_|

  . Manometric head: nominal    |_||_||_||_|

                     max.       |_||_||_||_|
```

The completion of the identification form is arduous, particularly for the first unit of a series of plants. Fortunately however, the standardization of nuclear plants in France allows direct copying, with small modifications, for the following forms.

9.3.2.2 The Operating Form
These are completed once a year for each component (1100 forms for a pair of units) and give:

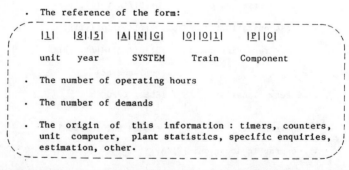

```
  . The reference of the form:

   |1|     |8|5|   |A|N|G|   |0|0|1|    |P||0|

   unit    year    SYSTEM    Train    Component

  . The number of operating hours

  . The number of demands

  . The origin of this information : timers, counters,
    unit computer,  plant statistics, specific enquiries,
    estimation, other.
```

Many automatic controls are performed on the SRDF central computer with a view to estimating the level of the data homogeneity between plants. For instance, one handbook estimates a statistical average of the operation time and of the number of demands for each component. These data can help the operator to complete the form when a specific data point is not available (a counter is out of order, for instance). They also serve for the automatic validation (control) of the data.

9.3.2.3 *The Failure Form*

This form is completed for a selection of the plant works orders (about 5%).

An average of 100–150 failure forms per year per unit are recorded in the plant computer: for 54 operating units more than 5000 forms/yr will be supplied to SRDF in the next few years. The following information is collected:

. Form reference:

|4| |8|3| |0|0|0|9|

    unit   year   chronological form number

. Component reference: |4| |R|C|V| |0|0|1| |P|0|

. Work order reference: |1| |0| |5| |8| |9| |2|

. Other references: Historical component isolation
               order No: |_|_|_|_|_|_|

. Failure discovery date: /|D| |D|/|M| |M|/|Y| |Y|

. Failure starting date: |D| |D|/|M| |M|/|Y| |Y|

. State of the component:

  .. |A| Stand-by
  .. |F| In operation
  .. |S| On demand
  .. |E| Maintenance
  .. |N| Normal operation
  .. |T| Test

. Summary of the failure:

|N| |0| |I| |S| |E| |A| |N| |D| |L| |M| |P| |0| |R| |T| |A| |N| |T|

|V| |I| |B| |R| |A| |T| |I| |0| |N| |S| |I| |N| |T| |H| |E|

|C| |0| |U| |P| |L| |E| |R| |R| |E| |P| |L| |A| |C| |E| |M| |E| |N| |T|

(251 characters)

. Cumulative repair time: |_| |2| |3| |8| |h|

. MAN.REM: |_|_|_|_|_|0|

. Reactor state before anomaly (8 states) |0| to |08|

. Consequences on the unit (11 consequences)
    |01| to |11|

. Failure degree:

  .. |C| Complete
  .. |A| Sudden
  .. |D| Partial
  .. |E| Progressive

. Failure mode: |_|_|_|_| coded number, see below

. Affected subcomponents:

|1| |0| |8|/|1| |0| |6|/|4| |2| |5|/|_|_|_|_|

. Failure cause:

|_|_|_|_| |_|_|_|_| |_|_|_|_| coded number

. Repair duration: |_| |1| |1| |5| h

. Failure duration: |_| |1| |3| |0| h

. Unit unavailability: |_|_|_|_|_|0| h

. Unit unavailability: |_|_|_|_|_|_|0| MW

. Actions taken: |_|_|_| 8 coded possibilities

The completion of this form is time consuming, and analysis by a specialist is needed. First, he must select, from all the works orders, those concerning SRDF, and to complete the form, he must consult:

- the repair dossier;
- the system or component disconnection orders;
- the plant operation log book;
- the plant computer records; and, mainly,
- the logical description of the failure: from the first statistical analysis of each SRDF component, a specific fault tree has been established, which gives the main general subcomponents affected and their principal failure mode and cause: this gives the operator only a small choice of component failure mode and cause possibilities. Figure 4 gives an example of a failure form logic diagram.

9.3.3 Information Processing

9.3.3.1 At the Local Level

In each plant, an agent who is at the executive level is responsible for the system. He is assisted by a technician, who is responsible for monitoring a pair of reactor units and compiles computer files in which all the information contained in the cards are stored. The data are input through a display keyboard connected to the site computer. Before any input the card is checked and the name of the person who completed it as well as the name of the person who checked it both appear on the card. This procedure is part of a wider structure, which was defined when the system was set up, to ensure a high standard of quality of the gathered information. As soon as the card is introduced, it is subjected to a number of tests, performed automatically, which allow one, for instance, to check the accuracy of the information which is judged to be absolutely necessary, the coherence of the information, the logical description of the failure, etc. From the information contained in the cards, the site computer makes up groups of identical equipment which will later be the subject of statistical processing. Periodically, a summary of the failures is made for each group of identical equipment. The input information can be checked, modified and completed at any time.

Software, called the Reliability Data Interrogating System (SIDF), allows one to consult the files through questions put in the form of Boolean equations. It is therefore possible to list the failures which occurred during a given period on a certain type of equipment which belongs to a given system. Such a system, because of its flexibility, quickly gives exact answers to the questions asked by the operating personnel.

9.3.3.2 Data Processing at the National Level

The data furnished by the nuclear plants are all gathered at the Calculation Center of the Research and Development Directorate, in Clamart. The files made up from

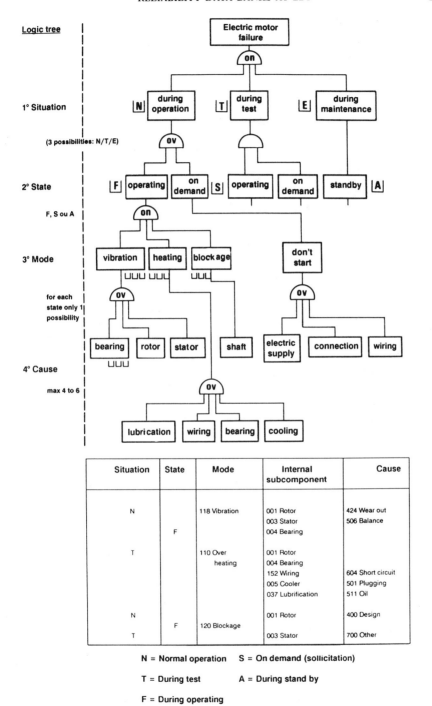

Fig. 4. Example of logic fault tree for electric motor, and coded table guide for operating situation.

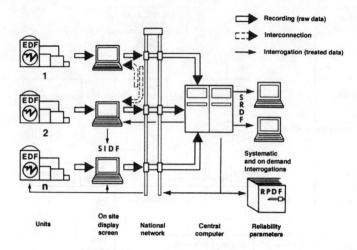

Fig. 5. Data collection organization.

these data can be reviewed at any time according to a range of classification criteria. Various types of processing on request permit the users to ask questions of a varied nature: reliability parameter calculation of a population of equipment of given characteristics, research into legislative aspects, research into the statistics which will be best adapted to represent the lifetime of a given set of equipment, etc.

For the time being, the main task consists of the yearly systematic processing. This processing, performed at the same time each year, aims to update completely all the files from the information gathered during the preceding year, and this information is published in the EDF reliability parameters' handbook: the RPDF (*Recueil Périodique de Données de Fiabilité*). A scheme of the general data collection or processing organization is given in Fig. 5.

9.3.4 Data Retrieval and Treatment

Obviously, all the combinations of coded characters can be interrogated in the data bank: this is done either by use of logic Boolean equations, or by use of the IBM data interrogative system DB2/SAS: it should be noted that, in particular, this latter system allows a search based on some words in a chain of characters, for instance, in the summary of the failure. These possibilities are used 'on demand' for very specific studies; for instance, research on the Reactor Coolant System (RCP), the steam generator component (GV) and the coordinates of all the plugged tubes (column number, row number). On the other hand, the simplest interrogation is the printing of the chronological events for a group of plants, a unit, a system or a component, between two given dates, with a selection of the printed characters. However, the most used tool is the systematic interrogation of practical menus elaborated as functions of current requests.

Let us look at one example of systematic interrogation on electric motors.

First Menu: sampling selection
For electric motors only two groups of sampling are proposed (a maximum of 13
group possibilities, depending on the component).

```
              Title: MO  electric motor

   Selection       Groups       GROUP TITLE

        X       |0| |1| |0| |1|   ELECTRIC MOTOR U = 380 V   P<200 KW
   or   _       |_| |1| |0| |2|   ELECTRIC MOTOR U = 6.6 KV  P>200 KW
        _           ____          ____  ____  ____  ____ __
        _           ____          ____  ____  ____  ____ __
        _           ____          ____  ____  ____  ____ __
```

Second menu: plants and systems concerned

```
      Title: |M| |O|  ELECTRIC MOTOR

      Group: |0| |1| |0| |1|   U = 380 V    P < 200 KW

   PLANTS  |F| |E| |S|  |B| |U| |G|  |T| |R| |I|   |G| |R| |A|  ...  ...  etc.

                  LIST                              CHOICE

   SYSTEMS    FROM NUMBER      TO        SYS      FROM        TO

   PTR*          001          002        __        __         __
   REA           001          004        X         001        002
   RPE           001          004        __        __         __
   TEG           001          002        __        __         __
   RAM           001          002        __        __         __
   RIS           021          022        __        __         ___
   etc            __           __        __        __         __
    __            __           __        __        __         __
```

Remark: All the characteristics of a given motor of a given system are completely
defined in the corresponding identification form, and in particular, the list of
subcomponents.

First treatment: general failures distribution
(example for all electric motors with $P < 200\,kW$). (For screen display see p. 183.)

Remarks

- Complete failures lead to the loss of the component mission: only these failures
  are taken into account for reliability or safety analyses. These failures can be
  sudden or progressive.
- The anomalies discovered during maintenance are only potential failures, but
  they indicate which spare parts are needed.

Title: |M| |O|

Group |0| |1| |0| |1| U = 380 V   P < 200 KW

Number of failures:

Situation	State	Nb	Mode	Complete failure Nb
32 N (N = during normal operation)	28 F (F = operating)	8	Sudden stop	7
		4	Loss of character- istic	3
		1	Over heating	0
		2	External leak	0
		13	Noise/Vibration	1
		1	Other	1
	3S (S : on demand)	3	Does not start	3
16E (E = during maintenance)	16(A) (A = during stand-by)	9	Maintenance	0
		7	Modification	

A second treatment: reliability parameters
(example: interrogration on the complete failures)

Title: |M| |O|

Group |0| |1| |0| |1| U = 380 V   P < 200 KW

No of complete failures	No of operating hours	No of demands (start up)	Duration		Failure rates	
			Repair	Unavail.	In operation	On demand
F S	X10^{+6}h	X10^3.d	h	h		
12 3	3.39	351	16	137	Mini.: * 2.0 E-6	.2 E-5
					Average: 3.6 E-6	.9 E-5
					Max.: * 5.8 E-6	2.3 E-5
					* level of confidence: 95%	

Remark: The two first treatments are given in the RPDF (*Recueil Périodique de Données de Fiabilité*).

Third treatment
This concerns the data edition, with choice of parameters (number of failures or

reliability parameters) and coded characters (affected subcomponents, listing of the failures, summary, causes) to be printed.

Figure 6 shows some valve failure rates and classifications extracted from SRDF.

At present, direct statistical graphics (bar graphs, pie-charts, etc.) or direct computation of evolution laws (normal, log-normal, Poisson, Weibull, etc.) statistical tests and confidence levels, are available through the IBM compatible programs SAS or DISPLA.

Analysis and synthesis software has been developed in parallel with the interrogative tools; for instance, multivariate analysis codes for the detection of particular features of a component or of one of its operating parameters, a trend analysis code which allows one to follow automatically with time or age the improvement or degradation of a component.

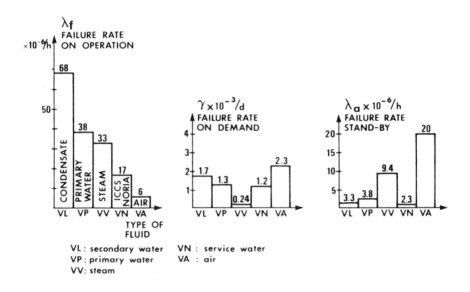

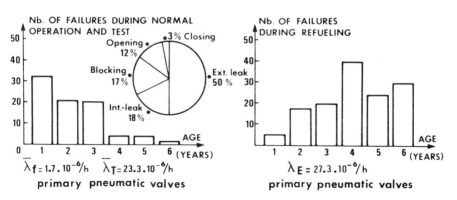

Fig. 6.   Example of valve data extracted from SRDF.

9.3.5 Subsequent Changes

The SRDF is a living and evolving tool; from the first pilot experiment, it has been tested since 1978 on six power plants for 800 components per pair of units, extended, from 1983, to all the EDF PWR units, with 1100 components monitored in each, and is now being implemented on the NERSA fast breeder reactor of Creys Malville (Super Phénix).

Analysis of the problems encountered in 1983 has given rise to:

- A total revision of the failure form (the logical failure analysis, etc), with the production of a guide[5] giving the procedures for completing the form, the logic fault tree (situation, state, subcomponent, mode and cause of failure), and the division of the coded subdivision of each component into subcomponents (an example is given Fig. 7). The 4000 existing failure forms, have been revised to take into account this structural modification.
- The redefinition of the operating time and number of demands collected per component, with a guide giving realistic values determined from special investigations on site.
- The categorization of the failure into several classes: complete or total, partial, sudden or progressive.

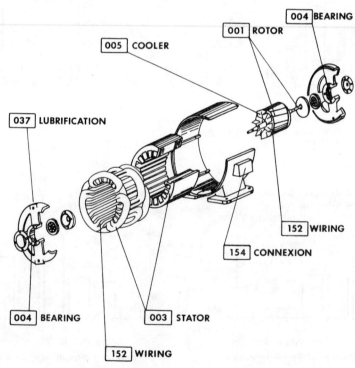

Fig. 7. Electric motor subcomponents.

The extension of SRDF in two ways is being discussed as follows:

- Extension of the components monitored.
- Extension of the record of maintenance operations: to include a summary of what is done, what is observed, difficulties, diagnostics and costs, for each maintenance action.

Also, EDF has decided to create a reliability parameters handbook for the grid and transmission system components, with a view to optimizing the overall availability and safety of the electricity distribution system. The SRDF and its direct product the RPDF will be the models of this future data bank.

One other change in the objectives of the SRDF data bank is the relative increase in its use for plant operation against the first safety objective: availability implementation, shutdown reduction, tests and maintenance optimization and component surveillance.

9.3.6 Some Examples of Studies Performed with SRDF

Much time is required between the decision to create a data bank and the ability to use the data for specific studies with high confidence. In fact, the first important use of the SRDF data was as late as 1983, when EDF launched the safety studies of the first 1300-MW Paluel unit's safeguard systems (14 systems studied). At the same time, the data have allowed confirmation of the previous 900-MW safety studies and refinement of the operating procedures, and have given an authenticated operating time for the plant before a component of a redundant safeguard system needs to be taken out of service. In 1986 general plant safety analyses were started at EDF. Priority was given to the use of SRDF data for this work. In the plant operating field, many actions have already been assessed or are under development, for instance:

- Estimation of the growth of the plant component reliability parameters with time or between plants.
- Plant ageing evaluation.
- Optimization of tests and maintenance.
- Elaboration of probabilistic procedures for in-service inspection, and decision analyses.

We will give one example of each of the above points:

Evolution of the reliability of the components: the experience feedback analysis at EDF has led to some modifications in the design or the operational conditions of components; for example, replacement of all the diesel generators' push rods because of bad design. On the other hand, the fuel cycle in some units has been extended from 12 to 18 months. In both cases, it is important to follow the consequences of such modification on the appropriate components' reliability.

Plant ageing is dependent, in particular, on the ageing of some critical components: systematic research into this ageing will allow preventive decisions to be taken, to limit operating transients and consequently the ageing factor (for example, modification of the water-level regulation of the pressurizer which limits the number of deviations; preventive replacement of components such as control rod tube guide pins).

First generation of diesel generators: For these components, tests are carried out with a periodicity of 15 days: this optimal periodicity has been confirmed by computing the time T_0, which leads to a minimum unavailability, I, of the generator. I depends on the different failure rates of the generator, during standby λ_a, in operation λ, and on-demand γ; on the corresponding repair times, τ_a, τ and τ_y; on the test periodicity, T; and on the test duration, σ, according to the following formula:

$$I \simeq \lambda_a \left(\tau_a + \frac{T}{2} \right) + \frac{\gamma \tau_y + \lambda \sigma \tau}{T}$$

In annulling the derivative of I, we obtain

$$T_0 = \sqrt{\frac{2(\gamma \tau_y + \lambda \sigma \tau)}{\lambda_a}}$$

T_0 has been computed with the reliability parameters observed for the Bugey and Fessenheim diesel generators, where the test periodicity, T, and the operating time, σ, were slightly different (respectively 450 and 306 h, and 1·9 and 2·9 h). The evolution of the two generators' unavailability vs their test periodicity is given in Fig. 8 and is compared with the first theoretical study, which defined the optimal periodicity from estimated failure rates. From the observed values for these plants, it is found that $T_0 = 550$ h (23 days), and that there are very small I variations over 1

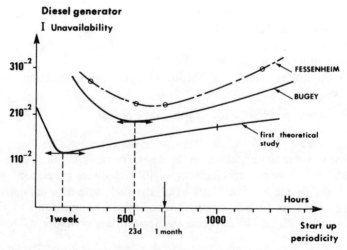

Fig. 8. Computation of diesel generator unavailability (first year of operation) vs the start-up periodicity.

month. In consequence, a test every month has been proposed to the safety authorities. It should be noted that the result of the study is strongly dependent on the failure rate during standby, λ_a.

EDF has developed a new methodology: causality analysis, which allows the determination, from the 'effects' of the observed types of failures (in operation, F_0, during tests, F_t, or during standby, F_s), of the real origins (causes) of the failures. Experts' judgements are given, to determine the probabilities matrix linking causes and effects of the failure. The computation of this matrix gives the real number of failures per type, F'_0, F'_t, F'_s, with the relation

$$\begin{Bmatrix} F'_0 \\ F'_t \\ F'_s \end{Bmatrix} = \begin{Bmatrix} P_{00} & P_{0t} & P_{0s} \\ P_{t0} & P_{tt} & P_{ts} \\ P_{s0} & P_{st} & P_{ss} \end{Bmatrix} \times \begin{Bmatrix} F_0 \\ F_t \\ F_s \end{Bmatrix}$$

where $P_{i,j}$ is the elementary probability that the observed failure effect 'i' is in reality owing to the cause 'j'.

Diesel generator failure rates have been significantly modified after this study; in particular, the failure rate during standby has been multiplied by a factor of about ten.[6]

Probabilistic procedures: An example is given for optimization of the steam generator tube bundle inspection; the tube bundle has been divided into five different zones affected by different kinds of degradation—intergranular stress corrosion cracking, U-bend stress corrosion, denting, mechanical damage by foreign object, and the rest of the tube bundle. For each zone the Weibull law, which gives the cumulative probability of tube degradation at a certain time, $F(t)$, has been established, using SRDF results relative to the older steam generators. This law is given in Fig. 9 for the small U-bend region.

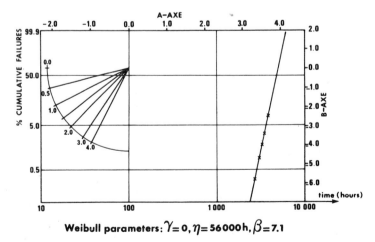

Weibull parameters: $\gamma = 0$, $\eta = 56000$h, $\beta = 7.1$

Fig. 9. Evolution of degradation with time for small U-bend tubes of steam generator.

It has been found that

$$F(t) = 1 - \exp\left[-\left(\frac{t-\gamma}{\eta}\right)^{\beta}\right]$$

$$F(t) = 1 - \exp\left[-\left(\frac{t}{56\,000}\right)^{7\cdot1}\right]$$

where

$\gamma = 0$ means that there is no latency at the beginning of the observation,
$\eta = 56\,000$ h means that 63% of the tubes are more or less degraded at this time,
$\beta = 7\cdot1$ means that once the degradation process begins, it proceeds very rapidly.

With this law, the leakage risk has been calculated for each cycle of the plant: this risk becomes significant (10^{-2}) for the fourth fuel cycle, and a specific inspection of the small U-bend tube is proposed only from this fourth cycle. The number of tubes to be inspected to detect the degradation process, with a certain level of confidence, is calculated using the relation:

$$\frac{C_D^0 \cdot C_{N-D}^n}{C_N^n} \leq \alpha$$

where n is the number of inspected tubes, D is the number of failed tubes and N is the total number of tubes in the zone considered. The number of tubes to be inspected is 20 in a population of 200 tubes for $\alpha = 5\%$ (95% chance of success). If only one out of 20 tubes is found to be degraded, the inspection is extended to the entire region, and a plugging policy is established. If no tube is degraded, the inspection of 20 tubes selected randomly is recommended for the next plant refuelling.

This probabilistic method has been used to determine the minimum number of steam generator tubes to be extracted at each plant refuelling for metallurgical analysis, to monitor the velocity of the degradation process once it is initiated.

9.3.6.1 Ageing and Maintenance Policy

Studies on diesel generators have been chosen to illustrate this approach. For diesel generators, the EDF Central Service, taking into account the feedback experience, has established a conditional maintenance policy which gives a periodicity of the maintenance interval, or inspection of the critical parts of the diesel, as a function of their state at the time of maintenance (Fig. 10).

The first generation of diesel generators experienced some design failures of the motor rods. This type of failure, which occurs at the beginning of the diesel life, has been corrected, and the rod design modified. The other failures, despite the periodic and conditional maintenance, affected principally three subparts of the diesel generators: the starting system, the lubricating system and the injection system; the failures of these three systems represented 54% of the total failures observed in the first generation of diesel generators. These failures were observed after a certain number of operating hours or start ups. Study of the failures' distribution with time

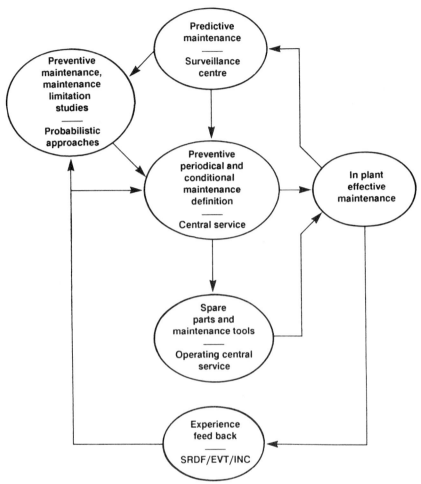

Fig. 10. Maintenance organization.

for these systems shows that:

- Random failures are observed in the injection system; in this case, the actual maintenance policy is well adapted.
- Failures developing with time are observed in the two other systems; a complementary preventive maintenance policy has been proposed.

For instance, Fig. 11 shows the cumulative distribution of the lubrication system failures vs time, from which is deduced the corresponding Weibull law:

$$F(t) = 1 - \exp\left[-\left(\frac{t + 1500}{5500}\right)^3 \right]$$

where

$\gamma = 1500\,$h means that the failure process starts before the beginning of the observation (commercial operation of the plant),

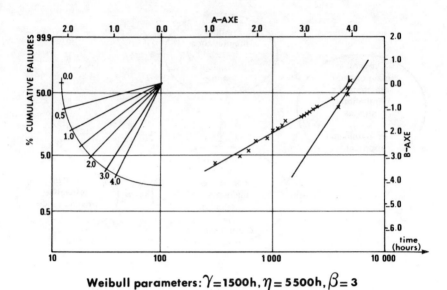

Weibull parameters: $\gamma = 1500\,h,\ \eta = 5500\,h,\ \beta = 3$

Fig. 11. Cumulative distribution of lubrication system failures with time for diesel generators.

$\eta = 5500\,h$ (here the characteristic operating equivalent hours is given by multiplying the number of diesel start-ups by a specific coefficient K and the number of effective operating hours),

$\beta = 3$ corresponds to a rapid degradation process.

The mean time before failure, M, is calculated from the relation

$$M = \gamma + \eta\Gamma\left(1 + \frac{1}{\beta}\right)$$

Γ is the gamma law and gives $M = 3400$ operating equivalent hours, corresponding to about five fuel cycles of the plant (each diesel operates about 700 equivalent hours per plant fuel cycle). A complementary maintenance on the lubrication pump (mainly replacement of all the seals) is therefore proposed after five plant operating cycles.

9.3.6.2 Evaluation of the Costs and Benefit of the Maintenance

It is relatively easy, in a plant, to evaluate the costs of the maintenance actions for a component, and the risk associated (human error, deficient spare part, etc.), with an analysis of the data collected in SRDF or in the plant; however, it is more difficult to evaluate the benefit anticipated for the life of the component when the same maintenance procedures are used in all the plants. Signal treatment methodologies, already applied, for instance, for analysis in public enquiries or in the biological domain, have been developed at EDF. These methodologies allow the following determinations:

(1) Is the maintenance periodicity well adapted to the component reliability?

For this, the conditional correlation coefficient C is computed, which links the discovery of a component failure at the time t_i, if one intervention has been performed before, at the time $t_i - \Delta t$. Thus, C is the conditional probability of having a failure at t_i, P_{ti}, relative to the probability of having made one intervention I at the time $t_i - \Delta t$, i.e.

$$C = P_{ti}/PI_{t_i - \Delta t}$$

Some typical observed results are the following:

- C is significant immediately after one intervention; we can deduce that the failures are the consequences of the intervention: human error, bad procedure, deficient spare part, etc.
- C is significant after a certain time of operation, but before the normal following programmed preventive interventions; if there is ageing between two programmed interventions, the periodicity must be revised. An example of ageing detected with this methodology is given in Fig. 12.

These two cases reflect a non-adapted maintenance (negative aspect).

- C is small between two programmed interventions; there is no correlation between intervention and anomalies, and there is good adaptation of the maintenance periodicity, but are the costs too high?

To answer this question, we have developed the second method.

(2) Is a benefit to be expected after one maintenance action?

To evaluate this benefit we compute the component availability variation function, D_t between two programmed interventions, compared with its mean availability, $\bar{D}$,

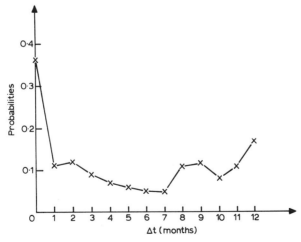

Fig. 12. Probability of failure after a maintenance action, for service water pumps at Bugey.

during a long period: $(D_t - \bar{D})$, relative to the distributive function of the interventions, $It - \Delta t$, compared with the mean frequency of the interventions, $\bar{I}$: $(I_{t - \Delta t} - \bar{I})$. The availability correlation coefficient C_{Di} between the periods of intervention, T, is given by the relation

$$C_{Di}(\Delta t) = \frac{1}{T} \int_0^T [D_t - \bar{D}].[I_t - \bar{I}_{t - \Delta t}]$$

This coefficient is normalized to one, taking into account the standard deviation of D (σD) and of I (σI):

$$C_{NDI}(\Delta t) = \frac{C_{Di}(\Delta t)}{\sqrt{\sigma_D^2 \times \sigma_I^2}} \qquad -1 \le C_{NDI} \le 1$$

For $C_{NDi} < 0$, the availability of the component decreases after one intervention and the anticipated benefit is negative. If $C_{NDi} > 1$ the benefit is positive, and the availability gain is compared with the maintenance cost to evaluate the maintenance policy.

This methodology is at present applied with success for the plant valves. It will be extended to other sensitive components.[7]

9.3.6.3 Evaluation of the Relative Costs of Different Designs
The principal correspondence component analysis allows direct estimation of the relative costs of different designs (as shown in Fig. 13 for feedwater pumps). A direct comparison is made between motor-driven pumps, used in some US nuclear plants, and the turbine-driven pumps which equip the French units. Axis 1 is correlated essentially with the number of incidents and plant shutdown, and axis 2 with the duration of the shutdown (cost).

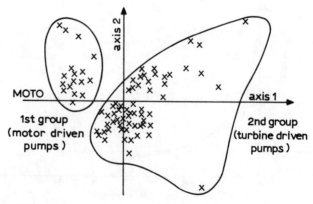

Fig. 13.   Principal component analysis for feedwater pumps of French and US PWRs.

9.4 CONCLUSION

All the examples given here are direct applications of the SRDF data bank: the possibilities of extension are very large and will be exploited in the near future at EDF. One should never forget the very considerable effort required to create a data bank before one is able to make use of it in the manner described above. Fortunately, at EDF, the rapid development of standardized nuclear plants, the voluntary limitation in the choice of components monitored, the homogeneity of the data collection, and the quality control imposed and verified, have been the main reasons for the SRDF success.

REFERENCES

1 NUREG, 0020 Vol. 1, No. 1. USNRC, Licensed operating reactors—Status summary report, from April 1974.
2. Larhant, C., EDF/SEPTEN—VE-SE/IA 79-00-04. Information appearing in the review *Atomic Energy Clearing House*.
3. *Nuclear Power Experience*, Vols PWR 1 and 2. Books 1–6.
4. STI/PUB/651. Operating experience with nuclear power stations in member states (year n). International Atomic Energy Agency, Vienna (year $n + 2$).
5. Aupied, J., EDF Rep. HP/219/84/25. Méthode d'analyse logique des défaillances— Applications au SRDF.
6. Procaccia, H. & Aupied, J. R., Use of a reliability data bank to analyse and quantify failure rates by a causality method. In EuReDatA Seminar, Chamonix, 1989.
7. Procaccia, H. & Lannoy, A., Impact of maintenance actions on the reliability and the availability of components cost–benefit analyses—application to nuclear valves and pumps. In EuReDatA Maintenance Seminar, 1989.

10

IAEA's Experience in Compiling a Generic Component Reliability Data Base

B. Tomic & L. Lederman

*International Atomic Energy Agency, Wagramerstrasse 5,
PO Box 100, A-1400 Vienna, Austria*

10.1 INTRODUCTION

Reliability data are an essential part of a probabilistic safety asessment (PSA). The quality of data can determine the quality of the study as a whole. Among all the data which are needed for performing a PSA study, component reliability parameters are those most frequently mentioned.

It is obvious that component failure data originating from the plant being analyzed would be most appropriate. However, in only few cases is complete reliance on plant experience possible, mainly because of the rather limited operating experience and usually limited number of failures for meaningful statistics. Nuclear plants, although of different design, often use rather similar components, so some of the experience could be combined and transferred from one plant to another. In addition, information about component failures is also available from experts with knowledge on component design, manufacturing and operation. Thus, use of component reliability parameters originating outside the plant being analyzed is rather common practice.

This brings us to the importance of assessing generic data. (Generic is meant to include everything that is not plant specific for the plant being analyzed.) The generic data available in the open literature can be divided into three broad categories. The first category includes the data base used in previous analysis. These data can be plant specific or updated from generic data with plant-specific information (the latter case deserves special attention). The second category is based on compilation of plants' operating experience collected through some kind of event reporting system. The third category includes data sources based on expert opinions (single or aggregate), or a combination of expert opinions and other nuclear and non-nuclear experience. If one is to utilize generic data in plant-specific PSA study, information on different aspects of generic data sources is essential.

Considering the need for generic data by PSA practitioners in its member states, the IAEA compiled the Generic Component Reliability Data Base[1] from the open literature. The data base is also a part of the IAEA-developed computer code package for fault/event tree analysis, PSAPACK, where it can be used in automatic retrieval mode. Therefore, some of the features of the data base, such as the dedicated coding system, are directly governed by the code requirements.

10.2 IAEA's GENERIC COMPONENT RELIABILITY DATA BASE

The final version of the IAEA's Generic Component Reliability Data Base contains 1010 different records, including practically all the components which are accounted for in PSA studies of nuclear power plants (NPPs). In addition to a dedicated coding system, a unique record form was developed for the data base. The selection of the data sources as well as selection of data points for inclusion in the data base was carefully performed. Finally, the data base input was quality controlled and a manual describing data sources and providing the listing of the data base was prepared. Some of the steps in compiling the data base as well as observations on possible problem areas when using generic data sources are described next.

10.2.1 Data Sources

To achieve coverage of different reactor technologies and different ultimate data sources, a total of 21 data sources have been included in the data base. The number of data points adopted from each of the sources is, however, substantially different. Some of the sources provide up to 180 different records, whereas one source provided only two data points.

The basic characteristics of the data source are essential in the data selection process. To highlight some of the basic characteristics of the sources included in the IAEA's data base, they can be divided into three basic categories, each of which has some unique characteristics.

Because of the different ultimate data sources, some of the sources fall into more than one category. A typical example is the 'German Risk Study', where some data points are derived from the NPP operational experience, some are combinations of data which also include nuclear operating experience, and the rest are from a combination of several different data sources, without nuclear experience. Thus, the source categorization is based on the majority of data from a particular source.

10.2.1.1 Plant-specific Data
Two subgroups exist in this category. The first is plant-specific data drawn directly from sources available at the plant (log-books, maintenance records, work orders, etc.), and the second is when generic data are updated with plant-specific information.

As the data could be traced all the way to individual components, the first subgroup is considered the best source of data. However, that is not necessarily the case when one uses these data at another plant. Sources exclusively containing this type of data are rarely found. The only source of this kind in the IAEA data base is NUREG 4550 (Vol. 3, Surry NPP) and it provides only 10 records. It should be noted that a number of other sources also provide data for operating experience at a single plant, but as most of the data provided belong to some other category, they are quoted elsewhere.

The second subgroup considers generic data updated with single plant operating experience. This procedure is usually applied when either limited plant-specific operating experience is available, or the data gathered are considered unreliable. In fact, in most of the recently completed PSA studies (which are not entirely based on generic data) the component reliability data base is derived in this manner. The IAEA Data Base includes several sources of this kind (e.g. Oconee NPP PRA, Zion NPP PSS and a source identified as 'Old W PWR').

In addition to the problems encountered in defining component boundaries and failure modes, the means of acquiring raw data at the plant have the greatest impact on the quality of reliability data derived. As this has the greatest impact on the data in the plant-specific category, some observations on this aspect are provided next.

There are basically two types of raw data sources at a plant: log-books and maintenance work orders. In terms of the quality of a component's reliability parameters derived from these sources both types have advantages and drawbacks.

Deriving raw data from the maintenance work orders is usually easier and less time consuming (especially when work orders are computerized), because every work order addresses an abnormal occurrence. Events related to a single component can be easily compiled. On the other hand, the quality of information found in the work orders is generally not very good. For example, work orders may be open for months or years, and work done on one component may be identified as done on another. Log-books, especially those compiled and filled by control room personnel, are more accurate, but deriving raw data from them is extremely time consuming.

Even if the raw data are drawn from the log-books or maintenance records, one is still not sure that all the failures of a particular component have been reported. If both sources are searched, the probability of failures not being reported is lower. Therefore it is understandable that the quality of component failure data is directly proportional to the quality of plant records. A dedicated reliability data collection system would be the best possible source of raw data.

In addition, the determination of the failure rate denominators (number of demands, or hours in standby or in operation), could also substantially influence the reliability parameter. In that respect, the actual number of demands is sometimes assessed on the basis of average time on power or calendar time. Also, trials subsequent to the successful start during tests are rarely identified.

Running experience of standby components is usually limited to a running time of about 1 h (common test running time). The failure rate based on that experience is also used (in the analysis) as a long-term failure rate. However, there is no evidence that the long-term failure rate is equal or comparable to the short-term one.

10.2.1.2 Data Extracted from Reporting Systems
A widely known NPP event reporting system is the Licensee Event Report (LER)

System used in the USA. As most of the safety-related events occurring at the NPPs have to be reported, it is possible to pinpoint failures of the safety-related components. The data base includes four sources of that kind, namely LER-derived reliability parameters for valves, pumps, instrumentation and control components and control rods. In some ways comparable to LER-based parameters are those published in the Swedish *Reliability Data Book*, which provides the reliability parameters derived from Swedish LERs, ATV system (The Swedish Thermal Power Reliability Data system) and information provided by the plant staff.

The advantage of reliability parameters derived through the event reporting system is that the actual component population covered is large, which guarantees more reliable statistics. The disadvantage is that the LER systems are event oriented and not component oriented, so actual component failure could be misinterpreted or overlooked. In addition, some of the component failures are never reported because their failures either did not cause any safety significant event or reporting was not required. Furthermore, a small percentage of events are not reported because of plant personnel's attitude towards reporting systems. All these factors may lead to possible overestimates in component reliability.

Similarly, plant-specific sources, the operating time and number of demands of the component are not easy to determine. The operating time is usually estimated on reactor operating time, and number of demands is estimated as an average also based on operating time. This can drive the reliability parameter in either direction.

Compilations of that kind tend to diminish differences in component design, operational practice and environment, all of which could greatly influence actual component reliability.

10.2.1.3 Data Based on Expert Opinion, Nuclear and Non-nuclear Experience

Categories in this group include single expert opinion, aggregate expert opinion, aggregation of non-nuclear sources and aggregation of operating experience of several NPPs. Usually, even a single data source includes several of these categories. It is clear that any aggregation of data (if properly performed) provides more reliable data than a single expert's opinion or single-source information.

The most widely known representative of this category is the IEEE Standard 500. Its 1977 version includes mainly expert opinion, where the 1984 version also includes nuclear and non-nuclear experience. Other examples of data sources which are included in the IAEA Data Base are NUREG 2728-IREP (Interim Reliability Evaluation Program which adopted a data base from EGG-EA-5887), NUREG 2815, PSA procedure guide (data from expert opinion combined with IREP data base), Sizewell B assessment (operating experience including nuclear and other industrial sources).

The WASH-1400 (a combination of expert opinion and data from non-nuclear and nuclear sources) also belongs to this category. Some of the sources included in the IAEA data base, such as NUREG 2886 and NUREG 3831, draw data for parameter estimation from a limited group of plants. Another example is the Shoreham NPP PRA-GE data, which are drawn only from General Electric Co. operating plants.

The quality of the reliability parameters provided by the sources in this category can vary substantially, depending on the ultimate data source.

10.2.2 The Data Base Record Form

To permit storage of different information from such a variety of sources in a systematic and consistent manner, it was necessary to define a unique data base record form. The record form was defined as having 21 input fields (lines), characterizing 10 categories of information (Table 1). A short description of information contained in each category is provided next.

(1) Every record has a code which is a unique combination of five alphanumeric characters. A detailed description of the coding system is presented later.

(2) Component type is described in four lines, namely: type, subtype, and detail types 1 and 2. *Type* characterizes basic component type (e.g. 'pump', 'valve'). *Subtype* characterizes more specifically the component category (e.g. motor driven (pump), solenoid operated (valve), pressure (sensòr), AC (motor)). Some of the components do not have information at this level (battery charger). *Detail type 1* contains information about the system in which the component is located, or other characteristics such as voltage, pipe diameter or valve type (e.g. gate, butterfly, etc.). 'General' means that further characterization is not possible. *Detail type 2* is the last entry of the component description. Usually, such a detailed division of component categories is not available. In some cases, the information about size or the system in which the component belongs is found in this line. Such a detailed division is used mainly for pumps, valves and transformers.

(3) The component's operating mode is, in particular, an important characteristic for pumps (standby, alternating or running). For other components this information is of less importance. Precise information of this type is seldom included in data bases. When the component operating mode is obvious (e.g. a safety injection pump is a standby pump), this information is included. In other cases 'all' operating modes was the default value chosen.

(4) Operating environment is the next entry, which, similar to the previous one, is rarely found in the literature data sources. Although it is obvious that the aggressive

TABLE 1
Record Categories

1. Code	1 line
2. Component type	4 lines
3. Operating mode	1 line
4. Operating environment	1 line
5. Failure mode	2 lines
6. Failure rate	5 lines
7. Repair time	1 line
8. Source	2 lines
9. Component boundary	1 line
10. Comments	3 lines

environment could influence the component failure rate, few data sources address that issue. For example, IEEE 500 provides multipliers for most of components listed for environments such as those with a high level of radiation, temperature, humidity or vibrations. WASH 1400 provides different failure rates for pumps and motors in an extreme, post-accident environment. A default value 'normal' was chosen for all cases where no other environmental condition was indicated.

(5) The failure mode category is presented in two entries, one describing 'generic' failure mode and the other citing failure mode as found in the original source. A generic failure mode was assigned because the coding system was not able to cope with the number and differences in failure modes found in the sources. The original failure mode was, however, left in the record for users' clarification.

(6) The failure rate is presented in five entries. The first entry is failure rate description, which gives information on the failure rate (mean or median), upper and lower bounds (percentiles of the distribution, low and high or maximum and minimum values), and defines the failure rate as per hour or per demand. The failure rate entry provides the actual numerical value for the mean, median, or best estimate value. Upper and lower bound entries also provide the respective actual numerical values. If the error factor is available it is given in the fifth entry. Upper and lower bounds and error factors are not always available, therefore n/a (meaning not available) is used as a default value.

(7) Repair time is the next category. It indicates the average repair time associated with a component failure. It is also very seldom found in the data sources adopted. Some sources provide duration based on recorded repair times; in others, repair times are a mean value of several maintenance durations on a particular component.

(8) Information on the data source is presented in two entries, one indicating the exact source (name of publication, page no., table no.) and the second giving information about the ultimate source of data (e.g. expert opinion, operating experience).

(9) Component boundary is one of the problem areas to be addressed later. Very few sources provide adequate information about component boundary. Whenever this information was not available, 'detail not available' was stated.

(10) Usually, all the information found in the source and considered relevant is provided in comment entries. This includes information about the prior use in updating, the operating experience (total population, number of demands or operational time, number of failures), additional failure rates relevant to the component (with or without command failures), etc. Practically all information which could in any way clarify failure rate, failure mode or component description is entered here. The comment category is therefore considered an integral part of each record.

Table 2 presents the complete record form.

10.2.3 Coding System

The coding system is the area where the **PSAPACK** code most strongly influenced the IAEA Data Base structure. In accordance with the requirements, each record

TABLE 2
Complete Record Form

MODE	10 spaces
TYPE	65 spaces
SUBTYPE	65 spaces
DETAILTY	65 spaces
DETILTY1	65 spaces
OPMODE	30 spaces
OPENVIRO	65 spaces
GENFAILMOD	50 spaces
FAILMODE	50 spaces
FRATEDESCP	30 spaces
FAILRATE	10 spaces
UPBOUND	10 spaces
LOWBOUND	10 spaces
ERRORFCTOR	10 spaces
REPAIRTM	10 spaces
SOURCE	30 spaces
ULTSOURCE	65 spaces
COMMENTS	65 spaces
COMMENTS1	65 spaces
COMMENTS2	65 spaces

code could have a maximum of four alphanumeric characters, and the fifth character describing the data source was used only for data retrieval purposes. Because each record must have its own unique code and there are component categories which should have the same code, a longer code (with more characters) would have been preferable. However, some of the fault tree analysis codes included in the PSAPACK limit identification of the basic event to eight alphanumeric characters. As it was felt that at least four characters are needed for further identification of components (including its physical position for eventual common-cause or dependence analysis), only four characters were used for basic component identification and failure mode description.

Originally, there were more than the 100 different failure modes. That number required two characters for coding, leaving only two characters for the component type. As the generic failure modes were designed, one character was sufficient to describe the component failure mode.

Three alphanumeric characters were then used for the component type. For component types with many subdivisions (for example, valves), the first character is unique for the component type, the second is unique for subtype (for example 'V' is valve and 'VM' is motor-operated valve). The last position characterizes the detail types 1 and 2. No firm rule exists for the last position. Usually, when the detail type is 'general' or no further division exists, character 'A' is in the third position. For

TABLE 3
Coding System Example

Component code	Description
K T A I W	fuse, general, fail to open, WASH 1400
P M D R T	pump, motor driven, centrifugal horizontal, flow rate 130–200 kg/s, fail to run, Swedish Reliability data book
R R A C E	relay, protective, all types, fail to close, IEEE 500
V C B O F	valve, self operated, check, less than 2-in diameter, fail to open, CANDU assessment

components with few subdivisions, the first two positions characterize the type (e.g. 'LT' is transmitter), and the last one characterizes the subtype or detail type, if any. For components which are 'one of a kind', all three positions characterize a single component type (e.g. 'XMC' stands for manual control device).

The data base contains about 450 different components listed by component identification code. They are divided into 76 types. As there is no space in the coding system for operating mode or environment, sometimes the same component is coded differently because of operating conditions (e.g. a motor-driven pump without further subdivision is coded 'PMB' when in alternating operating mode, and 'PMR' when in running mode).

10.2.4 Data Selection

After choosing the data sources and defining the record format and coding system, the actual data input was performed. Some of the sources (such as WASH 1400 or IREP) were reproduced in the data base entirely, whereas, in other cases (such as IEEE 500 or Old W PWR), data for inclusion were carefully chosen.

From some of the data sources, data for components which are plant specific and are not comparable with any other (e.g. emergency AC source-hydro unit) were excluded. Also, the data directly adopted from any other data source which has already been reproduced in the data base were excluded.

The IEEE Standard 500 provided single-source values and aggregate values. In the IAEA Data Base, depending on the particular case, single or composite values or even both (when particularly illustrative) were included. If 'per demand' and 'per hour' failure rates were provided, both were included, together with ultimate data source.

Sources such as NUREG's LER data for failure rates for pumps and valves usually offer two values, i.e. with command failures and without command failures. Values given in the failure rate entry are generally without command failures (clearly stated in the comment entry). The 'with command failure' rate is also cited in the comment entry.

These sources often divide data into categories in accordance with the NSSS vendor. In the IAEA Data Base usually the overall value is given, which is again described in the comment entry.

10.2.5 Data Extraction from the Data Base

The IAEA Generic Data Base was created using the IBM-PC software dBase III, so it can be stored as a data base or in plain text format. It exists, in computerized form as well as in the form of a book. Its use is by no means limited to the PSAPACK code.

The PSAPACK package provides users with the options for browsing and for retrieval of data from the IAEA Data Base. Retrieval of data can be accomplished by knowing the exact code of the record of interest. Then the complete record or the entries of interest can be retrieved. The second method of data retrieval is to view the data base record by record, and then retrieve information by entering the particular record number. The PSAPACK code also includes a small data base editor which allows the user not only to retrieve data but also to change, modify, add or delete any information. By retrieving data and combining them with data which were added or modified (if any) the PSAPACK forms its own small data base which is then used for solving a particular problem.

Using the dBase III code it is even easier to 'search' for or to 'locate' a certain code, type, subtype or any other relevant information. Browsing through the chosen fields, after locating a particular set of components of interest, one can easily compare any of the values included in the IAEA Data Base.

10.3 PROBLEM AREAS CONNECTED WITH USE OF GENERIC DATA BASES

Use of reliability parameters originating outside the plant which is being analyzed always introduces some uncertainty owing to judgement in the data selection process. Therefore, the user has to be aware of possible problem areas where misinterpretation can occur when generic data sources are being used. During the compilation of the Generic Component Reliability Data Base the following four problem areas have been identified, in decreasing order of importance:

—component boundary definition;
—failure mode definition;
—operating mode definition;
—operating environment definition.

However, those issues are not exclusively connected with use of generic data bases. Even when deriving failure rates from raw data from the plant being analyzed, some of the issues may lead to substantial errors in estimating reliability parameters. A detailed review of the data sources produces insight into how different data bases have addressed some of these issues. Possible ways of avoiding or solving such problems are addressed next.

10.3.1 Component Boundary

It is obvious that a major source of misinterpretation is the component boundary definition. Some experts agree that variations in component boundaries are the

primary reason for failure rate fluctuation between sources. Although that
statement seems to be too rigid, component boundaries could, depending on the
particular component, change failure rates substantially. Thus it is interesting to
observe how different sources address this issue.

Probably the best-defined component boundaries are in the Swedish *Reliability
Data Book*. In that source, practically each component category has a sketch
indicating the component boundary and points of interface with other systems or
components. In some of the NUREG LER rates the component boundaries are
outlined by precisely defining major interface points. Some other sources define a
component as being an 'off-the-shelf' item. This is an interesting and noteworthy
definition, as it assumes that 'off-the-shelf' has the same meaning everywhere.
However, that is not necessarily the case for all the components.

Data bases which are part of PSAs usually do not provide detailed definition of
the component boundary. This is understandable, because these sources were
compiled for specific use and a component boundary is actually defined in a fault
tree. When performing data updating, the component boundary gains importance
because of the need to match the prior with the plant-specific operating experience.
Sources which base their failure rate upon the combination of nuclear and non-
nuclear experience (or even expert opinion) do not provide detailed boundary
description. The level of similarity of different sources combined is not known, but it
is to be expected that certain differences exist.

For sources mostly based on expert opinion, the question of a strictly defined
boundary becomes more academic. However, cases such as whether or not
lubricating oil which is part of a diesel generator component or circuit breaker being
part of a pump boundary must be addressed to avoid significant (orders of
magnitude) variations in the failure rates.

One way of avoiding serious problems with component boundary definitions is to
define 'generic' component boundaries. That, of course, does not help in already
existing data sources, but could save considerable trouble in the future. However,
this is mainly applicable to data collection efforts undertaken during the
performance of a PSA. In that case, component boundaries should reflect two,
sometimes opposite, requirements: the level of detail needed (or wanted) by the
system model and the level of detail of plant records from which raw data are
retrieved.

There are generally three major interfaces to be defined in connection with the
component boundary definition:

—mechanical interface (including cooling system, lubricating system, etc., where
  appropriate);
—power supply interface;
—control system interface.

10.3.2 Failure Mode

Component failure mode definition is the second problem area dealt with. Failure
modes found in various sources show significant differences even when describing

similar failure. For example, in 21 sources included in the data base over 100 different failure modes were found. Some of these differences were basically in wording (e.g. 'fail to run' vs 'failure to run'). In other cases, it is sometimes difficult to understand properly the failure mode and compare it with other sources. To allow comparison of reliability parameters and to enhance the data base coding system, considerable effort was made to define generic failure modes.

In addition to the component design and function in the system, there are three basic component operating modes which affect the failure mode:

—standby;
—alternating;
—continuously operating.

There are also two distinct failure rate definitions. One is time related (further divided in standby and operating hourly rate) and the other is demand related. These were also taken into account while determining, for each single component (or group of components), possible ways (modes) of failure. These all served as the bases for defining generic failure modes. Finally, the original failure mode was included under one of the generic categories.

The disadvantage of the approach described is that it opens the way for inconsistencies in the grouping. For example, generic definitions 'failure to function' and 'failure to operate' describe basically the same failure mode, but whereas the first is defined as per hour, the second is per demand. Because some sources define 'failure to operate as a per hour value, whereas others define it as a per demand value, the same (in words) failure mode is listed in different generic categories. Another possible controversy comes from sources such as NUREG 2815, Baseline Data, where all failure rates are defined per hour, although some of them are actually demand related. Therefore a generic failure mode, such as 'fail to start' (which is defined per demand) includes a per hour failure rate from that source.

The failure mode 'all modes' deserves special attention because it is usually a composite failure mode, which actually contains several 'single' failure modes. The problem here is that each component usually has a different failure mode. Whenever possible, failure modes contained in 'all modes' are listed in the comment entry of the data base record form.

Generic failure modes as proposed in the data base are one of the possible ways of defining failure modes. This is, however, not the only solution, it would be possible to define them in several other ways. Altogether 28 failure modes were defined. The 19 which are considered to be the most important are shown in Table 4. Nine others cover a minor number of peculiar failures, such as 'overheated' or heat exchanger 'tube' or 'shell' leak.

10.3.3 Operating Mode

Component operating mode is important for active components, but generally has much less weight for passive components. Even for active components there are cases where the operating mode has more or less influence depending primarily on

TABLE 4
Generic Failure Modes

Failure mode	Failure mode code
ALL MODES	A
DEGRADED	B
FAIL TO CHANGE POSITION	C
FAIL TO REMAIN IN POSITION	D
FAIL TO CLOSE	E
FAIL TO FUNCTION	F
SHORT TO GROUND	G
SHORT CIRCUIT	H
OPEN CIRCUIT	I
PLUG/RUPTURE	J
SPURIOUS FUNCTION	K
FAIL TO OPERATE	L
FAIL TO OPEN	O
PLUG	Q
FAIL TO RUN	R
FAIL TO START	S
RUPTURE	T
OTHER CRITICAL FAULTS	X
LEAKAGE/EXTERNAL LEAK	Y

the mode and mechanism of the failure. Operating mode is of great importance for pumps and other components which perform their function by moving continuously. The operating modes for such components could be defined in three categories:

—standby;
—alternating (intermittent); and
—running (operating).

For components which perform their function by changing between discrete states (e.g. valves), the operating mode as defined above corresponds to the status of the system in which they belong. Operating mode pertinent to the component itself is, in these cases, normally open or normally closed.

The majority of the data sources included in the data base do not define the component operating mode. The only sources which define operating mode are some of the NUREG LER rates. The PSA studies usually define the system in which the component is located. As, for most of the systems, it is possible to determine the operating mode, this could be used for definition of active components' operating mode.

When determining the failure rate for standby components, failures which occurred during standby must be accounted for. As the failures are not revealed until a test or an actual component demand, these failures are usually included in the model as a demand-related failure. In these cases the demand-related failure should comprise those failures whose mechanism is purely related to the demand (e.g. high current to motor windings during start) and those related to the time which the component spent in a standby condition. If the data source provides a demand-related failure probability without indication of how long the component is in standby between two demands, the fact that component failure during standby is time related is overlooked. The component's failure probability could vary substantially with variation in time between tests or actual demands. Some of the sources have recognized this fact and provide an hourly failure rate for standby condition.

10.3.4 Operating Environment

The component operating environment is rather poorly defined in most of the sources. The majority do not address it at all, whereas some define environment as the normal power plant environment. This definition could basically hold for normal operation or accidents which do not change environmentally affected parameters. However, when performing a PSA one is interested in predicting the outcome of an accident in aggressive environments, which could in certain cases change component failure rates substantially.

The data sources which provide some information on the influence of aggressive environment are WASH 1400 (separate failure rate for post-accident situation for pumps and motors) and IEEE Standard 500 (environment multipliers are given for most of the components included, for effects such as high level of radiation, humidity, temperature and pressure).

Environmental effects could obviously affect component failure rate in different manners, so careful consideration should be given to this issue. Data from plant operating experience assume a normal environment, because operating experience data are normally either from normal operation or from test data, both of which are very different from accident conditions. On the other hand, the number and types of components affected by post-accident conditions are usually rather limited; their extent is greatly dependent on plant design and type of accident.

Another type of extreme environment condition which can occur in NPPs is a high-temperature condition occurring after the failure of room-cooling systems. For most electronic components or systems it is relatively easy to predict accurately the effects of high temperature, and experimental data are available. For mechanical components such as pumps, a high-temperature condition and consequently accelerated failure rates are relatively more complicated to predict.

10.4 CONCLUSION

Generic component reliability data are indispensable in any PSA. It is not unrealistic to imagine that all possible component failures and failure modes modeled in a PSA would be available from the operating experience of a specific plant in a statistically meaningful way.

The degree to which generic data are used in PSAs varies from case to case. Some

IAEA RELIABILITY DATA BASE

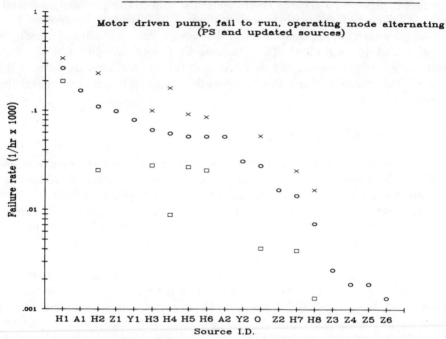

Fig. 1. Illustration of differences in reliability data from different sources (source Ref. 2). ×, Upper bound; ○, centre point; □, lower bound.

studies are totally based on generic data whereas others use generic data as prior information to be specialized by plant-specific data. Most studies, however, use a combination, where data for certain components come from purely generic data and for others from Bayesian updating.

The IAEA effort to compile a generic component reliability data base aimed at identifying strengths and limitations of generic data usage and at highlighting pitfalls which deserve special consideration. It was also intended to complement the PSAPACK package and to facilitate its use.

As it was the most comprehensive collection of generic reliability data publicly available, the Generic Component Reliability Data Base was greatly appreciated by many PSA practitioners. At present, more than 600 copies (about 500 hard copies and 100 diskettes) are distributed world-wide.

The follow-up activity on compilation of the data base was a survey of ranges of component reliability data. This survey, which was also published in IAEA's TECDOC series,[2] revises orders-of-magnitude differences (Fig. 1) in reliability parameters originating from different sources. As the influence on final PSA results when the failure rate of significant components is changed could be substantial,[3] proper selection of generic data is very important. To permit adequate data selection, causes of difference in reliability data have to be explained. In that respect, the IAEA initiated activity aimed at providing guidance on data selection process based on identification of causes of variation of component reliability parameters as seen in different data sources.[4]

REFERENCES

1. IAEA TECDOC 478, Component reliability data for use in probabilistic safety assessment. IAEA, Vienna, 1988.
2. IAEA TECDOC 508, Survey of ranges of component reliability data for use in probabilistic safety assessment. IAEA, Vienna, 1989.
3. Tomic, B. & Lederman, L. Data selection for probabilistic safety assessment. EuReDatA Conf., Siena, 1989.
4. IAEA TECDOC, Evaluation of differences in component reliability data. In *An Assessment of Variation in Reliability Data*. IAEA, Vienna, 1990.

APPENDIX: DATA SOURCES INCLUDED IN THE GENERIC COMPONENT RELIABILITY DATA BASE (IN ALPHABETICAL ORDER)

CANDU Assessment.

EPRI-NP-2433, Diesel-Generator Reliability at Nuclear Power Plants: Data and Preliminary Analysis. Science Application, Inc., Palo Alto, USA, 1982.

German Risk Study (Deutsche Risikostudie Kernkraftwerke). GRS, Verlag TÜV, Rheinland, Köln, FRG, 1979.

IEEE Standard 500, IEEE Guide to the Collection and Presentation of Electrical, Electronic, Sensing Component, and Mechanical Equipment Reliability Data for Nuclear-Power Generating Stations, Appendix D, Reliability Data for Nuclear-Power Generating Stations. IEEE, New York, 1984.

NUREG/CR-2728, Interim Reliability Evaluation Program Procedure Guide. Sandia National Laboratories, USNRC, Washington DC, 1983.

NUREG/CR-1205, Data Summaries of Licencee Events Reports of Pumps at US Commercial Nuclear Power Plants. EG & G Idaho, USNRC, Washington DC, 1982.

NUREG/CR-1331, Data Summaries of Licencee Event Reports of Control Rods and Drive Mechanisms at US Commercial Nuclear Power Plants. EG&G Idaho, USNRC, Washington DC, 1980.

NUREG/CR-1363, Data Summaries of Licencee Event Reports of Valves at US Commercial Nuclear Power Plants. EG&G Idaho, USNRC, Washington DC, 1982.

NUREG/CR-1740, Data Summaries of Licencee Event Reports of Selected Instrumentation and Control Components at US Commercial Nuclear Power Plants. EG&G Idaho, USNRC, Washington DC, 1984.

NUREG/CR-2815, Probabilistic Safety Analysis Procedure Guide. Brookhaven National Laboratory, USNRC, Washington DC, 1984.

NUREG/CR-2886, In-Plant Reliability Data Base for Nuclear Plant Components: Interim Data Report, the Pump Component. Oak Ridge National Laboratory, Oak Ridge, TN, USNRC, Washington DC, 1982.

NUREG/CR-3831, In-Plant Reliability Data Base for Nuclear Plant Components: Interim Data Report, Diesel Generators, Batteries, Chargers and Inverters. Oak Ridge National Labratory, Oak Ridge, TN, USNRC, Washington DC, 1985.

NUREG/CR-4550, Analysis of Core Damage Frequency from Internal Events Surry, Unit 1. Sandia National Laboratory, USNRC, Washington DC, 1986.

NASC 60, OCONEE PRA, A Probabilistic Risk Assessment of Oconne Unit 3. The Nuclear Safety Research Center, EPRI, and Duke Power Co., Palo Alto, USA, 1984.

Old Westinghouse PWR reactor.

Shoreham Nuclear Power Station Unit, Probabilistic Safety Assessment, Long Island Lighting Co., Science Application, Inc.

PWR/RX 312, Sizewell 'B' PWR Pre-Construction Safety Report, Component Failure Data for PWR System Reliability Assessment. NNC, 1982.

RKS 85-25, Reliability Data Book for Components in Swedish Nuclear Power Plants. RKS, SKI, Stockholm, Sweden.

WASH-1400, Reactor Safety Study, An Assessment of Accident in US Commercial Nuclear Power Plants. USNRC, Washington DC, 1975.

Zion Nuclear Power Station, Probabilistic Safety Study. Commonwealth Edison Co., Chicago, Illinois, 1981.

The CANDU assessment and Old Westinghouse PWR are not individual publications. The data indicated as coming from those sources has been compiled by the IAEA in the framework of various activities including workshops and technical visits. The source name is being used for illustrative purposes only.

11

The European Reliability Data System—ERDS: Status and Future Developments

the late S. Capobianchi

Commission of the European Communities, Joint Research Centre, Ispra Establishment, 21020 Ispra (Va), Italy

11.1 INTRODUCTION

As part of the Nuclear Safety Programme of the JRC (Joint Research Centre) of the Commission of the European Communities, a project was carried out to create a centralized data system to collect and organize information related to the operation of nuclear power plants (NPPs): this system was called ERDS (European Reliability Data Sytem). At present, ERDS is exploiting information already collected in national data systems and information derived from single reactor sources.

The four data sub-systems constituting ERDS are:

—Component Event Data Bank;
—Abnormal Occurrences Reporting System;
—Operating Unit Status Report;
—Reliability Parameter Data Bank.

The structure of these data banks and the facilities which the JRC implemented to deal with them are described, and current and future developments are outlined.

11.2 GENERAL DESCRIPTION OF ERDS

11.2.1 Aims of the System

A lack of organized collection and exploitation of operational records in NPPs leads to large uncertainty ranges in probability estimations for risk assessment studies. It is sufficient to recall the uncertainty band that affects the results of the most well-known risk studies and the criticism of this by various review groups[1] to understand how decision-makers are often left in such a state of uncertainty that they do not rely on probabilistic methods, even if these are judged to be the most suitable for safety analysis. Moreover, without the implementation of continuous feedback between power plant operating experience and risk assessment, it is impossible to ensure the necessary control, improvement and updating of risk estimates; thus the confidence of a decision-maker in the technical assessment of the risk, made by experts, can also be a matter of considerable uncertainty.

These considerations were behind the launching of a project to create the European Reliability Data System—ERDS;[2] this is a centralized system whose purpose is not only the procurement of reliability data for probabilistic risk assessments (PRA) but also the setting-up of an organized collection of event information to ensure the necessary feedback from reactor operational experience (e.g. the capability of developing models for failure mechanisms, so as to permit an improved prediction of component behaviour and a deeper understanding of how a fault can appear and develop).

The use of this data system should improve confidence in the safety standards of reactor operation and should allow correct 'risk management' by the plant operators.

ERDS collects, homogenizes, organizes and processes various types of information (component reliability data, abnormal event reports and plant performance data) on NPPs and, more specifically, on Light Water Reactors (LWRs); the original aim of ERDS was to include data for reactors located in the European Community countries, but this was extended to include non-Community data; for example, data from the USA and Sweden.

11.2.2 Information Content of ERDS

On the basis of a feasibility study for the implementation of ERDS, which was successfully terminated at the end of 1979, the information content and the design of the system were defined; the collection of the information to be managed by ERDS is based on data supplied by the power station managements of various utilities and on data from existing national or international data systems, on the basis of agreements with international organizations, with licensing authorities (e.g.NRC in the USA and CEA in France) and with utilities (e.g. ENEL in Italy).

In general, ERDS contains information on two main topics:

—operational data;
—reliability data.

The first topic, operational data, concerns the continuous collection and organization of data on events occurring in nuclear plants (raw data), relevant to the safety and availability of operation: component failures, repairs, abnormal occurrences, changes in power production, etc. Most of these data are collected as an aid to plant management from the points of view of safety and productivity.

The second topic, reliability data, concerns the problem of the availability of generic failure and repair rates for similar classes of components; such data are needed, in the field of reactor safety, for the estimation of the probability of failure of complex, redundant systems, through the use of itemizing techniques such as fault trees, etc. These data can be derived from operational data of plants, through appropriate filtering and processing techniques; they may also be derived from more generic experience and from expert judgements.

To be able to supply ERDS with the various types of information mentioned above, approaches were made to utilities, research centres, licensing authorities, manufacturers and international organizations; these contacts led to a very fruitful co-operative exercise that involved:

—acquisition and analysis of the information handled by the existing data systems;
—elucidation of the requirements of the end-users;
—comparison of the information stored in the different data systems and the definition of suitable reference classifications, to homogenize the content mentioned above.

11.2.3 General Architecture of ERDS

The general architecture[3] of this system was designed to take account of the different nature, the different level of detail and the different aims of the various kinds of information which must be stored in ERDS. The system was therefore subdivided into four main sub-systems (see Fig. 1).

11.2.3.1 Component Event Data Bank—CEDB
The purpose of this sub-system is the merging of data from different European sources on reactor component operational behaviour.[4,5] For each component the engineering characteristics are specified, together with the operational duties, the environmental conditions, etc.; the related failures are also reported in detail. Data managed by this sub-system are coded according to the Common European Reference Classifications.[6-9]

11.2.3.2 Abnormal Occurrences Reporting System—AORS
The purpose of this sub-system is the collection of information on safety-related abnormal events from NPPs in Europe and the USA, to provide a service and a tool for safety analyses.[10,11] This information is collected at present by the national authorities and is mostly in the form of computerized data banks which are based on different data base management systems (DBMSs), languages, organizations and reporting principles. Therefore the AORS comprises two types of bank:

(1) the AORS Data Bank, in which the relevant information from the national data files is stored homogeneously,[12] according to a common format and to the European Reference Classifications;
(2) a set of satellite data banks, in which original data supplied by different countries are stored unmodified, according to their specific classification and format.

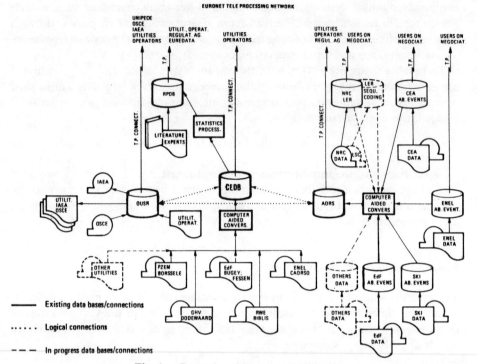

Fig. 1. General architecture of ERDS.

11.2.3.3 Operating Unit Status Report—OUSR

The purpose of this sub-system[26] is the collection, organization and dissemination of information on the productivity factors and on outage data for European NPPs Stored data consist of

—detailed information on outages;
—reactor performance information, allowing the evaluation of productivity factors for each reactor.

11.2.3.4 Reliability Parameter Data Bank—RPDB

The purpose of this sub-system is the collection, organization and dissemination of reliability parameters for similar classes of components operating in similar conditions. These parameters should be obtained by means of an analytical process (which is still in the definition phase), combining parameters extracted from the technical literature with the corresponding data derived from CEDB through its inquiry data-processing procedure.

11.2.4 Data Homogenization

As has previously been outlined, the main role played by the JRC in the development of ERDS was the following:

—to assemble information from different sources, homogenizing its classification and formats;

—to create a computerized structure, capable of handling information in a rational way and of putting it at the disposal of the data suppliers and other authorized organizations;

—to create the software tool (statistical and analytical process, on-line queries, etc.) for accessing and processing data in an intelligent way.

To achieve the first goal, the major problem to be dealt with was the definition of a set of common 'Reference Classifications', which would permit, on the one hand, the merging of information stored and codified in the national data systems, without losing any significant information, and, on the other hand, a correct interrogation of ERDS and an easy pooling of data to be retrieved when computing statistical parameters.[5-9]

These two aspects were difficult to manage because of the different philosophies and methods underlying the various data collection systems and the unequal level of detail adopted by the different national classifications. The set of Reference Classifications developed at Ispra is the following:

—a Plant Classification Scheme, used to characterize the context in which an event occurs (plant type, plant functional structure, plant items);

—a Reference System Classification, providing a breakdown of an NPP into homogeneous functional systems;

—a Component Family Reference Classification, identifying categories of components which have similar engineering characteristics;

—a Component Failure Reference Classification, providing the identification of the failure event in a coded form;

—an Event Reporting Scheme, for the general characterization of an abnormal occurrence and of its pathway for accident or safety significant data banks (e.g. AORS);

—a Common Classification Description List, identifying through literal descriptors or parameter ranges some engineering characteristics which are common to various component families.

More detailed information on the Common Reference Classifications is given in Section 11.3.3.2.

11.2.5 Software Aspects

The ERDS computerized structure has been developed using the ADABAS DBMS (Adaptable Data Base System, version 1.4, of the Software A.G.[13]), installed on an AMDAHL 470-V8 computer, under the IBM, MVS-SP-1.3 Operating System.

The ADABAS data banks can be interrogated through the ITAPAC data transmission network; as query language, ADACCL (an extended version of ADASCRIPT, the query language supplied with ADABAS) may be used for all the banks, under the TSO/ISPF.

CEDB can also be interrogated through an *ad hoc* query language, as will be described later.

The programming languages used to build up ERDS are:

—COBOL ANSI language, enlarged by the Direct Call Feature for access to the ADABAS files;
—NATURAL, a fourth-generation interactive programme language, particularly oriented to the treatment of ADABAS files;
—ADAMINT, a macro-language used in conjunction with COBOL to speed up and standardize the data base access.

11.2.6 Conclusions on ERDS

As was described above, ERDS topic characteristics are the following:

—ERDS manages data which were not created within the JRC services; its main tasks are therefore to merge the information supplied by other organizations, adding to it the supplementary value derived by the homogenization in the centralized management, and to make available sophisticated software facilities.
—The general ERDS architecture, based on four loosely coupled subsystems, is the consequence of the situation existing in the countries of interest from the reliability data collection point of view. The general ERDS structure (even if not the best from a theoretical angle) tries to match practical needs as much as possible and to follow reality closely.
—ERDS is operative at present as far as CEDB and AORS are concerned. For the time being, CEDB stores operational histories of about 5500 components with the related failures (more than 3800), and the AORS Data Bank stores more than 30 000 events, covering 760 reactor-years of experience from 134 reactor units (the AORS information is equivalent to 21% of the world-wide experience gained to date in this environment). ERDS is therefore an important tool, for which many developments are already envisaged as part of the JRC multi-annual research programme on reactor safety.

From the various sub-systems composing ERDS, CEDB has been chosed for a more detailed description: in fact, the CEDB (Component Event Data Bank) may be considered the central, topical sub-system of ERDS (as shown in Fig. 1). It is interconnected to all the other sub-systems, either via logical pointers to OURS and AORS (because the same event may be relevant from both the safety and the productivity point of view), or via a direct feeding of the RPDB (it is envisaged that parameters resulting from statistical processes on the CEDB raw data will be stored directly in RPDB).

CEDB handles data on component characteristics, operational behaviour and failure-event representation; it is therefore the richest source of information in the ERDS framework.

11.3 THE COMPONENT EVENT DATA BANK (CEDB)

11.3.1 General Description of CEDB

As stated above, CEDB is an organized collection of events for major NPP components (mainly for LWR components at present), the technical specifications of which are given, together with their operational and environmental conditions. CEDB relies, for its operation, on the systematic exploitation of the reliability data acquisition systems running in various European countries and on *ad hoc* data collections performed at those power stations for which an information system is not yet operative (see Fig. 2).

The centralized and homogenized set of raw data stored in CEDB may be processed in a homogeneous way,

—to improve the credibility of the estimated reliability and availability parameters by assuming the necessary feedback from the reactor operation;
—to provide a solution to one of the major problems of the reliability analyst by assessing, methodically, well-founded parameters which might assume the value of 'reference' or standard parameters;
—to satisfy the requirements of licensing authorities, architect–engineers, utilities, etc., through the different computerized processes (statistical and analytical–qualitative) to which CEDB data may be submitted (e.g. distribution of failure rate with time, human error analysis, common-mode and common-cause failures, maintenance optimization, influence of environmental conditions, etc.).

11.3.2 Content of CEDB

The component is the focal point of CEDB; each component is uniquely identified so that it is possible to follow a given component during its life-span.

The data bank content[5,14,15] is therefore based on sets of information where each individual datum is related to a given component or to a failure of that component.

CEDB handles the following types of information:

11.3.2.1 Fixed Information on the Component

● The component's internal identification code, used by CEDB to identify a component uniquely; this is represented by a progressive number.
● The component's external identification code, which is added to the component identification code as used by the data supplier to identify a component uniquely within a reactor plant; this consists of the IAEA reactor code and a component progressive number. The latter code is needed for those utilities which identify a component by its position in the reactor map at a given time; the progressive number allows singling out of the different components which follow one another in the same position.
● The engineering characteristics (up to 20 attributes of two types: coded values and nominal values.[5]

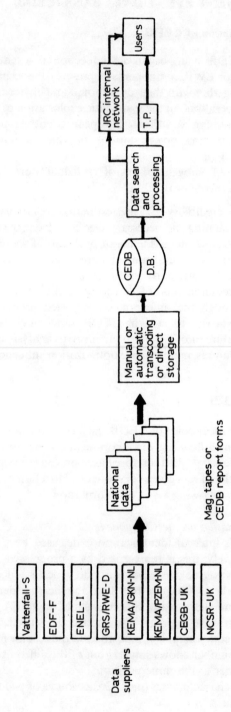

Fig. 2. General structure of CEDB.

- The functional system under which a given component operates (identified on the basis of the Reference System Classification[5,6]).
- Information on the manufacturer (manufacturer identification code, serial number for the given component, date of construction).
- In-service date and scrapping date (date on which the component was removed from service or replaced).
- The safety classes defined on the basis of existing standards, giving an indication of the quality level of the component.

11.3.2.2 Historical Information on the Operating Characteristics under which the Component Operates[5]
- Installation environment, e.g. pressure, temperature, humidity, corrosion, vibration, type of industry in which the component is used, etc.
- Operation mode and duty-related attributes, giving an indication of the type of stresses to which the component is subjected.
- Maintenance type and schedule, giving an indication of the regime of monitoring and periodic checking.

This group of information constitutes an 'operation' status, identified by an operation date at the beginning.

11.3.2.3 Historical Information on the Operating History
- Per year: the operating hours or number of cycles or demands for each component.

11.3.2.4 Failure Information[5,7]
- The failure code, used by CEDB, and represented by a progressive number.
- The failure external code, used by the utility to identify a failure uniquely.
- Unavailability time for the failed component and repair time.
- Failure modes and means of detection.
- Failure causes, failure descriptors and parts failed.
- Reactor status before the failure and failure effect on the reactor operation, on the system in which the failed component is installed and on other systems.
- Actions taken, corrective and/or administrative.
- Operating hours or number of cycles/demands for the failed component at the failure time.
- Other related failures (identified with their identification codes).
- A narrative failure description.

Temporal links between these various groups of information on the component, its operation conditions and history and the possible failures are established by a set of dates which allows a check of the correctness of the order in time of the different events. The most significant dates are the in-service and the scrapping date of the component, the date identifying a new operational 'status', the failure date and the unavailability date.

11.3.3 Input Procedure for CEDB

11.3.3.1 Data Collection
In summary, each reportable event may be thought of as being composed of three main issues:

(a) identification of the item involved in the event and of its characteristics (component engineering pedigree, operating and installation conditions);
(b) identification of the type of event and of its characteristics and consequences;
(c) identification of the operating history of the component.

The (a) information must be reported when monitoring of the component starts (engineering pedigree information is provided only once during the life of a component) and when the operation conditions are changed. The (b) information must be reported each time a failure occurs on a monitored component. The (c) information must be reported, for all the monitored components, on an annual basis.

To make the reporting operation easier, four report forms[4,5,15] were designed which were suitable for the Reference Classifications defined at Ispra:

—the component report form (Fig. 3);
—the operation report form (Fig. 4);
—the failure report form (Fig. 5);
—the annual operating report form (Fig. 6).

With the exception of a small amount of information automatically added by the system, the completion of these reports would supply CEDB with all the information required. In reality, only a few organizations supply their data using these forms; most European utilities manage their own data collection systems and send data to Ispra (on magnetic or paper tape) which are collected and codified according to specific methods, structures and classifications. In practice, the input information for the most part must be converted to the European format and classifications through a transcoding activity which at present is performed manually with the help of a small computerized support.

The current development of a semi-automatic transcoding system is described in Section 11.3.6.[16]

11.3.3.2 Reference Classifications
One of the most complex problems to be solved in the creation of a suitable and correct CEDB was the drawing up of a set of Reference Classifications to allow, on the one hand, the merging of information already coded in the various national data systems, without losing any relevant information, and, on the other hand, the construction of easy to interpret and easy to use intelligent codifications.

By analysing the coding methods used by almost all the existing reliability data systems in Europe and in the USA, a set of Reference Classifications has been developed,[5] which represents a fairly original and new set of codings, the usefulness of which may be envisaged to cover not only the needs of the ERDS project, but also

EUROPEAN RELIABILITY DATA SYSTEM - ERDS
COMPONENT EVENTS DATA BANK - CEDB

COMPONENT REPORT FORM

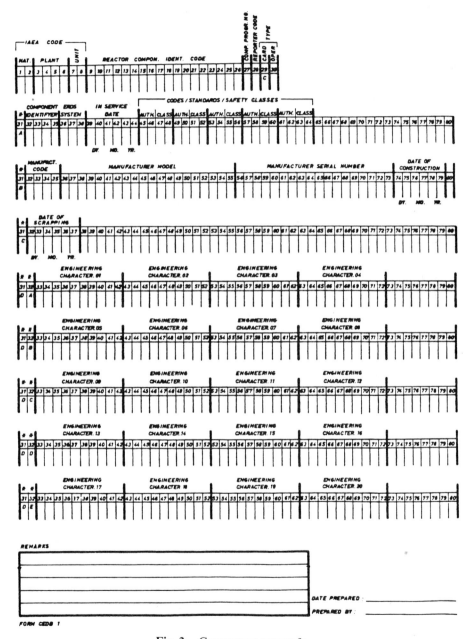

Fig. 3. Component report form.

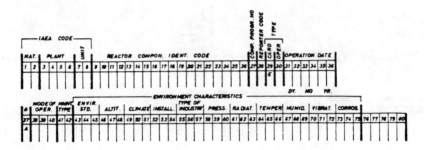

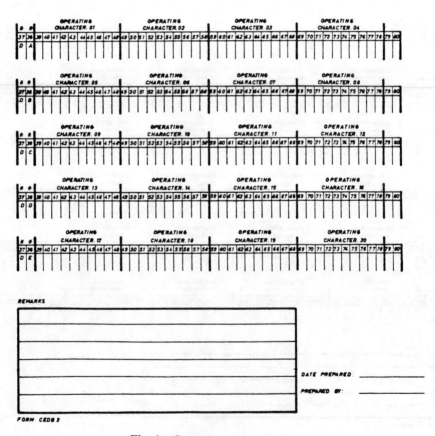

Fig. 4. Operation report form.

EUROPEAN RELIABILITY DATA SYSTEM – EROS

COMPONENT EVENTS DATA BANK – CEDB

FAILURE REPORT FORM

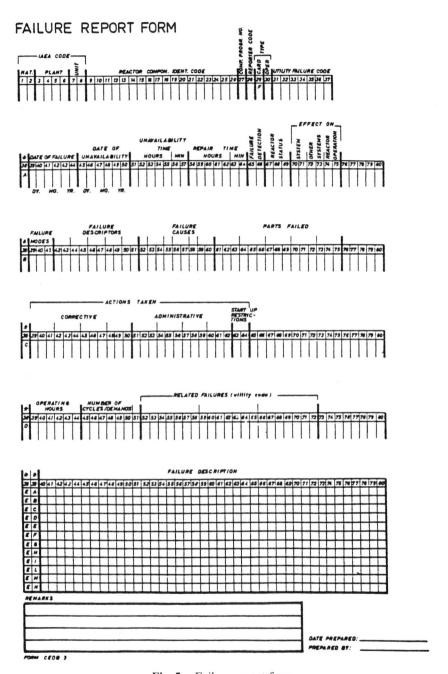

Fig. 5. Failure report form.

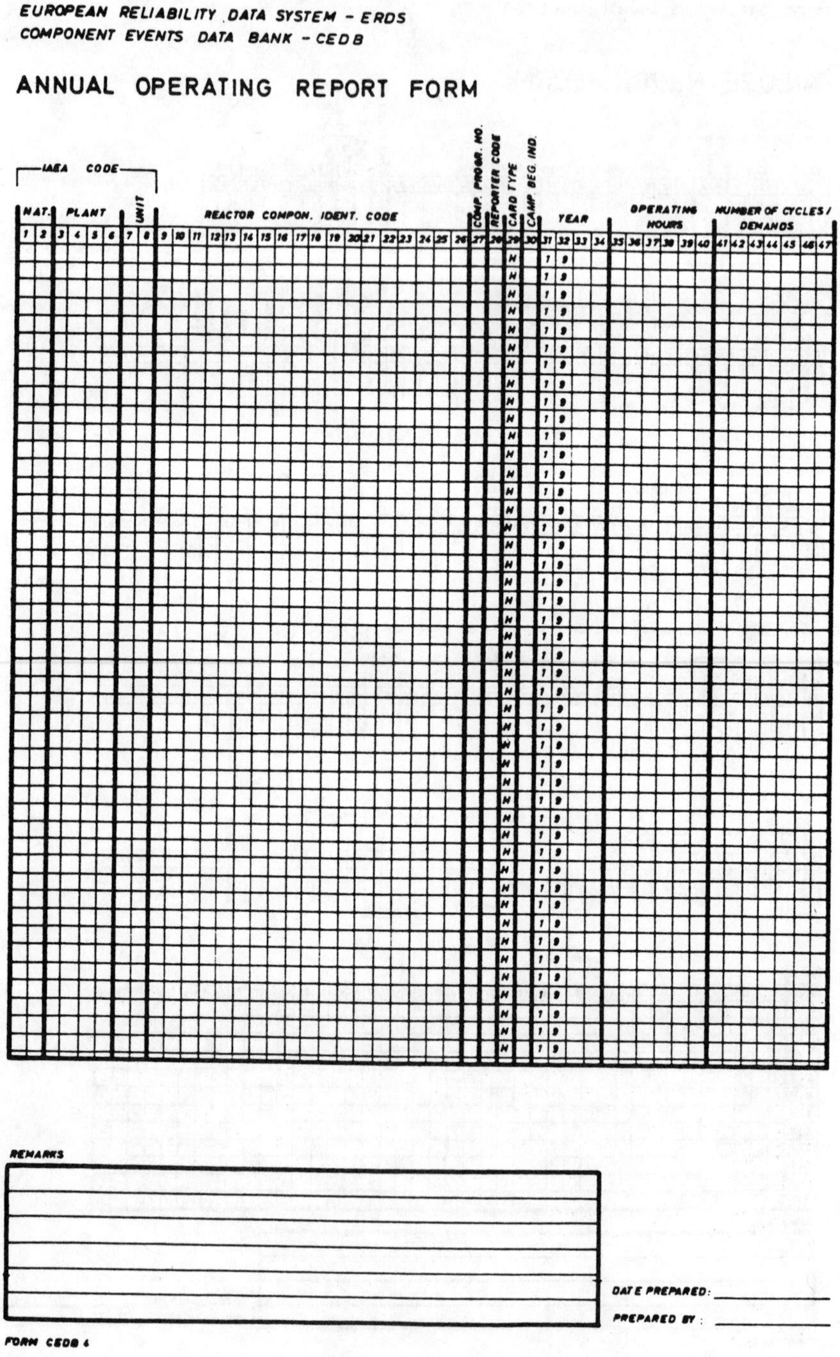

Fig. 6. Annual operating report form.

those of safety authorities and industry. Before describing in detail these classifications, some basic definitions are given here to clarify the logical environment in which they were developed:[8]

—A *component family* code identifies a category of components having similar engineering characteristics (e.g. pump; see Fig. 7).

—A *component* is a structure, or equipment, considered as an aggregate of mechanical or electrical parts, constituting a well-identified element in the plant.

—The *component engineering and operating* characteristics constitute the minimum set of attributes required to assess the reliability of a component.

—The *component mode of operation* or duty identifies the operational regime of the component in a specific plant system. A component can be called upon to perform a function continuously, cyclically or on demand.

—The *component failure* is defined as the termination or the degradation of the ability of a component to perform a required function; it is a component malfunction which requires some repair.

—The *failure mode* is defined as the effect by which a component failure is observed. Failure mode types are correlated with the component operation mode. Failure modes are subdivided into two general classes:

● '(not demanded) change of operating conditions (or state)' for components asked to accomplish a function during a certain time;
● 'demanded change of state not achieved, or not correctly achieved' for components which are called to operate on demand.

—A *system* is a set of mechanical, electrical or electronic components uniquely identified by whether:

● it accomplishes a clearly defined function in the plant;
● it accomplishes more than one function but in different plant-operating modes (i.e. cold-shutdown, emergency, normal operation).

—A *system grouping* is a set of NPP systems characterized by common properties, such as:

● functions which can be framed in a more general 'logic' function (i.e. protection and control system);
● functions related to the accomplishment of general plant-operating services (i.e. auxiliary systems).

As far as the Reference Classifications are concerned, the most important are the following.

The reference system classification. This classification defines 'functional systems' on the basis of a functional breakdown of NPPs (pressurized water reactor (PWR) and boiling water reactors (BWR) at present) to identify each plant engineering system according to its function in the plant.[8]

ACTE	Electromechanical Actuator	ELHE	Electrical Heater
ACTH	Hydraulic Actuator	ELMO	Electric Motor
ACTP	Pneumatic Actuator	ENGI	Internal Combustion Engine
AMPL	Amplifier	EXCH	Heat Exchanger
ANCT	Annunciator Module/Alarm	FILT	Filter
BATC	Battery Charger	FUSE	Fuse
BATT	Battery	GENE	Electrical Generator
BLOW	Blower/Fan/Ventilator	INCO	Instrumentation–Controllers
BOIL	Boiler	INST	Instrumentation—Field
CKBR	Circuit Breaker	INSU	Insulator
CLTW	Cooling Tower	MOPU	Motor–Pump Unit
CLUT	Clutch	PIPE	Piping/Fitting
COMP	Compressor	PUMP	Pump
CPCT	Capacitor	RECT	Rectifier
DLGE	Diesel-Generator set	:	::
DRYE	Air, Gas Dryer/Dehumidifier		

Fig. 7.   Component family reference classification list.

In drawing up the Reference System Classification, the first step was the establishment of hierarchical levels for categorization of the plant. The chosen hierarchy is based on three levels: component, system and system grouping, defined as above. The next step was the analysis of plant layouts of commercial nuclear power stations and of the related process flow-sheets and operating mode, to identify a set of functions which, if accomplished, ensure a safe and continuous plant operation. Four fundamental 'families' of functions were singled out:

- functions essential to plant operation;
- safety functions;
- nuclear island auxiliary functions;
- BOP (balance of plant) auxiliary functions.

After a subdivision of these families (logic tree analysis) into their elementary functions it was possible to identify each system according to the function it accomplishes inside the plant. Thirteen system groupings were coded using an alphabetical character, from A to O (see Fig.8) together with 180 systems belonging to those groupings. The systems are identified by an alphanumeric code (see, as an example, Fig. 9). Each system has an associated sheet (Fig. 10), containing:

—a comprehensive description of the system function(s) and of the main system boundaries;
—a description of the plant operating modes (normal, emergency, etc.) linked to the various system functions;
—a list of the main interfaces to the system;
—a list of the main components of the system, with the corresponding Safety Class.

The main advantage of this functional breakdown of a nuclear plant into systems is that it enables the analyst to interrogate CEDB on the failures related to a particular

A   Nuclear heat system: plant systems involved in nuclear heat generation, exchange and transport.
B   Engineered safety features: plant systems providing accident-consequences limitation (i.e. to avoid release of fission products to the environment).
C   Reactor auxiliary system: nuclear-island systems which are essential to normal and cold shutdown operation.
D   Fuel storage and handling system: plant systems involved in nuclear fuel management (i.e. relocation of fuel elements and storage, cooling and purification of fuel-pools).
E   Radioactive waste management system: plant systems accomplishing the collection and treatment of solid, liquid, gaseous radioactive waste resulting from plant operation.
F   Steam and power conversion system: plant systems involved in steam-and-feedwater cycles inside the nuclear power station (i.e. steam expansion in turbines, steam condensation).
G   Power transmission system: plant systems providing mechanical/electrical energy conversion, and electrical energy transmission to HV station and plant MV–LV distribution lines.

Fig. 8.   System groupings—list and definitions.

Code	System
B	Engineered safety features
B1	Reactor containment system (PWR)
B2	Reactor containment system (BWR)
B3	Containment spray system
B4	Containment isolation system
B5	Containment pressure suppression system (BWR)
B6	Pressure relief system (PWR)
B7	Hydrogen venting system
B8	Post-accident containment atmosphere mixing system
B9	Containment gas control system
B10	Auxiliary feedwater system (PWR)
B11	Reactor core isolation cooling system (BWR)
B12	Emergency boration system (PWR)
B13	Standby liquid control system (BWR)
B14	Residual heat removal system (PWR)
B15	Residual heat removal system (BWR)
B16	High-pressure coolant injection system (PWR)
B17	Accumulator system (PWR)
B18	Low-pressure coolant injection system (PWR)
B19	Nuclear boiler overpressure protection system (BWR)
B20	High-pressure core spray system (BWR)
B21	High-pressure coolant injection system (BWR)
B22	Low-pressure core spray system (BWR)
B23	Low-pressure coolant injection system (BWR)

Fig. 9.   Functional systems belonging to the 'engineered safety features' system grouping.

System C7—Primary loads service water system

This system is designed to remove heat from various components of the nuclear system, such as the PCCW heat exchangers, the diesel generator heat exchangers and various HVAC units. Under normal conditions, the primary loads are cooled by the service water system; under emergency conditions the service water system is isolated and the primary loads service water system pumps are started to transfer heat from the essential loads to the ultimate heat sink system. The system is a closed cooling water line, from the cooled component (excluded) to the cooling towers (ultimate heat sink system), and return (see Fig. 2).

Mode of operation: the system is operating on emergency conditions

Main interface systems:
• Engineered safety features systems (B1–2–3–4–5–6–7–8–9–10–11–12–13–14–15)
• ECCS systems (B16–17–18–19–20–21–22–23)
• Primary component cooling water system (C5)
• Ultimate heat sink system (C8)
• Control room building HVAC system (M12)
• Diesel-generator system (H5)
• Engineered safety features actuation system (L3)
• Fuel building HVAC system (M13)
• Service water system (N1)

Main components	Safety class
• Pumps (centrifugal)	3
• Motors (three-phase, induction)	3
• Piping	3
• Valves (check, globe, butterfly, other)	3
• Isolation valves	2
• Instrumentation and controls	
• Cables	

Fig. 10.   Example of a sheet for an engineering system.

Boundary definition:
Component boundary is identified by its interface with the electric power source and plant equipment, i.e.

—cable terminal (included)
—coupling devices (excluded), connecting the electromechanical actuator to the driven item.

Auxiliary devices:

—positioner
—other devices, when they are essential to the component operation, are included within the component boundary, as far as they are dedicated to the unit.

Protection and trip devices (limit switches, overload, locked-rotor protection, winding temperature, other local protection devices) are included within the component boundary. Instrumentation/alarms for the monitoring of the status of the component are included within the component boundary.

Fig. 11.   Electromechanical actuator (ACTE).

1	Enclosure
18	Stator
19	Stator windings
20	Rotor
21	Rotor bars
22	Insulation
23	Flywheel
24	Ring collector
25	Brushes
26	Excitation devices
27	Stator terminals
16	Instrumentation/monitors/recorders
51	Commutator (DC motors)
80X	Lubrication devices
81X	Cooling system
82X	Protection devices

Fig. 12. Electromechanical actuator (ACTE); piece part list.

function accomplishment; this is a great help for the analyst when studying plant operation behaviour from the point of view of safety and availability, but can be extended to serve the needs of design, procurement, construction and operation of any nuclear power station.

The component family reference classification.[5] This classification aims at regrouping into homogeneous families components of similar engineering characteristics, to allow the merging of similar components of the same or of different plants and to achieve a sample size which justifies a successive statistical treatment. Almost 60 components types have been identified and coded (see Fig. 11). An example of the Component Family Reference Classification is given in Fig. 7. For each component family the following information is given:

—an exact definition of the component boundaries and of the auxiliary devices (see Fig. 11);
—a piece part list, i.e. a list of the main component parts which form the component itself (see Fig. 12);
—a series of up to 20 engineering attributes, internally hierarchically coded up to a maximum of three levels, which provides an exhaustive identification of the component from an engineering point of view (see Fig. 13). By combining these attributes it is possible to interrogate CEDB at various levels of detail, so allowing CEDB users to create the 'family' they require for their particular needs.

Almost 200 different engineering attributes are identified at the time. Because some of the attributes providing an engineering characterization are common to various component families, they have been coded as 'Common Descriptors'; these are identified by a two-character alphabetical code and handle two groups of information:

- literal descriptors (e.g. lubrication type) (see Figs 14 and 15);
- parameter ranges (e.g. temperature ranges) (see Figs 16 and 17)

these may be used by any component type.

Dealing with features which are common to more than one component type, makes possible the analysis of the influence of certain engineering attributes on the performance of various pieces of equipment (e.g. investigation on the performance

ACTE	ELECTROMECHANICAL ACTUATOR
ACTE01	TYPE
ACTE0101	DIRECT CURRENT
ACTE0101ZZ	N.O.C.
ACTE010101	PERMANENT MAGNET
ACTE010102	SERIES WOUND
ACTE010103	SHUNT WOUND
ACTE010199	OTHER
ACTE0102	AC, SYNCHRONOUS
ACTE0103	AC, INDUCTION
ACTE0103ZZ	N.O.C.
ACTE010301	SQUIRREL CAGE
ACTE010302	WOUND ROTOR
ACTE010303	REPULSION START
ACTE010304	SPLIT-PHASE
ACTE010305	DRUG CAP
ACTE010399	OTHER
ACTE0199	OTHER
ACTE02	CURRENT TYPE
ACTE0201	DIRECT
ACTE0202	A.C. MONOPHASE
ACTE0203	A.C. THREEPHASE
ACTE0299	OTHER
ACTE03	APPLICATION
ACTE0301	INSTRUMENT-SERVO
ACTE0302	VALVE-OPERATION
ACTE0399	OTHER
ACTE04	ROTATION
ACTE0401	REVERSIBLE
ACTE0402	NOT-REVERSIBLE
ACTE05	NUMBER OF POLES
ACTE0501	BIPOLAR MACHINE
ACTE0502	MULTIPOLAR MACHINE
ACTE06	COOLING TYPE
ACTE0601	AIR COOLING
ACTE0601ZZ	N.O.C.
ACTE060101	NATURAL VENTILATION

Fig. 13. Partial list of the attributes defining the electromechanical actuator component family.

AT   Actuation
BL   Blading type
BT   Bearings type
CD   Cylinders disposition
CN   Cylinder number
CO   Connection type
CT   Cooling type
CY   Current type
DC   Delivery control/regulation
DR   Driver
DS   Disposition
ET   Excitation type
FA   Fabrication type
IC   Insulation classes
LT   Lubrication type
MA   Materials
MH   Medium handled
NS   Number of stages
PA   Protection mode 1 (against ingress of foreign bodies)
PB   Protection mode 2 (against liquid ingress)
⋮   ⋮

Fig. 14.   Common descriptor list.

****(AT)   ACTUATION
****(AT)01   DIFFERENTIAL PRESSURE/SPRING
****(AT)02   ELECTRIC MOTOR/SERVO
****(AT)03   EXPLOSIVE
****(AT)04   FLOAT
****(AT)05   HYDRAULIC
****(AT)06   DIRECT MANUAL
****(AT)07   MECHANICAL TRANSMISSION
****(AT)08   PNEUMATIC,DIAPHRAGM/CYLINDER
****(AT)09   SOLENOID
****(AT)10   THERMAL
****(AT)11   DYNAMIC-SENSITIVE
****(AT)12   REMOTE MANUAL
****(AT)13   ELECTROMAGNETIC
****(AT)14   THERMAL-MAGNETIC
****(AT)15   INDUCTION
****(AT)16   ELECTRONIC
****(AT)17   VOCAL
****(AT)99   OTHER

Fig. 15.   Values possible for the AT (Actuation) literal common descriptor.

AY	Accuracy class	PR	Pressure
CA	Capacity	PS	Particle size
CF	Compression factor	PW	Power/heat rating
CP	Capacitance	RC	Rupturing capacity
CS	Conductor size	RE	Efficiency
CU	Current	RS	Rotational speed
ER	Electrical resistance	RT	Response time
FO	Developed force	SC	Short-circuit ratio
FR	Frequency	SK	Stroke
FS	Fluid speed	TE	Temperature coefficient
GA	Gain	TH	Height
LO	Load/Pound	TN	Tube number
MF	Mass flow	TQ	Torque
NC	Number of operational cycles	TR	Torque ratio
OD	Tube outside diameter	:	:
PF	Power factor		

Fig. 16. Engineering parameter list.

of sealing devices working in different media for a sample including pumps and valves). In the same way, the set of common parameter ranges, covering the numerical parameters defined in the Family Classification, is a useful guide for CEDB users when pooling data for evaluation of reliability characteristics.

Failure reference classification. This classification aims to provide complete reporting and identification of a failure in a coded form, to allow users to perform an in-depth analysis of this information. In fact, different classes of users are concerned with the failure data:

—safety/reliability analysts, mainly interested in the effects of failures on the component state;

—utilities, who are interested in operating conditions and maintenance influence on component availability, to optimize maintenance frequency, spare part management and productivity indices;

—licensing authorities, who wish to identify recurrent or abnormal failure patterns which may invalidate previous safety assessments (e.g. malfunctions because of common-cause failures, etc.);

—manufacturers, interested in the cause of component failures, failed parts, etc.

The Failure Classification[5,7] was therefore subdivided into many reference classifications, each specifically oriented to a particular aspect of the problem, as follows:

(1) *Failure mode*, describing the effect by which a failure is observed on the failed component; this effect consists of a variation of the status of the component which results from the failure. Two different, mutually exclusive, 'failure modes' exist, according to the following:

   • a change of status, when requested, is not (completely) fulfilled (failure on demand);

****(CS)	CONDUCTOR SIZE (METER)
****(CS)01	UP TO 1.0 E$-$5
****(CS)02	1.0 E$-$5 TO 1.0 E$-$4
****(CS)03	1·0 E$-$4 TO 1·0 E$-$3
****(CS)04	1·0 E$-$3 TO 1.0 E$-$2
****(CS)05	1.0 E$-$2 TO 5.0 E$-$2
****(CS)06	5.0 E$-$2 TO 1.0 E$-$1
****(CS)99	MORE THAN 1.0 E$-$1

****(CU)	CURRENT (AMPERE)
****(CU)01	UP TO 1.0 E$-$3
****(CU)02	1.0 E$-$3 TO 1.0 E$-$2
****(CU)03	1.0 E$-$2 TO 1·0 E$-$1
****(CU)04	1.0 E$-$1 TO 1.0 E$+$0
****(CU)05	1·0 E$+$0 TO 1.0 E$+$1
****(CU)06	1.0 E$+$1 TO 5.0 E$+$1
****(CU)07	5.0 E$+$1 TO 1.0 E$+$2
****(CU)08	1.0 E$+$2 TO 5.0 E$+$2
****(CU)09	5.0 E$+$3 TO 1.0 E$+$3
****(CU)10	1.0 E$+$3 TO 2.0 E$+$3
****(CU)11	2.0 E$+$3 TO 6.0 E$+$3
****(CU)12	6.0 E$+$3 TO 1.2 E$+$4
****(CU)99	MORE THAN 1.2 E$+$4

****(ER)	ELECTRICAL RESISTANCE (OHM)
****(ER)01	UP TO 1.0 E$-$4
****(ER)02	1.0 E$-$4 TO 1.0 E$-$3
****(ER)03	1.0 E$-$3 TO 1.0 E$-$2
****(ER)04	1.0 E$-$2 TO 1.0 E$-$1
****(ER)05	1.0 E$-$1 TO 1.0 E$+$0
****(ER)06	1.0 E$+$0 TO 1.0 E$+$1
****(ER)07	1.0 E$+$1 TO 1.0 E$+$2
****(ER)08	1·0 E$+$2 TO 1.0 E$+$3
****(ER)09	1.0 E$+$3 TO 1.0 E$+$4
****(ER)10	1.0 E$+$4 TO 1.0 E$+$5
****(ER)11	1.0 E$+$5 TO 1.0 E$+$6
****(ER)12	1.0 E$+$6 TO 1.0 E$+$7
****(ER)13	1.0 E$+$7 TO 1·0 E$+$8
****(ER)14	1·0 E$+$8 TO 1.0 E$+$9
****(ER)15	1.0 E$+$9 TO 1.0 E$+$12
****(ER)16	1.0 E$+$12 TO 1.0 E$+$15
****(ER)99	MORE THAN 1.0 E$+$15

****(FO)	DEVELOPED FORCE (NEWTON)
****(FO)01	UP TO 5.0 E$+$1
****(FO)02	5.0 E$+$1 TO 1.0 E$+$2
****(FO)03	1.0 E$+$2 TO 2.5 E$+$2
****(FO)04	2.5 E$+$2 TO 5.0 E$+$2
****(FO)05	5.0 E$+$2 TO 1.0 E$+$3
****(FO)99	MORE THAN 1·0 E$+$3

Fig. 17.   Numeric ranges for a sample of engineering common descriptors.

- a change occurs when the component is in operation (failure in operation).

For the 'failure mode on demand' a suitable set of codes was defined, specifying the status which was not achieved (e.g. 'Won't open'; 'Fails to stop'; etc.); for the 'failure mode in operation' the suddenness of the change in conditions (e.g. 'incipient' failure) and the degree of seriousness of the failure itself (e.g. 'outside specifications') are described.

(b) *Failure cause*, describing the original causes of the item failure, i.e. the circumstances during design, manufacture, assembly, installation or use which led to failure. This classification is hierarchical and was defined for engineering, manufacturing, maintenance, abnormal services, etc. errors (e.g. 'incorrect procedure, or incorrect instruction for maintenance').

(c) *Failure descriptors*, reporting—through numerically codified keywords—information on attributes of the failure event that can be deduced on the basis of the knowledge of the failure mechanism and of the physical phenomena involved. These codes have been grouped into classes:

- descriptors related to instrumentation failures (e.g. '29': instability/oscillation);
- descriptors related to electrical failures (e.g. '22': short circuit);
- descriptors related to material failures (e.g. '18': corrosion/erosion);
- descriptors related to external foreign causes (e.g. '34': liquid ingress);
- descriptors related to design/construction causes (e.g. '41': misalignment);
- etc.

(d) *Failure detection*, reporting the way and means by which a failure was discovered. The codes are organized so as to distinguish between the failures detected during maintenance and those detected during normal operation (e.g. 'routine surveillance').

(e) *Part failed* codes, reporting the parts involved in the failure. These parts must previously have been included in the list for each component family.

(f) *Action taken*, providing an exhaustive description of the action to be taken by the maintenance staff. This action can be corrective (e.g. 'repair with partial disassembly', 'replace part', etc.) or administrative. In the latter case, the information on the action to be taken is based on three hierarchical pieces of information:

- repair schedule (e.g. '1U': urgent repair);
- alteration of plant operation (e.g. '2P': power reduction required);
- type of documentation (e.g. '3M': failure submitted to national licensing authority).

The possible start-up restrictions imposed by licensing authorities following an enforced stop caused by a component failure have also been coded (e.g. 'LR': request licence revision).

(g) *Status of the reactor*, providing information on the status of the plant at the time of the failure occurrence (e.g. 'I1A': in testing phase; 'J1': shutting-down).

(h) *Effects of failure*, reporting the consequences of a failure on:

- the system to which the component belongs (e.g. 'D': degraded system operation; 'R': loss of redundancy);
- other systems or components (e.g. 'FO': failure of other systems/ components);
- reactor operation (e.g. 'C': delayed coupling; 'P2': power reduction).

11.3.4 Architecture of CEDB

As was mentioned in Section 11.2.5, CEDB was implemented on an AMDAHL 470-V8 computer, under the OS/MVS, using the features offered by the DBMS ADABAS of the Software A.G.

On the basis of the information content of CEDB and of the requirements expressed by users, a main relational *structure*[14] was chosen, to design the architecture of this sub-system; it is a central descendant relation, practically hierarchical, the root of which is the 'component'. The successive levels are the 'operation and environment data' and the 'failure' (see Fig. 18).

There are other multiple relations in the data bank which allow access to the

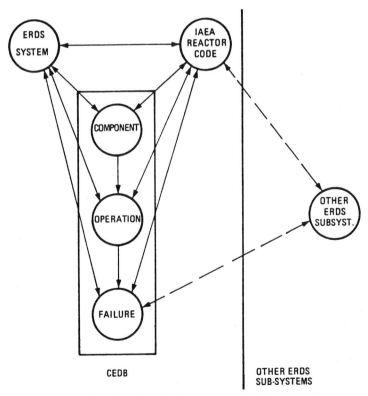

Fig. 18. Relational structure of CEDB.

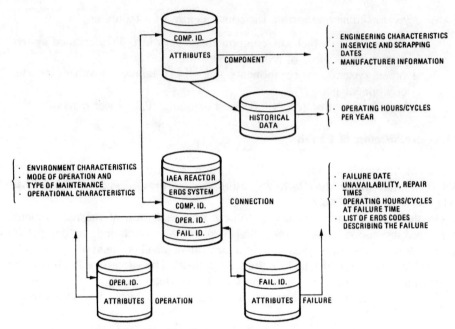

Fig. 19. Physical-logical structure of CEDB.

stored data by any logical entity represented in this figure: i.e. access to the data bank through the Reactor IAEA code, through the ERDS System Reference code (functional systems) or passing from the failure to the component involved. At the same time, these access routes may be used by other ERDS sub-systems (AORS, OURS) to link them to all the data available in CEDB.

Figure 19 shows the *physical–logical* structure,[14] which was implemented to realize the rationale of the relational structure mentioned above. Its three main logical entities ('component', 'operation' and 'failure') and their attributes are subdivided into four physical files, but they must be closely related. This is achieved by means of a 'connection file', which provides adequate links between the three logical entities.

The connection file uses internal codes (identifiers) to identify uniquely each component, operation and failure handled by CEDB. These identifiers (progressive numbers) allow the user:

—to homogenize the different national identification codes, which are generally very long (up to 33 characters for a failure);
—to reduce redundancy and to permit a two-directional link (saving an average of 25 characters with regard to national codes);
—to allow direct links with other ERDS sub-systems which use different external identifiers as implemented by the national data collection systems.

In the connection file the internal identifiers are supplied with external national identification codes, which differ from each other in format and nature; by storing these codes, the CEDB sub-systems are also capable of giving the national data suppliers data identified according to their own coding method.

The full physical structure of CEDB also requires two service files:

—IAEA reactor file, which holds information on all the NPPs installed world-wide. CEDB is continuously connected to a special version of this file, designed at Ispra;

—tables file, in which all the tables concerning the Reference Classifications and a set of other useful tables[17] are stored.

11.3.5 Software Considerations

11.3.5.1 Validation and Data Input/Update Procedure

The update procedure currently running[5,15] has been implemented in batch mode, bearing in mind the large amount of information to be treated and the difficulties caused by the transcoding operation (either performed manually or computerized). Input data are submitted to a series of controls at two levels:

—formal checks, such as checks for the presence of mandatory data, agreement with coding in the reference tables, values included in ranges, etc.;

—coherence checks, such as checks for the correct succession of events, correctness of temporal sequences, checking of data credibility, consistency of data, etc.

These coherence checks are fundamental in guaranteeing data validity and quality.

Depending on error severity, various actions are taken; adequate lists are supplied to support users in correcting the errors detected and in monitoring the status of the sub-system.

From a software point of view, the updating procedure is composed of several modular programs. The techniques used in these programs are the following:

—top-down programming;

—structured programming reflecting the problem;

—division of the program into self-contained blocks;

—use of state diagrams.

An important characteristic of the updating procedure is that it can be automatically restarted at any point.

11.3.5.2 Outputs of CEDB

CEDB outputs are of two fundamental types:

(a) Printed listings, reporting data extracted by the data base or the results of statistical and analytical processes;

(b) Displayed information, reporting 'on demand' on a video-screen any possible selection of raw data and/or the results (analytical or statistical) of a data processing.

This type of output is generally supplied to the authorized users by means of an *ad hoc* Query and Analysis System which was designed and implemented specifically for CEDB.

Data and statistical–analytical reports (batch reports). These reports present the contents of the data base, complete or partial (according to various criteria), unchanged or elaborated. Among these reports the following general ones may be quoted:

—a report on all the components with their operational characteristics and
  failures;
—a report on component engineering characteristics;
—a failure report for specific families of components;
—reports periodically producing statistical parameters, including a constant rate
  distribution and a time-dependent distribution analysis;
—special reports concerning analytical studies on the content of CEDB (this
  aspect will be presented in the following sections, because the printed results
  may be considered as a by-product of an on-line treatment).

On-line enquiry and treatment. On-line access to CEDB is technically available via ITAPAC, the Italian network connected to the other teleprocessing national networks; Ispra users can query CEDB via the JRC internal network (see Fig. 2). Access to CEDB is protected against unauthorized entry by means of a password mechanism, and the potential CEDB users (who are not data suppliers) must meet specific requirements to be entitled to free access to the bank.

Because of the complexity of the CEDB structure and content, and to avoid problems or misinterpretation by users, an original 'Query and Analysis System' has been designed and implemented.[4,18,19] This system makes possible the selection of any desired information sample (according to the basic descendant relationship: component–operation–failure) and its submission to multiple types of qualitative and quantitative analysis.

The general logic of the enquiry tends to favour the presumed most frequent enquiry, which has the aim of computing statistical parameters of reliability, and it therefore follows the descendant relationship: component–operation–failure (see Fig. 20).

The selection of a given subset of information stored in CEDB is therefore a three-step search by criteria on components, operations and failures, which produces at least three sets of components and a set of failures. The first set of components retrieved by the Query and Analysis System is uniquely identified by the component characteristics; the second set of components is a subset of the first, obtained by stepwise refinements applied to the operational/environment characteristics, and the last (the third set) is a subset of the second component set, obtained by stepwise refinements applied to the characteristics of the failures which occurred to the components belonging to the second subset. At this third level one set of failures and one of components are retrieved, and the computerized treatments are applied to these last significant sets of the selection.

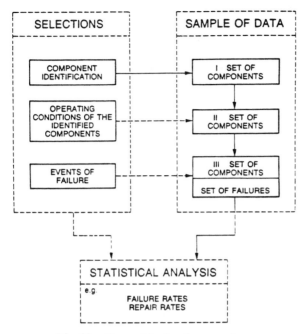

Fig. 20. General logic of an enquiry.

Many criteria may be taken into account when selecting, for example, a set of components, and very often the end-user refines his question in a stepwise way. It is therefore usual for a user to retrieve many component (and failure) sets before he is satisfied.

On the other hand, in a new selection, one can refer to any of the sets of components identified from an earlier selection, and use them as a starting point for further enquiries (see Fig. 20). Figure 21 shows the commands which can be used during a session. These commands have the following structure:

ACTION   [OBJECT]   [PARAMETERS]

ACTION   name of the command;
OBJECT   of the action; this can be omitted in the case of a default or when it does not exist for some actions;
PARAMETERS   depending on the action; some can have a default.

Examples:	ACTION	OBJECT	PARAMETERS
	SELECT	Component	WITH identifier = valv
	STAT	S01	CLE
	DISPLAY	S01	

where S01 is the name of a selected set, given automatically in the selection step, and where CLE is a statistical parameter defining the classical estimation.

SESSION INQUIRY COMMANDS

I° STAGE	II STAGE		III STAGE		IV STAGE
OPENING OF THE SESSION AND GENERAL INFORMATION COMMANDS	SELECTIONS		STATISTICAL ANALYSIS		CLOSING OF THE SESSION
	MAIN COMMANDS	OTHER COMMANDS	MAIN COMMANDS	TEST COMMANDS	
LOGON					
HELP DISPLAY					
	SELECT { with criteria / OR / Snn END SELECTION	CANCEL DELETE DISPLAY DISTRIBUTION HELP SHOW DISTRIBUT + SHOW			
			STAT { CLE / BAE	STAT ENT	
					LOGOFF

Fig. 21.   Session enquiry commands.

The commands are of three main types:

—general commands of a session (LOGON and LOGOFF, HELP, DISPLAY...)
—commands of a selection (SELECT...)
—statistical commands (STAT...)

Help facilities are provided at any time during the enquiry, allowing, for example, the consultation of codification tables, engineering characteristics classifications and the history of the previous selections. The 'STAT' COMMAND (statistical processing command) is of particular interest for users. It must be used, if statistical results are required, after a 'SELECTION' operation has been performed; at this time a set of components (e.g. S01) is available together with a related failure set. The user can then launch different types of computerized processes according to the requirements of his problem and to the assumptions that can be made on the retrieved sample. Two examples are given here of the way the STAT command may be used:

—If the user assumes that the S01 component set has a constant failure rate and he wants to estimate its failure rate by the classical method, the COMMAND to be given is:

STAT S01 CLE.

In this case the system will display the mean value (MU) for the failure rate, the standard deviation (STD) and the 90% symmetrical confidence interval; the parameter 'CLE' means 'CLASSICAL method'. The answer of the computer may be, for example, as follows:

STATISTICAL SAMPLE: 117 COMPONENTS WITH 35 FAILURES
CLASSICAL METHOD, CONST. FAILURE RATE ON S01

$N = 2006643$ $R = 35$

RESULTS: MEAN VALUE $= 1.74E - 05$, STAND. DEV. $= 2.95E - 06$

90% SYMMETR.CONF.INT. $= (1.29E - 05; 2.31E - 05)$

where N is the total number of operating hours and R is the number of failures.
—If the user assumes a constant failure rate but wishes to estimate a failure rate
by the Bayesian method, he must use the 'BAE' parameter instead of 'CLE' and
specify a prior distribution and its parameters. In this case, the STAT command
may be:

STAT S01 BAE WITH PRIOR $=$ BETA, $A = 2$, $B = 1000$

where the parameters A and B define the prior distribution.

The statistical analysis methods operative with the Query and Analysis System[20]
are shown below.

(a) *Point and interval estimation* (complete and censored samples)

   (a1) *Constant reliability parameters* (time-independent failure rates, time
      independent repair rates, constant unavailabilities): exponential
      distribution;

   —Bayesian approach (parametric; beta, log-normal, log-uniform priors,
   histogram, …);
   —orthodox approach (maximum likelihood, confidence interval).

   (a2) *Non-constant reliability parameters* (time-dependent failure rates,
      time-dependent repair rates, non-constant unavailabilities):

   —Bayesian approach (non-parametric);
   —orthodox approach (maximum likelihood, confidence interval; distribution considered: Weibull, log-normal, gamma).

(b) *Tests of hypothesis*

   (b1) *Tests of hypothesis* (complete samples)

   —constant failure rate (exponential distribution);
   —increasing failure rate;
   —decreasing failure rate;
   —Weibull distribution:
   —log-normal distribution;
   —gamma distribution.

   (b2) *Tests of hypothesis* (censored sample).

In addition to the main retrieval processing, which aims to provide a quantitative
analysis, other special enquiries have been included in the Query and Analysis

System, which aim to perform qualitative analysis, often supported by graphical
tools. Some of the graphical tools available are:

—graph of an observed time-dependent failure rate;
—graph of prior and posterior distribution (Bayesian parametric approach);
—graph of observed and hypothetical distribution (Bayesian non-parametric
    approach);
—graph of estimated quantities and Bayesian interval (Bayesian non-parametric
    approach);
—graph of smooth distribution (Weibull, log-normal, gamma, etc.).

The following example (Fig. 22) shows one type of qualitative analysis applicable to
the CEDB data and how this analysis may be supported by a graphical tool; in this
example, the enquiry seeks the selection of a particular subset of values and the
analysis of the distribution of the related failures according to the failure descriptor
parameter. The resulting distribution may be directly displayed on a video screen

Select component with eng-char = valv Ø1Ø8 . —→ gate valves
S1 – 7Ø COMPONENT FOUND

End Selection
S1 – SELECTION 1 STORED

Distribution into failure descriptors
S1 – GRAPHICS READY

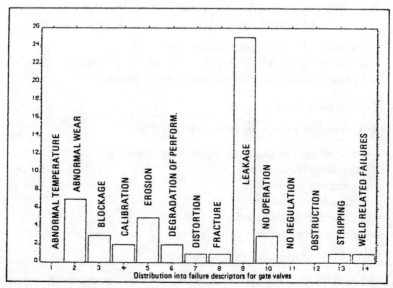

Fig. 22. Example of enquiry: qualitative analysis.

using the histogram format or, alternatively, printed on paper. This latter facility (i.e. the possible choice of printing the results of the interactive Query and Analysis System in batch mode) is a general characteristic of this system.

The main lines of investigation (currently carried out or planned by the JRC), which aim at fully exploiting the knowledge included in CEDB, to achieve the main objective of assisting analysts in their safety studies, are summarized in the next section.[21]

Lines of investigation for the analysis of the CEDB content. As stated above, CEDB stores operational histories of about 5500 components pertaining to 11 LWRs (September 1986); the sum of their monitoring times is about 24 000 component years of observation and the total number of failure events is about 3800. Most of the components being monitored by CEDB are mechanical or electro-mechanical, belonging to about 10 component families and some tens of functional systems; most of them are items which have an important function in the plant operation behaviour and, as such, are specifically taken into account in PRA models and plant availability studies. The volume (and quality) of the information stored in CEDB is now suitable to allow the development of a systematic programme of analysis investigations. This programme may be subdivided into four lines of investigations: qualitative or semi-quantitative, strongly interconnected and complementary.[21] Each of them complies with one or more of the general objectives of CEDB and differs from the others only in the techniques used.

The lines of investigation mentioned above are:

(a) *Study of linked multiple failure events (MFEs).* A critical examination of failure events, performed through a systematic screening of the raw data, has been undertaken, with the aims of identifying the many types of links (random, modal, temporal, structural, etc.) which may exist between failures and classifying and, possibly, theoretically modelling these related 'multiple failures'. The current studies developed at Ispra[22,23] are very promising.

(b) *Application of discriminant function analysis techniques (DFA).* The application of these techniques gives a useful, compact overview of all the coded data stored in CEDB and has the potential for elucidation of the essential underlying structure in the data, and for the identification of trends and patterns in the failure event space, and relationships between the data. In the case of CEDB, DFA has been used to investigate the influence of various variables (such as parameters expressing working conditions, stresses, environmental factors for mechanical components) semi-quantitatively on pre-defined groupings.[24,25]

(c) *Failure mechanism modelling.* This investigation will be implemented on mechanical and electro-mechanical component types, to model, for various classes of components, the physics and dynamics of their failure mechanisms and to predict their behaviour even in operating conditions beyond the design limits. Input to this line of research will be the correlations between attributes obtained from the two lines of investigation (a) and (b) above. Understanding the effect of loading and of environmental factors on a component's operational behaviour is a particularly complex and relevant task, especially when the safety analyst is interested in reliability parameters estimated for components working in post-accident conditions.

(d) *Contribution to the establishment of the reliability parameter data bank* (*RPDB*). This bank, designed as a support for PRA, is in a definition phase. It is a collection of reliability parameters which should result from combination of the reliability parameters obtained as output from CEDB with analogous figures derived through a search in the technical literature. These sources of parameters are, in general, fairly heterogeneous, in the sense that they characterize both the component and the associated failures by making use of different attributes or of attributes defined in a different way. As a consequence, the combination of these two types of sources produces uncertainty and imprecision.

One of the lines of investigation undertaken to deal with the problem caused by this uncertainty is based on the current studies on:

(a) fuzzy sets and possibility theory for the representation of fuzzily known attribute values in relational data bases;[27,28] and on
(b) the definition of a query language where fuzzy specifications are allowed for attributes identifying a given component (such as 'high nominal power') and a failure mode (such as 'complete loss of operation').[28]

The line of development being followed at setting up a computerized interface system, capable of:

(1) understanding fuzzy questions;
(2) interrogating the data bases representing the literature sources;
(3) obtaining from CEDB suitable reliability parameters, aggregating in an 'intelligent' way the items of information so retrieved.

11.3.6 Current CEDB Developments

CEDB requires an adequately large support staff at JRC to set up all the computerized tools which are available at present; e.g. a general 'table management' data base system has been implemented,[17] simply to handle the very large number of complex tables which are necessary for CEDB.

Other important developments are, nevertheless, being carried out; they mainly concern two projects which attempt to use artificial intelligence (A.I.) techniques in the field of reliability data bases.

11.3.6.1 Semi-automatic data transcoding system

This project is aimed at developing a generalized semi-automatic transcoding system capable of converting into a target data system the information defined and handled by a source data base system.[16] The relevance of this project for CEDB (and, generally, for ERDS) is obvious because of the huge amount of data from the different national data banks which has to be converted into the corresponding European formats and classifications. In fact, the logical information entities

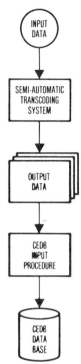

Fig. 23. Data flow from a national data base to CEDB.

existing in the various national 'event' data banks do not necessarily correspond to the CEDB content, because of the different design philosophies of those data banks and their different aims. Consequently, the transcoding work does not simply consist in finding a correspondence between analogous codes, but also in representing in the target system the information which was described in the source system according to a completely different method. This is a very demanding and time-consuming task because it requires from the people concerned a very complete and precise knowledge of the source data bank, of the target data bank, of the relationships between source and target data (not limited to the one-to-one relationships but, generally, more complex and represented through conditional expressions involving transcoding algorithms) and of the nuclear environment.

The project being developed by the JRC is based on the methodology of the well-known 'expert systems';[30,31] however, that method cannot be applied in an orthodox way because of the peculiarities of the problem. The general scheme of data flow from a national data bank towards CEDB is shown in Fig. 23; as is indicated in this figure, the semi-automatic transcoding system produces, as output data, CEDB input forms, which are then submitted to the normal input procedure and become part of CEDB.

The knowledge required by the system to perform its tasks is composed of models and transcoding rules:

— the models describe the different structures of the data involved in the transcoding process;

—the rules lay down the correct values to be assigned to each element of the output transcoded information, on the basis of the relationships existing between source and target data.

The transcoding program, which can be seen as a kind of 'inference system' (in the sense of the A.I. terminology), makes decisions on the use of that knowledge and performs an automatic transformation of the input data; when the available knowledge is not sufficient to take a final decision among many options or to reach a correct conversion of the input data, the system displays the relevant information on the video screen, and asks for a human action. The choice made by the user is subsequently checked by the system, which, in any case, gives a trace of its reasoning, of the rules used and the human decisions. The overall transcoding system architecture is shown in Fig. 24. To recapitulate, the knowledge of the system is based on models and rules which must be specified for each pair of source and target data banks; this modelling operation makes the transcoding system independent of its specific use and therefore applicable, in a generalized way, to any pair of data banks. To support users (in general, engineering-analysts, who are not expert in programming) in supplying the system with the required knowledge (models and rules), an easy-to-use language has been designed for the rule definition and two user-friendly input procedures have been implemented; the function of these procedures is similar, in fact, to the knowledge acquisition module of the typical 'expert system' architecture.

The semi-automatic transcoding system became operative in September 1990.

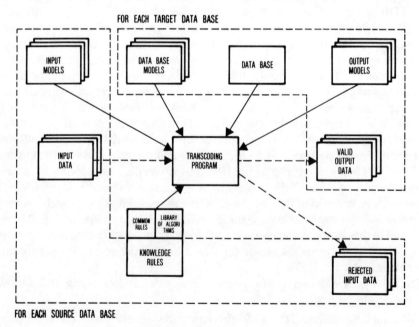

Fig. 24. Overall transcoding system architecture.

11.3.6.2 An Intelligent Interface for ERDS Interrogation

This project concerns the design and the implementation of an intelligent interface aimed at assisting end-users in accessing ERDS as a whole, in a friendly, correct and effective way. The interface should include both natural language understanding and expert capabilities, to meet the requirements of technical and non-technical users.[16,29]

11.3.6.3 Description of the Problem

At present, end-users can interrogate each ERDS sub-system *independently* (e.g. the CEDB sub-system may be interrogated with the *ad hoc* Query and Analysis System, AORS with the ADACCL query language, and so on), even if the query operation is not very simple because of the large number of items of information composing each sub-system, the multi-file structure of these sub-systems and the specific expertise necessary to use the available query languages. However, it is practically impossible to interrogate ERDS as a whole. Queries of the type: 'which failures to gate valves for borated water caused a decrease of safety level and productivity?' involve three sub-systems and do not find any direct, computerized answer at present; in fact, no available query language allows queries on more than one independent (or loosely connected) data bank at the same time. In any case, even if the users were allowed to interrogate the whole system, seen as a unique, large and complex data bank, they would be faced with several difficulties concerning:

(a) the formulation of 'meaningful' queries; and
(b) the correct interpretation of the answers received from the system.

The first type of difficulty involves the following aspects:

—the user cannot rely, in formulating his requests, on a high-level problem-oriented view of the stored data, but he must refer to the lowest level of information corresponding to raw data definition as explicitly 'known' by the data bases;
—the user must learn a formal query language which has little in common with the language he speaks and writes;
—the user must be acquainted with the logic structure and with some of the technicalities of the data banks, and must be knowledgeable about the information stored as well its meaning and use;
—user queries generally involve both data that can be directly retrieved and used and information that may be obtained only be means of appropriate processing on the set of elementary data extracted from the data bank.

The second type of difficulty is a result of the gap existing between the user's expectations and the generally very poor level at which the answers are formulated by the DBMS; answers of the type: 'eight records found' are obviously not meaningful for non-expert end-users. In many cases, moreover, user's desiderata are more qualitative than quantitative and should be expressed via conceptual problem-oriented questions. Only very rarely can they be satisfied with the query languages now available.

11.3.6.4 Specification of the Intelligent Interface (I.I.)
For all the reasons mentioned above, the design of an I.I., acting in a co-operative manner, capable of supporting a dialogue in English and offering assistance to the user similar to that which may be supplied by human experts has been undertaken. A feasibility study was carried out in 1983 to assess the feasibility of the project and to devise basic technical design criteria.[32] At present, a prototyping activity is being developed, aiming at acquiring experience and at experimenting with the solutions which were arrived at after the user's profile and his requirements and expectations had been analysed in depth. The users can be described as

—Technical users: mainly safety engineers interested in designing, maintaining and managing NPPs. They are fully acquainted with the domain and generally with the statistical application programs applicable to ERDS. Nevertheless, only a few of them know the logical structure of CEDB and of the other sub-systems, the Query and Analysis System, ADACCL and how to navigate inside ERDS.
—Non-technical users (casual users): mainly managers, who occasionally access ERDS and are not fully acquainted with its domain and technical aspects.

As a result of the analysis mentioned above, it was clear that coping with such problems required the design of a global interface, adequate for both technical and non-technical (casual) users, consisting of a natural language interface and of a complex expert system.

Taking into account the difficulties involved in such an approach, the global interface has been split into three simpler and more specialized interrelated interfaces (see Fig. 25):

—a Natural Language Query Interface (NLQI), designed to convert non-technical or casual users' questions, written in English, into a Problem Description Language (PDL) and to support the user in defining his requests through a natural language dialogue; this interface should act as a front-end to an Expert Interface;
—a Technical User Interface (TUI), reserved for technical users as an alternative to the direct use of English (the technical users are expected to know how to formalize their requests in a Problem Description, expressed in Problem Description Language (PDL)); this interface should also act as a front-end to an Expert Interface;
—an Expert Interface (EI), designed to deal with the output coming from the NLQI or from the TUI, i.e. with questions written in English and previously converted to the PDL format or with questions written by technical, well-trained and experienced users through the PDL (using the TUI). The EI is designed to assist users in accessing the ERDS data banks, acting as an intelligent human intermediary.

The architecture of the I.I. has up to now been described taking into account the problems involved in dealing with user's questions, but, to meet the user's requirements, it is also necessary to pay particular attention to the expressiveness,

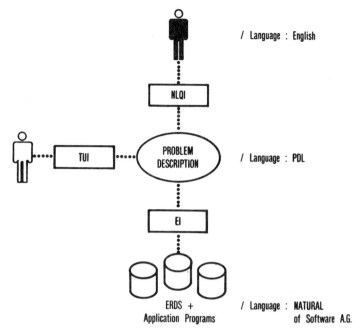

/ Language : English

/ Language : PDL

/ Language : NATURAL
of Software A.G.

ERDS +
Application Programs

Fig. 25. Basic architecture of the Intelligent Interface.

completeness and conceptual adequacy of the responses given by the system and to their appropriate presentation. The formulation of the answers in terms useful for the user's requirements (e.g. qualitative responses) represents a difficult and challenging task. A reconstruction activity has therefore been envisaged, starting with the raw data extracted from ERDS, to give the answers the same conceptual level as that used by the enquirer when he formulated his questions. This reconstruction activity will be the job of the EI, which will then direct the responses to the user via one of the two alternative routes (NLQI or TUI).

REFERENCES

1. Lewis, H. W. *et al.*, Risk Assessment Review Group Report on the USNRC WASH 1400. NUREG/CR-0400, 1978.
2. Mancini, G., Amesz, J., Bastianini, P. & Capobianchi, S., The European Reliability Data System—ERDS: an organized information exchange on the operation of the European nuclear reactors. *Nuclear Power Experience*, Vol. 2. IAEA CN 42/311, Vienna, 1983.
3. Capobianchi, S., The general informatic structure and software facilities developed for the ERDS. 4th EuReDatA Conf., Venice, 1983.
4. Balestreri, S., The European Component Event Data Bank and its uses. P.E.R. 1059/85. JRC, Ispra, 1985.
5. Balesteri, S. (ed.), *Component Event Data Bank Handbook*. T.N. 1.05.Cl.84.86. JRC, Ispra, 1984.

6. Melis, M. & Mancini, G., LWR Reference System Classification for the ERDS. EUR Report EN, CEC. JRC, Ispra, 1982.
7. Mancini, G., Stevens, B., Le Coguiec, A. & Dosi, F., Failure classification. T.N. 1.06.01.81.116. JRC, Ispra, 1983.
8. Besi, A., Reference classifications for event data collection. P.E.R. 1166/86. JRC, Ispra, 1986.
9. Luisi, T. (ed.), Reference classification concerning component's reliability. EuReDatA Project Rep. 1. Distributed by CEC. JRC, Ispra, 1983.
10. Amesz, J. & Kalfsbeek, H. W., *Abnormal Occurrences Reporting System—Handbook.* T.N. I.05.Cl.86.09. JRC, Ispra, 1986.
11. Amesz, J. *et al.*, Status of the Abnormal Occurrences Reporting System (AORS) of the CEC. IAEA Technical Committee on the National Incident Reporting System, Vienna, 1985.
12. Kalfsbeek, H. W. *et al.*, Merging of heterogeneous data sources on N.P.P. operating experience. 5th EuReDatA Conf., Heidelberg, 1986.
13. *ADABAS Instruction Manual.* Software A.G., Darmstadt, FRG, 1979.
14. Carlesso, S., Bastin, F. & Borella, A., Principal achievements in the development of the Component Event Data Bank. 4th EuReDatA Conf., Venice, 1983.
15. Bastin, F., Carlesso, S. & Capobianchi, S., CEDB: input procedure. T.N. I.05.01.83.43. JRC, Ispra, 1983.
16. Bastin, F., Capobianchi, S., Carlesso, S., Koletsos, A. D. & Barbas, T., Artificial intelligence techniques for the European Reliability Data System (ERDS). 5th EuReDatA Conf., Heidelberg, 1986.
17. Bastin, F. & Cocco, A., Sistema generalizzato per la gestione di un data-base di tabelle. T.N. 1.05.01.83.26. JRC, Ispra, 1983.
18. Bastin, F., Carlesso, S. & Jaarsma, R. J., CEDB analysis and query system. T.N. 1.05.01.84.25. JRC, Ispra, 1984.
19. Balestreri, S., Carlesso, S., Bastin, F. & Jaarsma, R. J., Inquiry and statistical analysis of the CEDB by means of a terminal. T.N. I.05.B1.85.128. JRC, Ispra, 1985.
20. Colombo, A. G., Calculation of time-independent reliability parameters from event data. T.N. I.05.01.83.01. JRC, Ispra, 1983.
21. Besi, A., Analysis of the Component Event Data Bank (CEDB) of the ERDS: general lines of investigation and objectives. 5th EuReDatA Conf., Heidelberg, 1986.
22. Games, A., Amendola, A. & Martin, P., Exploitation of a Component Event Data Bank for common cause failure analysis. Int. ANS/ENS Topical Meeting on Probabilistic Safety Methods and Applications, San Francisco, 1985.
23. Games, A., A methodology for detecting multiple related failure events in the ERDS Component Event Data Bank using CEDB interrogative procedures. T.N. I.05.C1.85.146. JRC Ispra, 1985.
24. Sayles, R. S., The use of discriminant function techniques in reliability assessment and data classification. *Reliab. Engng*, No. 6 (1983) 103–24.
25. Sayles, R. S., Harries, C. J. & Moss, T. R., Discriminant function analysis in ERDS valve data. Final Report, Contract 2261-83-12 ED ISP I, JRC Ispra, 1984
26. Bastianini, P. & Soro, J., Operating Unit Status Report (OUSR)—a pilot experiment for a centralized data bank. T.N. I.06.01.82.32. JRC, Ispra, 1982.
27. Prade, H. & Testemale, C., Representation of software constraints and fuzzy attribute values by means of possibility distributions in data-bases. 1st Int. Conf. Fuzzy Information Processing, Kauai, USA, 1984.
28. Prade, H. & Testemale, C., Databases with fuzzy information and their summarization in the framework of possibility theory. 2nd IFAC/IFIP/IFORS/TEA Conf., Varese, 1985.
29. Bastin, F., Capobianchi, S., Carlesso, S., Mancini, G., Guida, G., Somalvico, M. & Tasso, C., An intelligent interface for accessing a technical data base. 2nd IFAC/IFIP/IFORS/IEA Conf., Varese, 1985.

30. Hayes-Roth, F., Lenat, D. & Watermann, D. A., *Building Expert Systems*. Addison–Wesley, Reading, MA, 1983.
31. Rutgers, U., Weiss, S. M. & Kulikowski, C. A., *A Practical Guide to Designing Expert Systems*. Rowman & Allanheld, Totowa, NJ, 1984.
32. Guida, G., Somalvico, M. & Tasso, C., Feasibility study of a natural language interface for accessing the ERDS data bank. Final Report, Contract 2125-83-06 EP ISP I. JRC, Ispra, 1983.

12

Development of a Large Data Bank

A. G. Cannon
2 Colletts Close, Corfe Castle, Dorset BH20 5HG, UK

12.1 INTRODUCTION

The following description of the development of a large data bank system shows the steps that were taken to gather the necessary data to meet two requirements. The system as it developed is unique in that it grew to meet an urgent need which presented itself with changes in terms of reference, so that the time was not available to decide what data and what level of sophistication were wanted; rather, it had to be decided whether there were any data available which might provide the information required. The data bank was able, in a very short time, to answer a large number of the queries put to it. In some cases, the information was good; at the other extreme, the information was poor. As one learns from such investigations, techniques improve and greater interest is generated in industry, so that the quality of the information improves beyond recognition; at that point the question arises of what one should do with the now-ageing data. It is suggested that there is a case, at least for a while, for storing them so that they are still accessible but on a slightly longer time-scale, in order not to inhibit future developments. It will become evident when the data become valueless, and then perhaps erasure is appropriate, although, for historical reasons, samples would be of great interest.

In Chapter 13, Cross and Stevens discuss the problems presented by such a large system, bearing in mind the less than ideal conditions in which, and from which, its operators worked in the system's formative years. The fact that, in computer terms facilities had to be used which were designed for other conflicting purposes imposed severe restrictions. Data had to be adapted from maintenance records rather than from records specifically designed for reliability purposes; this constrained the operation considerably, but did provide the impetus for further development.

In the UK, over a quarter of a century ago, the Act of Parliament which set up the nuclear industry required it to minimise harm and danger in its operation and, resulting from this, a number of actions were taken to meet the requirements.

One of these was to monitor maloperations which occurred in reactors and chemical plants. The logging of these events, at first on cards in literal form, was a crude commencement to the data bank system, but it quickly showed the benefits that could accrue from a disciplined recording of faults. These records were soon extended to include the types of faults typical of maintenance activities and abnormal operation which are an inevitable part of the day-to-day functioning of the type of plants concerned. Unwanted events were thoroughly examined, to learn from them and to provide a feedback to design.

This pattern of data retrieval, analysis and interpretation was carried on within the early nuclear industry for a decade or so, by which time the advantages to be gained from such a system could be seen. During the latter part of the 1960s the records up to then were computerised. It was difficult to justify the effort in terms of the results of the exercise, but subsequent developments have clearly indicated the advantages of keeping this information on a computerised data base management system.

After a decade or so of data bank operation within the nuclear industry, the unit operating the bank was set up to offer a consulting service, so that the lessons learned from the nuclear industry could be applied to obtain improvements in the reliability of conventional industries. At that time, it was difficult to envisage applying the data from the nuclear industry directly to conventional industry largely because of the differences in environment (i.e. the conditions external to but acting on process components). To approach this problem, the co-operation of industry was sought, especially from those industries which had maintenance records covering a number of years of operation. This led, over several years, to a considerable flow of information to the data bank, concerned with a very broad spectrum of items of equipment in a number of industries.

Much information owed its existence not to reliability needs but to maintenance and operational needs, and was derived from maintenance job cards, operations log-books, permits to work, clearance certificates, stores requisitions and, to a lesser degree, stores withdrawals, etc. This data bank information was divided roughly equally between electronic, electrical and mechanical items. Most electronic information in the data bank derived from experience in the nuclear and chemical industries, which was matched, contrasted and compared with information such as that derived from MILSPEC or RADC handbooks. There was a need for caution in the use of such information because of marked differences in performance in some industries. This information was statistically good and, apart from the reservation indicated above, could be applied successfully throughout the field of interest. Electrical information was derived almost entirely from electrical generating organisations within the UK, and consisted of data from a well-disciplined operating regime. In addition, samples of comparable data from organisations throughout Europe and the USA provided useful anchor points for data comparison. This information was statistically adequate, operating and mainten- ance conditions were clearly defined, and the data could be applied quite well in the reliability/availability sense for assessing new systems or for other purposes.

Mechanical data were very mixed and were drawn from a very broad spectrum of operating/environmental conditions, including onshore industries, North Sea operations and oil-production facilities. The statistical value ranged from fairly good to extremely poor. Good samples of data were available for valves, pumps, motors, etc. Poor data arose for example, for a few very large units of equipment and some specific smaller items which were either few in number or very reliable.

12.2 THE DATA BANK SYSTEM

The bank comprised a number of computerised data stores:

(i)   The Generic Reliability Data Store contained processed reliability data obtained from published information, manufacturers, data collection exercises, etc.

(ii) The Event Data Store contained raw data from specially structured collection schemes set up in association with plant operators.

(iii) The Accident Data Store.

(iv) The Human Reliability Data Store.

(v) The Maloperation Data Store.

12.3 STUDENT COLLECTION SCHEME

One major difficulty of the data collection was that it was expensive to obtain this type of information, even in relatively small amounts. Such expense was not readily justifiable because it was often not clear that data collection was of immediate use to the various parties concerned. It was often difficult to find the effort to collect necessary data within the resources of the site operational or maintenance staff. Extended negotiations and compromises were often necessary to put a formalised data collection system into operation. It was in this atmosphere that a search was made for methods and effort to expedite the flow of information.

Enquiries revealed that there were several possible staff categories who could be suitably employed to meet this requirement. The most promising were student assistants. These students were recruited from the sandwich courses of universities or polytechnics in the geographical areas of interest. Initially, trainee mechanical engineers were involved, but the trawl was extended to include trainee electrical and chemical engineers, physicists and industrial technologists.

When it was clear that sufficient information was available and that the staff of a firm were willing to co-operate in these exercises, a formal agreement was negotiated. This agreement was, in the main, simple and asked that while the student was on the site the host firm would take care of him, making sure that he came to no harm in the health and safety sense. A special point was to ask the firm to give the student a satisfactory grounding in site safety requirements and in the use of any protective equipment which he must use or wear without question. It was important that site and trade unions were informed, and appreciated the reasons for the student being there and for the exercise being carried out. In turn, the information from the exercise remained confidential and was not revealed to anyone without the written consent of the host firm.

Although relatively inexperienced staff were used, the results they produced were extremely useful and valuable. The exercises themselves have been shown to result in financial savings and to improve the efficiency of the plants concerned. They have provided reliability information for the data bank which would have been difficult to obtain by other means.

12.4 THE ITEM INVENTORY

Whatever degree of simplicity or sophistication was chosen, it was important to be clear at the outset about the items of plant for which data were to be collected and provided. This was normally achieved by agreeing an item inventory. The items chosen would normally be assemblies such as pumps, motors, valves, etc., but equally they could be components such as bearings or glands. In all cases, a small amount of basic technical information on each inventory item was desirable to identify it by manufacturer, range, size and type. Thus no matter what form the ultimate collection system may take, its output would be associated with well-defined items of plant. For the more modest data collection scheme, the inventory data included an 'operating time function' or 'operating cycles function' (unless it was agreed to work on calendar time rather than operating time). These factors were simple relationships between the operating time (or number of cycles) of a plant item and its total time as a part of the plant. They allowed a sufficiently accurate estimate of operating time or cycles to be made, as it was unlikely, except in elaborate schemes, that recourse would be made to elapsed time counters or other devices. Table 1 lists typical item inventory technical data.

Once the item inventory and its associated technical data were agreed, the next key document was the event report (shown in Fig. 1). The content was adjustable to local needs. The information on it had a strong resemblance to the 'job cards', 'work orders', etc., in common use in industrial plants, and in some cases existing form with little or no alteration or addition could be used. The codes and computer input

TABLE 1
Item Inventory Technical Data

Inventory no.	Quality
Item description (words)	Circuit type
Identity (mark; type)	Material of composition
SRS item code no.	Environment
Manufacturer	Application
Designer	Maintenance interval
Serial no.	Operating time function
Design year	Operating cycles function
Commissioning data	Population
Range/size	Entry date into system

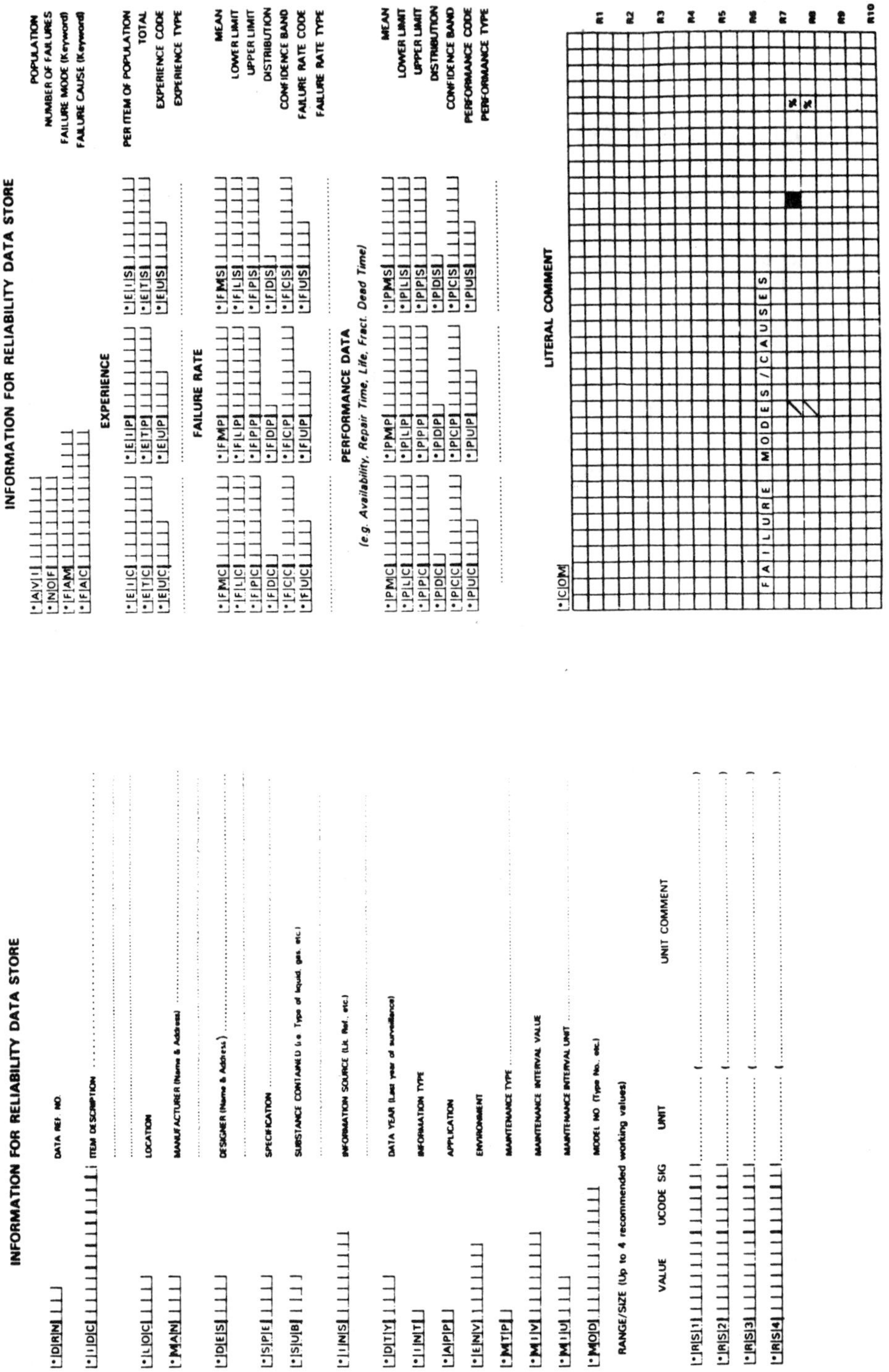

Fig. 1. Information for reliability data store.

stationery permitted these event data to be stored on computer files related to the inventory item and to the system and installation of which it was part.

12.5 CODED STORAGE

The codes used for storage of event data were detailed and comprehensive, and contained ample space for extension to accommodate novel items of plant or the special reporting requirements of individual contributors. They were basically a mixture of alphabetic, numeric and alphanumeric codes, but facilities for plain text entries were also included. The main codes in use were numeric, keyword and hierarchical.

Arrangements for coding and processing contributors' event data were extremely flexible, subject to certain commercial safeguards. They ranged from a complete coding/retrieval service to the relevant sections of code being made available to the contributor for use at his own plant.

12.6 OUTPUT DATA

Table 2 lists the output data available, given that the event data were suitable. The information, presented in tabulated and graphical form, allowed operation and maintenance engineers to assess:

(i)   overall equipment performance and reliability;
(ii) effectiveness of maintenance;

TABLE 2
Performance and Reliability Information Obtainable from the Data Bank

Equipment
1. Mean time between failures
2. Mean time to repair (breakdown)
3. Minimum and maximum repair (breakdown) times
4. Mean time between maintenance
5. Mean time to maintain
6. Minimum and maximum maintenance times
7. Mean man-hours per maintenance
8. Minimum and maximum man-hours per maintenance
9. % Reliability (relative to t = Mean time between maintenance)

10. % Availability $= \dfrac{\text{operating time} + \text{availability-for-operation time}}{\text{total time}}$

11. Number of modifications
12. Mean man-hours (breakdown + maintenance) cost
13. Mean materials/parts cost
14. Operating cost $(12 + 13)$

(iii) correctness of maintenance periodicities;
(iv) correctness of materials/components holdings;
(v) economics of equipment maintenance;
(vi) the need to investigate and modify equipment.

Efforts could then be directed towards equipment maintenance optimisation relative to plant operation demands. The information was also valuable to the manufacturer, design authority and customer (specification and design assessment).

12.7 GENERIC RELIABILITY DATA OUTPUT ENQUIRY AND REPLY SERVICE

The data bank system aimed to offer a service providing data for hazard risk assessments, reliability/availability purposes, etc., and to this end queries were received for data relating to a very broad spectrum of equipment. To meet this demand, a general procedure was developed using a search profile for the equipment item data on an appropriate enquiry form. In addition, three main computer program outputs were used. These were:

(i) (Generic data) output, which listed all generically homogeneous data statistically derived from the data samples per equipment item code in the data bank. The 14-digit code with six separate sub-field demarcations of each item code were scanned separately and in combination. All combinations of equipment failure 'modes and causes were similarly separated and statistically treated.

(ii) Failure listing and reliability data output, which alloted one line to each item description. The entire contents of the data store, or a specified selection of the stored items, could be printed out. The printout was largely in code but the most significant part of the literal description was included. The principal parameters listed were: item description code, fault mode, source reference, number of items, sample size, number of faults, mean failure rate, and several minor entries indicating that additional information was available in store for that item. This printout was intended as a first interrogation of the reliability data store, to identify the items of interest.

(iii) The basic record (and therefore amplification) was of a single line of information. One page of computer printout was obtained for each entry in the reliability data store. Most entries were based on consideration of a number of items (generally a small population) operating in a specified plant for a period of time (typically 1 or 2 years). Information on plant location, item manufacturer, information source, etc., was available in addition to numerical data. These data were supported by a brief description of the item, and of the system operating and environmental conditions which were thought to affect the item's reliability. Commercially sensitive information was suppressed.

12.8 RELIABILITY IMPROVEMENTS

During the process of data collection it was common to become aware of a number of faults in the system under examination. These faults were often far-reaching, and their close examination had a marked bearing on many aspects of plant operation. Many cases could be quoted as examples, but here we propose to examine one briefly. The case was that of a small chemical plant for which rebuilding was contemplated. Examination of the fault rates of the items concerned indicated that both maintenance and operation were not functioning as efficiently as was desirable. In maintenance, this was illustrated by the often-repeated instance that as soon as a repair was affected, the item was on-line again for only a very short period before a further failure occurred. This was brought about because the failure of one item led to the degradation of others to such an extent that a second failure in a short time could resonably be expected to occur. Steps were therefore taken to produce parameters for gauging the wear for all items such that if, on checking, these values were exceeded, then that item, though not a contributor to failure, was also replaced. These parameters were included in a thorough rewriting of maintenance

TABLE 3
Some Performance Data on Motors Obtained from One Site

Horsepower	Kilowatt	No. of items	No. of failures	History		Operating		
				Time (yr)	Failures/ item/yr	Time (yr)	Failures/ item/yr	
0·5	0·373	2	14	5·67	2·47	3·58	3·91	S
0·25	0·186 5	68	95	135·84	0·7			
0·5	0·373	3	1			3·08	0·32	
0·5	0·373	6	6	12·0				
1·1	0·820 6	8	81	34·38	2·36	30·94	2·62	S
1·0	0·746	2	2	11·5	0·17			
2·0	1·492	10	14	36·53	0·38	21·23	0·66	
4·0	2·984	1	4	4·54	0·88	3·77	1·06	S
4·0	2·984	2	3	11·5	0·26	4·3	0·7	
5·0	3·73	1	1	5·8	0·17			
5·0	3·73	576	107	5 760·0	0·02			
8·0	5·968	1	2	4·0	0·5	2·28	0·88	S
7·5	5·595	3	1	12·4	0·08			
7·5	5·595	576	134	5 760·0	0·02			
20·0	14·92	1	14	4·54	3·08	4·09	3·42	S
25·0	18·65	8	17	46·0	0·37	20·8	0·82	
26·0	19·396	12	2	120·0	0·02	27·4	0·07	
100·0	74·6	1	8	4·54	1·76	4·09	1·96	S
100·0	74·6	3	9	17·3	0·52	11·5	0·78	

Electric motors marked 'S' are at the site referred to in the text.

TABLE 4
Before and After Performance Data After Action had been Effected Based on Data Collected
on the Site in Question

Description	No. of items	No. of failures	History		Operating		%[a]
			Time (yr)	Failures/ item/yr	Time (yr)	Failures/ item/yr	
Pumps							
1970–1974	7	200	30·0	6·7	16·1	12·4	
1977	7	22	7·0	3·1	3·76	5·8	46·8
Worm conveyors							
1970–1974	4	158	17·13	9·2	11·41	13·8	
1977	5	24	5·0	4·8	3·67	6·5	47·1
Elevators							
1970–1974	2	139	8·56	16·2	5·47	25·4	
1977	2	52	2·0	26	1·47	35·4	139·4
Fans							
1970–1974	5	116	21·41	5·4	14·45	8·0	
1977	5	15	5·0	3·0	3·67	4·0	50·0
Product screens (Sizers)							
1970–1974	4	191	17·13	11·2	11·26	17·0	
1977	3	4	3·0	1·33	2·2	1·8	10·6
Rotary drum dryer							
1970–1974	1	427	4·28	100·0	2·67	166·0	
1977	1	114	1·0	114·0	0·73	155·0	96·3
Attritor mill							
1970–1974	1	93	4·28	21·7	2·9	32·1	
1977	1	3	1·0	3	0·73	4·1	12·8

[a] The ratio (expressed as a percentage) of the later (1977) to the earlier (1970–1974) operational failure rates.

instructions for the procedures to be adopted in future. The effect of this was dramatic. Not only was the availability improved, but the workload was reduced and the staff operated under less pressure. Closer examination of the pattern of records showed, for example, that the bearings on which the kiln was mounted failed in pairs, and often in fours. Examination of plant logs highlighted repeated entries recording shutdown for the removal of accretions (large masses of material built up eccentrically on the walls of the kiln). Adhesion of this type suggested stickiness; i.e. the feed material was possibly too moist. Examination of the actual operating procedures, as opposed to written instructions (which were not as lucid as desirable), indicated that the former were very different from those recommended by the licensee of the process. Attention to this detail led to rewritten operating instructions which were readily understood by the staff concerned, and this, together with a staff training programme tailored to fit the particular case, removed the problem of build-up on the kiln wall. The failure rate of the bearings was reduced to the point where few breakdowns occurred, wear was detected on inspection, and repairs were effected at these periods.

It was estimated that the effect of this investigation and the related corrective action produce a saving such that the cost per annum of investigative effort was being recovered each week.

Table 3 shows a comparison between motors on this site and those at another site with better environmental conditions. Table 4 shows some comparative figures for a 'before-and-after' situation. The improvements in reliability are evident in a number of cases, and were brought about by the approach described above.

Most of the above must be regarded as a personal view of the state of the art. The experience which underlies these words would not have been achievable without the very enjoyable time the author spent with Systems Reliability Service (SRS), and he is most grateful for that. None of the comments must, however, be regarded as owing in any way to that organisation. It is very gratifying to have participated in a development which appears to be a foundation stone for the future. The flexibility built into the data bank has stood the test of time and enabled it to progress to keep abreast of future needs.

The above description deals with the early development of one of the pioneering engineering data banks, which had the aim of providing a service to a customer (an industrial organisation). This trend has continued, and, indeed, has accelerated so much that, based on the experience and successes of the early efforts, operating procedures were evolved which formed the foundation for the present service, which is commented upon by Stevens and Cross in Chapter 13.

Additionally, considerable effort was put into reviewing all the data and, where possible, updating them to the then available standards wherever possible, at which point it was found expedient to issue the data source as a floppy disc to members of the organisation for their individual interpretation and use. This, of course, reduced the need for the labour-intensive answering scheme which had been developed as described above. It also took the stress from the problem of whether or not to store the large volume of accumulated data. This is clearly one answer to such a problem, but it is obvious that each case has to be treated on its own merits, and it is by no means certain that the same answer applies in every case. Indeed, it is likely that because of the uniqueness of this system its solutions also are likely to be unique.

13

Reliability Data Banks—Friend, Foe or a Waste of Time?

Andy Cross & Barry Stevens

National Centre of Systems Reliability, AEA Technology, SRD, Wigshaw Lane, Culcheth, Warrington WA3 4NE, UK

13.1 INTRODUCTION

For over ten years the authors of this chapter have had an interest in the application of reliability data bank technology. This interest has ranged from data bank user (for fault tree, event tree, FMEA studies, etc.); data collection supervisor (field studies for inventory and event data); database administrator (provider of database software) and data bank manager (responsible for data collection, analysis, storage and output).

The NCSR Reliability Data Bank is often referred to as being one of the oldest and largest in the world—it might well be; but this is seldom a source of comfort to those who operate it, and it frequently causes despair to the users when they find that it is not omnipotent. Its age has meant that, until recently, development has been slow and difficult because of the limitations of the original database model, developed in 1968, and software design. These problems were exacerbated by using a remote, shared, mainframe facility which was designed for scientific use, with poor facilities for users who require data-processing capacity. The size of the Reliability Data Bank has meant that there has been a huge inertia against any change.

The intention of this chapter is to examine the major problems that bedevil the development of any reliability data bank, large or small.

13.2 THE PERSONALITIES

The personalities involved with reliability data bank technology fall into one of the following groups:

(a) those who want to use the reliability data;
(b) those who possess the basic information that can be converted into the required reliability data;

(c) those who attempt to obtain the reliability data from group (b) and pass the data on to group (a);

(d) those who provide the computing facilities to group (c).

Group (a) usually expect data to be available to a degree that will allow them to match design, operational and environmental parameters exactly. There is an increasing demand for high-quality data to satisfy the increasing requirements for licensing procedures. Frequently, reliability consultants are asked to examine the effects of data uncertainty, for which they require information about the likely distributions for the component failure rates; such studies can be more 'complicated' where 'engineering judgement' has been used to establish the basic data parameters.

Group (b) usually want to get on with the job of running the plant and producing the goods; any effort that has to be diverted to other tasks, such as filling in additional report forms, is wasted effort (at least that is what we usually hear from the plant operators). Another problem area raised at some sites is the attitude of the shop-floor staff to the detailed observations that have to be made. Large, multi-site, organisations can create special problems if different sites are involved in a single data collection study; local management policy can often work against corporate strategy.

Group (c) have two major problems. The first is to find ways of persuading group (b) to co-operate with the data collection activities; invariably this means that we must, at least, show the possibility of a cash return. This cash return may be expressed in terms of reduced maintenance, lower capital investment on spare parts, higher availability, etc. It is often very difficult to predict, at the initial stage of discussion, the exact nature of the benefits to be gained. Experience has shown that good-quality data can be produced where there is close co-operation between the data collectors and the site staff. In fact, the more active the site participation, the greater the benefit to the site and the better the data quality. It is usual to find that real cash benefits do result from the data collection, but not always in the ways originally predicted. The second major problem for group (c) is to explain why we seldom have the exact information that group (a) requires (even when we can supply data that are probably good enough in at least 90% of cases). It is sometimes very difficult for the data users to grasp the basic fact that reliability data might have to be generated by extrapolation or interpolation, or even by reasoned engineering evaluation.

Group (d) provide the facilities for data input, storage and retrieval. In environments where the computing facilities are provided by a large mainframe computer, often shared by a number of sites, there is usually a dichotomy of interests. The reliability database administrator will require a database management system (DBMS) that is suitable for his particular purpose, whereas the manager of the mainframe may only want to install a DBMS that is suitable for accounting and personnel use (this appears to be the number one priority in most companies!). If the organisation is particularly security conscious, further problems of access control and data security are evident.

The growth in the availability of DBMSs over the past few years has produced its own problems, rather than making the task of package selection easier. The database administrator can be easy to slick salesmen keen to unload their product by promising to solve all his current problems. In far too many cases, after they have sold a package, the salesmen either get out as fast as possible or look forward to a regular maintenance contract. The high cost of package development makes it essential that the package is ported to as many different machines as possible. Invariably, thorough testing is sacrificed in the effort to put the product on the market as soon as possible.

13.3 THE DATABASE DESIGN

In the introduction to this chapter the original NCSR mainframe database model was referred to. This model was not based on the true 'real-world' relationships of the data items, but was totally dependent on the best computing technology that was then available; i.e. fixed-length records stored serially on magnetic tape. Today, we have more elegant ways of storing the data. These are supplemented by an extensive range of sophisticated DBMSs which allow us to use these facilities with ease. It may have been more prudent to have said 'should allow us to use...' because incorrect selection of a DBMS package can cause a multitude of problems associated with the nature of the data. DBMSs are based on one of three basic mathematical models:

(a) hierarchic;
(b) network;
(c) relational.

Each of these models presents its own difficulties and problems in use. It is essential to undertake an analysis of the 'real-world' relationships of the data to be handled before selecting the DBMS.

Unfortunately, classification of commercially available DBMSs into the above three categories is only indicative of the nature of the data structure that can be 'easily' implemented. If a 'hierarchic' DBMS does not prohibit an entity or record having more than one owner or parent, then it becomes possible to implement a network structure. However, this may well introduce data entry problems, or processing problems, at a late stage in the design phase.

If we consider the minimum basic requirements for a reliability data bank, it is possible that we would have only three files arranged in a hierarchy as shown in Fig. 1. This structure represents the heart of all reliability data banks; it is expanded only as the requirements of the end-users increase.

The major problem that we face as database designers is that our database design must be 'all things to all men'. We are often required to store information which might have very low frequencies of use, but is essential information in some of the latest analysis techniques that are being now applied.

The current design of the NCSR Reliability Data Bank has over 50 entities, some having as many as 30 attributes. The complexity of the design is demonstrated in the 'softbox' diagram shown in Fig. 2. This diagram is not the definitive model, but a

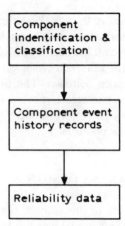

Fig. 1. The basic reliability data bank structure.

version that was current for a few weeks during the early development of a new database to replace the original NCSR implementation.

Examination of the diagram shows that the hierarchic model is no longer appropriate. With the full range of set relationships in the model, we must use a DBMS capable of handling recursive and 'many-to-many' relationships, as well as the hierarchic structure. It is good practice to 'normalise' the data model to remove all 'many-to-many' relationships. However, there are occasions when the complexity of data retrieval paths makes it necessary that these are retained. The penalty of this is to limit the choice of DBMSs; particularly for the larger microcomputers.

This was the situation that we found ourselves in about three years ago. Before we purchased the system that we now use, we designed a test which was thought to be truly representative of the required working data bank. With hindsight this assumption has proved to be very wrong indeed.

The main purpose of redesigning the data bank was to provide a better service to our users. Hence, all trials were based on retrieval times for the most popular access paths by our customers. These trials showed that retrieval times on the microcomputer database were 10–20 times faster than the current mainframe implementation.

It was on this single type of trial that the decision to buy a particular combination of computer and DBMS was made.

The first signs that all was not well came during the testing of the user interface on the full database. Retrieval times were nothing like those experienced in the trials; in fact, a complete reversal had occurred, in that the mainframe was now 14 times *faster* than the new system! Investigations showed that the database security system (which had not been used during the trials) was causing the trouble. Its design allowed us to store *all* our data in one database, but access to the various users was controlled by way of sub-schemas at the top entry point, and also by security codes on the individual data items at the lowest level. The problem was caused by the method that was used to manage pointers internally in the DBMS.

Information on the inner workings of DBMSs is not usually supplied by the

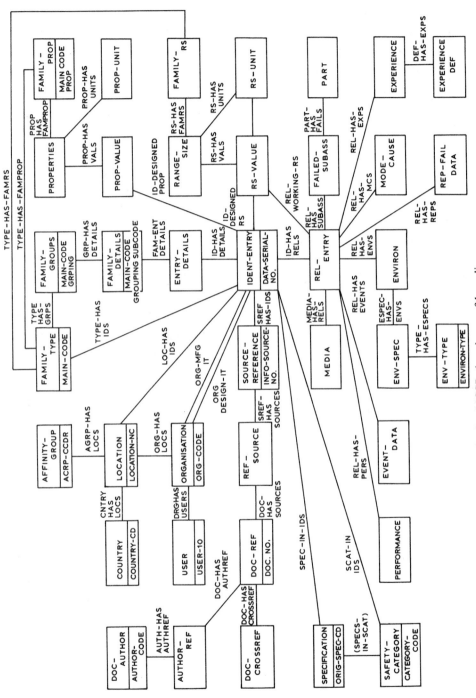

Fig. 2. NCSR data base softbox diagram.

vendors, and generally this should not cause any trouble to the users. Unfortunately, when combined with our complex security requirements and diverse information requirements, it caused major problems. To achieve the required improvements in access times we had to adopt a totally different philosophy for the security system to overcome the limitations of the DBMS. This resulted in a totally new schema being designed, with the inevitable delays.

Many DBMS's designed in the past 3–4 years have provision for multi-user access, with a wide range of security privileges, which are compatible with most user requirements. It is important that the processing time overhead on these facilities is clearly recognised.

Later in the testing phase we had the first indications that even bigger problems were about to strike. As the data sets grew in size we started to lose pointers to related sets. Our first thoughts were that our data loading routines were to blame. This was quickly disproved and the major task of finding when and why the pointers were being deleted was started. This took several weeks of exhaustive testing, using newly written programs to load data and examine the state of the indices. With this technique we were able to pinpoint the region that was causing the problem. Without the source code of the DBMS we had to send our findings to the vending company complete with the database itself. At the time of writing, nearly 2 years after being informed of the problem, we have not received a working version of the package from the vendors. Even with a maintenance contract to cover these eventualities, the maxim to observe is 'buyer beware'. We were victims of the haste to port to many computers (to expand the possible sales base) and then only support and develop the package on the most popular computer!

To ensure that our considerable capital investment was not totally wasted, it has been necessary for us to redesign the database schema so that any one group of pointers never becomes too large. This is not an elegant solution but it is the only one we have. The major penalty of this approach is the reworking of the user interface (i.e. rewriting of most of the in-house software), which caused even more delays to the full implementation of the new data bank. This approach was successful and we have achieved better response times because of fewer disk accesses.

In parallel with the development of this database, others were being designed and implemented on similar super-microcomputers using a relational DBMS. This work, we are pleased to say, has been relatively problem free.

In a microcomputer environment, the complexity of the schema that can be modelled with a relational DBMS is limited, and processing times can be long if complicated retrievals are required. These limitations are more than offset by not having to maintain files of pointers, and by the ease with which new data items or tables can be added to the database.

13.4 THE COMPONENT INVENTORY DATA

Inventory data deal with how groups of components are designed and operated. This section of the database must therefore handle physical descriptions, numeric information and the relationships between the components and the plant.

The first major problem is how to define the component boundary. A particular pump/motor combination might be unique; but one site could have 10 such combinations with, say, eight on active duty and two spares. If the motors can be removed from the pumps, it is likely that the various combinations will change throughout the plant life. Recent NCSR experience has shown that equipment combinations (e.g. pumps/motors, valves/actuators, etc.) can lead to loss of important data at a later date. At the same time, we must retain important information at the sub-component level, e.g. if the only data we have on flanged joints come from information gathered on mechanical valves, we must isolate those data and keep them as a separate record.

The next major problem is the component classification system. The NCSR component classification system (item description code) began life as a nine-digit code. It very soon became clear that this was totally inadequate, and it was replaced by a 14-digit code (a main code of five digits; three sub-codes of two digits and three sub-codes of one digit). Even with 14 digits, it is difficult to describe the physical features of some component types (e.g. mechanical valves), especially when some of these digits are wasted in trying to provide some of the design parameters (e.g. temperature, pressure).

With the current database design we are able to use a main code to describe the basic component class, and an unlimited number of sub-codes to describe the physical features of each component type (each main code and sub-code being of, almost, unlimited length). The 14-digit item description codes were developed over a number of years by a succession of committees; as such, each group of codes reflects the composition of the committee at a particular time. A major effort is being put into the redesign of the codes, using the new format that is now available. Much of this effort will be needed to divide inventories of existing equipment combinations (particularly valves/actuators) which describe one half of the inventory fairly well (the valves), but which give practically no information about the other half of the inventory (the actuators). The main guidelines for this effort come from the NCSR contributions to EuReDatA[1] and the EEC Component Event Data Bank at Ispra.[2]

Design and working parameters are now stored in separate fields, outside the item description code, which can be searched independently after the item description code has been used to identify a given component type. Additional fields containing information related to materials of construction, media contained, manufacturer, specification standards, etc., are also available. Wherever possible, coded fields are used to ensure correct spelling or format, but free text fields are also provided to reduce the need for complex codes. Numeric data are now stored in 'real' fields, rather than in the coded fields which represented ranges of numeric values.

The development of the existing NCSR inventory model has been slow and expensive. The primary aim of the existing model is to give a facility that is easy to use for data input and storage, and which is also simple to use for end-users, i.e. those who need the data. The development of the inventory part of the database has not yet finished. The current database structure allows us to go down to individual plant component/location levels. This in itself presents us with a very difficult problem; do we try to follow the histories of individual components as they move between various plant locations, or do we follow the histories of locations and ignore the movement of components between plant locations? At present, the abilities of the DBMS to handle this extension of the database structure have yet to be proved, so we do not yet have to provide an answer.

When it comes to providing the actual component information for such a model, we are often faced with one basic problem: the lack of adequate plant records.

It is incredible how poor the average plant inventory records are. One would assume that the operators of a newly completed plant would possess a complete record of the equipments fitted; unfortunately, this is not always the case. Modifications during design, construction and commissioning might often be completed in a hurry to avoid cost penalties; updates to drawings and schedules are often forgotten. After plant operation has begun, the main objective is to keep the plant running; if a change of components is required in a hurry, there is no urgency to update records when the plant has resumed production. Hence, when dealing with a 15-year old plant, the drawing records have to be treated with 'respect'. The primary rule for NCSR staff collecting plant data is 'check the plant; not the drawings'. This has meant that we have spent many hours looking for items that are no longer there; following pipes that only lead to cut ends; and trying to identify a component that does not appear on any drawing (not an easy task when the 'component' is just a bulge in a lagged pipe).

The local identification of plant components can also cause a great deal of confusion. We have evidence of one plant using three totally different methods for the identification of one set of valves. The valve schedule identified one such valve as 'FC 8/1'; on the plant it was actually labelled 'WT 6543'; in the plant log-books, the operations and maintenance staff always referred to it as the 'PCB Cooler Inlet Valve' (the plant layout drawing showed the valve, but did not identify it in any way).

One final area of concern is the corruption of design parameters for the plant components. Designer 'A' specifies that a pump is required to operate at 150°C and 200 bar, etc. This information is passed on to the main contractor 'B', who orders the pump from manufacturer 'C', who then provides drawings for a pump that can operate at 200°C and 250 bar, etc. The main contractor 'B' then modifies the drawings to show the 'required' design parameters, and passes them on to the designer 'A'. Ten years after the plant has started operation, NCSR staff have to recognise that the drawings contain 'nominal plant design parameters' and hope that the manufacturers can provide the real design parameters. Fortunately, if the manufacturers are still in business, we have found that *their* records are usually very good.

13.5 THE COMPONENT HISTORY DATA

The history data record all events that affect the performance of items of equipment on the component inventory. As before, there are two basic problem areas; the design of the database, and the actual plant records.

Some modern plants, using 'state-of-the-art' computer records, can provide excellent plant histories, because the shop-floor staff are willing and able to complete the initial paperwork needed for such systems. In such cases, all preventive and breakdown maintenance is fully recorded and it is usually possible to log the complete history of each plant component. Most modern plants, with or without computer records, suffer from a basic lack of shop-floor co-operation; either because management do not know how to obtain it, or because management do not want to risk any conflict. The fact that good co-operation between shop-floor and management often leads to improved plant performance, increased profits and higher take-home pay does not always provide enough incentive.

It should be possible for the average 'job card' to give sufficient information about a particular event (whether it be preventive or breakdown maintenance), to identify the component in question, what happened to it, when it happened and why it happened. In practice, the 'average' job card seldom provides enough information to do more than identify the component in question, roughly when the event took place, and possibly give some idea of the failure mode (Figs 3a and 3b show the actual information contained on a typical job card from one site). Examination of the plant operating log-books can often reveal additional information, but this can be a very tedious job when the log-books are written in some unknown form of shorthand, and the entries concerning one failure/repair event are spread over several days or weeks; when there are several log-books (Mechanical Shift, Electrical Shift, etc.); and when no-one has summarised the actions carried out by the various departments.

Even when good-quality historical records are available, there remains the problem of classifying the failure modes and causes. During the early days of the NCSR Reliability Data Bank, failure modes and causes were entered using a 12-character code. Unfortunately, there was no provision for free text comment fields, and there was always the tendency for data entry staff to demand new codes to satisfy their 'unique' requirements. This resulted in over 120 Failure Mode codes and over 160 Failure Cause codes.

The EuReDatA Group made a bold attempt to resolve the problems of failure classification[1] by proposing short lists of Failure Mode and Failure Cause codes, together with a new Failure Descriptor code. For nearly 3 years, NCSR staff on field data collection duties have been using the EuReDatA codes. Experience has shown that it is easier to handle the 13 Failure Modes and the 21 Failure Causes proposed by EuReDatA than it was to use the old NCSR codes. Unfortunately, the 64 Failure Descriptors proposed by EuReDatA have not been easy to use—at times there are too many codes, at times there are not enough.

As a direct result of these observations, for current NCSR Reliability Data Bank operation, we have reduced the list of Failure Mode codes and Failure Cause codes to about 25 of each; but we have provided free text fields to allow further descriptions of the Failure Modes and Causes. This has already caused some protests by those whose prime concern is the analysis of the data records, and who therefore want every event coded down to the finest detail (before it comes to them), but our main concern is to provide accurate information about the events—hence the minimum number of coded fields and the provision of free text fields.

The structure of the database for the historical records can be of two basic types:

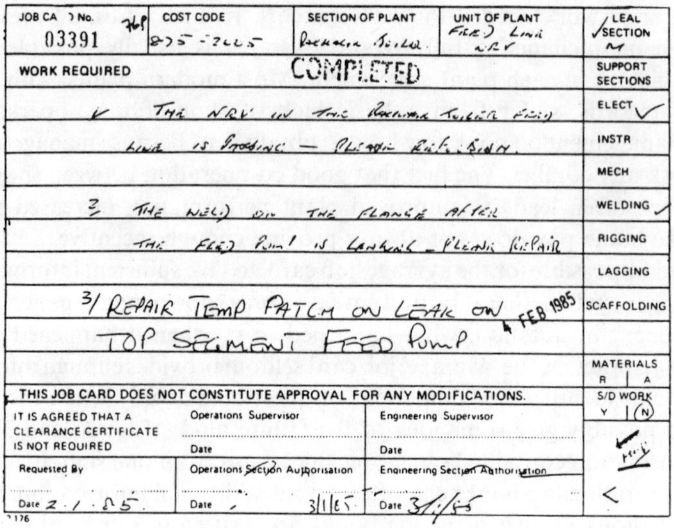

JOB CARD No. 03391 | COST CODE 875-2225 | SECTION OF PLANT | UNIT OF PLANT Feed Line NRV | LEAL SECTION

WORK REQUIRED COMPLETED

1/ THE NRV IN THE ... FEED LINE IS ... — PLEASE ...

2/ THE WELD ON THE FLANGE AFTER THE FEED PUMP IS LEAKING — PLEASE REPAIR

3/ REPAIR TEMP PATCH ON LEAK ON TOP SEGMENT FEED PUMP

4 FEB 1985

SUPPORT SECTIONS: ELECT, INSTR, MECH, WELDING, RIGGING, LAGGING, SCAFFOLDING; MATERIALS R A; S/D WORK Y N

THIS JOB CARD DOES NOT CONSTITUTE APPROVAL FOR ANY MODIFICATIONS.

IT IS AGREED THAT A CLEARANCE CERTIFICATE IS NOT REQUIRED | Operations Supervisor / Date | Engineering Supervisor / Date

Requested By / Date 2.1.85 | Operations Section Authorisation / Date 3/1/85 | Engineering Section Authorisation / Date 3/1/85

Fig. 3a. Typical job description.

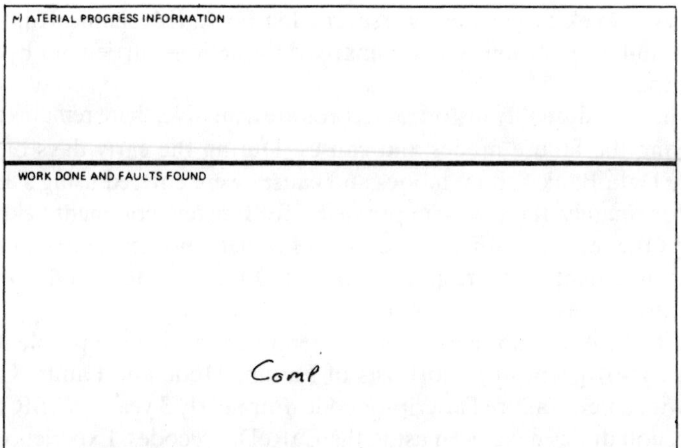

MATERIAL PROGRESS INFORMATION

WORK DONE AND FAULTS FOUND

Comp

ACCEPTED BY: DATE: 12/2/85

Fig. 3b. Typical description of work done.

summary format, containing the total number of events together with a breakdown of the Failure Modes/Causes; or complete record format, containing full details of each failure event. The original NCSR database was of the former type; the current database is of the latter type, with provision for the retention of the old format.

13.6 DEPENDENT FAILURES

There is clear evidence that the early attempts by NCSR to collect field-reported reliability data usually masked the fact that not all of the events represented independent failure events. The classic case is represented by four cast-iron valves, carrying seawater, that failed at about the same time because they had not been rubber lined (as specified). The original data bank paperwork produced for these events made them look like four random failures.

Over the last 3 years, NCSR staff have been engaged on a major project to study dependent failure events for the boiler feed systems at three power stations, and a pilot project has also been completed for a chemical process plant. The study of dependent failures has covered three aspects: (1) to modify the data collection procedures, to identify the equipment populations that could be affected by the various types of dependencies; (2) to improve the event records, to identify those events which could be related; and (3) to improve the modelling of dependent failure analysis.[3]

As a direct result of the experience gained from the above studies, steps are now being taken to modify the standard data collection procedures to ensure that dependent failures from future field data collection studies are identified.

13.7 DATA ANALYSIS

Standard treatment for NCSR data sets has, until recently, simply involved dividing the total number of failure events by the total experience (calendar time; operating time; demands, etc.), followed by a simple application of the Poisson distribution to give upper and lower limits (95 and 5 percentiles).

Over the past few years, a number of academic studies have been carried out using field-reported data from NCSR Reliability Data Bank sources.[4] These studies have generally highlighted a number of problem areas:

  (a) Many data sets are too small for any statistical analysis. Even when the population size is reasonable, say greater than 10, the observation period is often too short to reveal any significant trends.
  (b) The quality of the event data makes it difficult to demonstrate any real relationship between failure modes and failure causes.
  (c) Many of the trends that have been found using techniques such as proportional hazards modelling have often been distorted by a lack of engineering appreciation. In part, this reflects the need for a more detailed examination of the engineering implications of the event data before any statistical analysis is carried out.

Over the past year, NCSR staff, in conjunction with a member of the Australian Atomic Energy Commission on secondment to NCSR, have been carrying out detailed examinations of a number of the old field-reported data sets. These studies have shown that many of the old data sets have failure rates which are too high. Repairs are often carried out in two or more passes, e.g. a leaking flange might initially be tightened, then furmanited, and finally repaired by replacing the gasket; these might well have been treated as three separate failure events. In some cases, we have also been able to show that routine maintenance events have not been recorded (but we cannot prove whether or not the maintenance was actually carried out). It will take some time to review all of the old field-reported data sets, but in the mean time we can try to ensure that the current data collection activities are analysed correctly.

13.8 POOLED RELIABILITY DATA

The Associate Membership scheme established by the Systems Reliability Service (SRS), was intended to provide a facility whereby the individual members of the club could pool their reliability data (anonymously) for the mutual benefit of all of the members. Unfortunately, less than 10% of the data held in the current NCSR Reliability Data Bank has come via this route, and what has been supplied is usually in summarised form (no detailed event data) and seldom gives enough information about the components involved.

If such schemes are to succeed, the membership must recognise that they have an obligation to contribute data to an agreed standard. The effort required to combine information from a wide variety of sources is considerable, as the various members of the EEC Component Event Data Bank (CEDB) are finding out. The control of such a data bank is a difficult, and often thankless, task.

13.9 THE SUCCESSES

We have carried out several large-scale data collection projects over the last 4 years. Each of these projects has been supported by its own custom-designed database, with a common data format and DBMS.

One of our current major projects is the Advanced Manufacturing Technology Association. This project is jointly funded by the UK Department of Trade and Industry and participating manufacturing companies. The project is scheduled to run for at least 3 years. Membership of the Association is growing steadily and we now enjoy the co-operation of 28 sites where we collect data from advanced manufacturing technology systems.

The database that we have designed is a true event data bank and is based on a relational model. We have found this to be ideal, as it allows us to tailor the model to suit the available data at each site. This requires only the simple expedient of supplying additional tables or data fields, without the necessity of down-loading the data or modification of existing application programs for other sites.

We are delighted with the efficiency of the data collection/data analysis cycle. The time lag before data are resident on our database averages 2 weeks, and this is dictated by the frequency at which the contributing sites require reports on their machines. We are currently introducing local personal computers with a data collection package installed, to eliminate paper records, etc. This has resulted in improved quality of data and a marked reduction in turn-round time.

We have done a considerable amount of work in developing an extensive suite of programs for the analysis of the data. These programs automatically generate all the required reports for the sites. Again, a very short lead time is achieved.

The final phase of the database development has just been completed with integration of four computers (two super-microcomputers operating under 'Unix', and two PCs operating under DOS) linked by a local area network with a distributed file system. This has enabled us to take advantage of the best software available for each operating system to improve the quality of reports and generate an extensive range of generic data books for circulation to members of the Advanced Manufacturing Technology Association. Figure 4 shows the integrated system configuration and Fig. 5 shows the report generation route.

To give an indication of the size of the project, we are monitoring the performance of over 1100 systems, ranging from stand-alone CNC lathes to fully integrated flexible manufacturing systems. These may include robots, machining centres, automatic wire-guided vehicles, computerised tool stores, automated

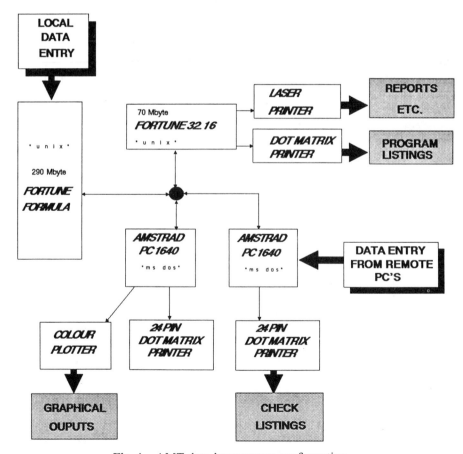

Fig. 4. AMT data base; system configuration.

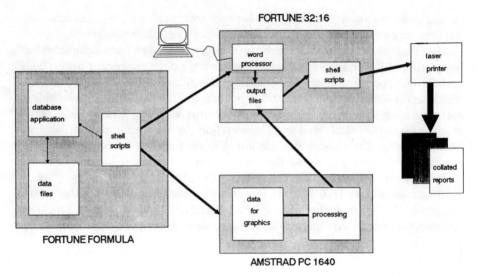

Fig. 5.   Report generation route.

finished component stores, etc. The economic viability of all these systems depends on achieving a high system availability (typically 98%). Actual achieved availability ranges from the high eighties to low nineties. Almost all participants have experienced a growth in availability since joining the Association, by applying knowledge gained from the data collection and analyses. To date, over 33 000 events have been analysed and stored on the database.

The main causes of unavailability can be roughly divided into three categories:

(1) inherent design faults leading to long outages;
(2) failure of low-cost items used in large numbers;
(3) incorrect spares holding.

In the first category, it has been possible to use the collected data to identify inadequate design that has led to major outages, and to recommend the design changes needed. One project member has included one of these specialised reports with his order for a new machine, and has stated that the order will not be confirmed until design changes have been made. He also requires a guarantee for achievable availability. Another member has made minor changes to his compressed air supply, which has made considerable improvements to the performance of his machines by eliminating systematic failures.

Category two is really the manufacturer's dilemma; does he use a low-cost component that is suspect in operation, or a high-cost component with high reliability? If a single machine contains a large number of these components, to choose the latter every time would probably make this product uncompetitive. Typical components from this aspect are microswitches and proximity switches. A possible solution for this dilemma is to install the high-reliability components in those areas that experience the higher stress/duty levels, and hence could be prone to higher failure rates. To improve existing equipment, or to predict the performance of future equipment, we must have a reasonably sized population of similar machines from which to gather data. A project of this sort provides the correct atmosphere to promote data collection from firms who might normally be competitors, but can see the overall benefits to be obtained from data exchange. This then provides us with the required population.

Finally, category three is symptomatic of the introduction of new technology, when it is hard to decide what spares are needed? During a pilot study for the current project,[5] downtimes were up to 30 times the repair times. This was generally because of unavailability of the correct spares. Data from the project will provide a method of accurately defining the spares holding.

The project is proving that this type of reliability data base can be a real friend, to the data collector and the end-user, rather than a foe! However, it does require that the DBMS is selected with great care and that the computer is adequate for the application.

The success of this project is the result of complete co-operation between all those involved, good communications within each organisation to inform all levels of the workforce of the aims of the data collection, and feedback of results, especially to the men operating the machines and systems.

13.10 CONCLUSIONS

Friend? If the correct hardware/DBMS package has been selected to suit the database to be constructed, if the plant has accurate records of the components fitted, and if the plant operators keep accurate records of all maintenance actions, data collection and analysis can be a pleasure. Despite all of the problems associated with a poor choice for our current DBMS, the new NCSR Reliability Data Bank can produce much better results than did the old mainframe data bank. In part, this is because the structure of the database allows more detail and more flexibility; in part, the simpler (in-house) routines for changing the database contents make it easier to update the old records and provide more information. Figure 6 shows a fictitious data bank record that demonstrates the type of data format that we expect from our more recent data collection activities, using the report generation route (cf. Fig. 5).

Foe? If you are stuck with a hardware/DBMS package that has been supplied with no thought to the end-user, or you have made the wrong choice and cannot change your system; if the component inventory has to be compiled by a process of check, re-check and hope; if the collection of the component histories requires the issue of a meerschaum pipe and deerstalker hat, data collection is a nightmare and data analysis is likely to be almost impossible. Another data bank foe is the databank that is dominated by extracts from other data banks, or published data, where 'environmental factors' have been used to change the numeric parts of the data. Such data can cause major problems when they are compared with the original data, if the link is not known to the user.

DATA SERIAL NUMBER 12556   DATA QUALITY GOOD

Valve (Mechanical, EXCLUDING Actuators)

VALVE TYPE	Gate, Parallel Slide with Single By-Pass/Equalising Valve
METHOD OF ACTUATION	Motor, Electric Rotary
TRIM MATERIAL (SEAT AND DISC)	Nickel Alloys (Monel, Inconel etc.)
FUNCTION	Isolation/Stop; Inlet, Outlet, Line Isolation etc.
STEM MOVEMENT	Rising Stem, Outside Screw
STEM SEALING	Compression Packing
END CONNECTIONS	Butt Weld
NORMAL VALVE STATE	Fully Open

SOURCE REFERENCE NUMBER	0 Demonstration Source Reference
DATA REFERENCE NUMBER	1
COMMISSIONING DATE	1 Apr 1984
AVERAGE NUMBER OF ITEMS	4 Valves
INDUSTRIAL GROUP	Generation and distribution of electric power
MANUFACTURER	Bloggs & Sprockett Ltd. Fiction Lane, Monkey Works, Hartlepool.
DESIGNER	UKAEA
MODEL NUMBER	PSV Mark 24
LOCATION	Paper Moderated Fast Reactor Power Station; Risley, Lancashire

DESIGN PARAMETERS

DIAMETER	(EQ) 250 Millimetre - Nominal Bore
DIAMETER	(EQ) 200 Millimetre - Throat diameter
PRESSURE (ABSOLUTE)	(EQ) 280 Bar - Maximum Feed Pressure
PRESSURE (ABSOLUTE)	(EQ) 300 Bar - Seat Test Pressure
PRESSURE (ABSOLUTE)	(EQ) 375 Bar - Body Test Pressure
TEMPERATURE	(EQ) 345 Celcius - Maximum Feed Temperature
COMPOSITION	(EQ) 0.300 Percent - Maximum Carbon Content Body Material
DIAMETER	(EQ) 20.0 Millimetre - Nominal Bore of By-Pass Valve
MEDIA(1)	Boiler Feed/Polished Water - De-aerated
MEDIA(2)	Air - During shutdown
SPECIFICATION(1)	BS 1504 - 161 Grade A
SPECIFICATION(2)	BS 1400
SPECIFICATION(3)	AISI-316
MATERIAL(1)	Cast Carbon Steel - Body & Bonnet
MATERIAL(2)	Bronze/Gunmetal - Disc
MATERIAL(3)	Austenitic Stainless Steel - Stem

WORKING PARAMETERS

PRESSURE (ABSOLUTE)	(EQ) 160 Bar - Normal Full Power Pressure
TEMPERATURE	(GE) 150 Celcius - Lower Working Temperature Limit
TEMPERATURE	(LE) 225 Celcius - Upper Working Temperature Limit
DUTY REQUIREMENT	(EQ) 100 Percent Duty - For Normal Plant Operation

Fig. 6.

RELIABILITY DATA

INFORMATION TYPE _ _ _ _ _ _ _ _ _ Field reported event data
DATA YEAR _ _ _ _ _ _ _ _ _ _ _ _ _ 1986
APPLICATION _ _ _ _ _ _ _ _ _ _ _ _ Average (industrial)
MAINTENANCE TYPE _ _ _ _ _ _ _ _ _ Scheduled; planned plant shutdown, components not required
                                          to function
MAINTENANCE INTERVAL _ _ _ _ _ _ _ 1.00 year
MAINTENANCE DETAILS _ _ _ _ _ _ _ General overhaul of Valve followed by functional test.
TESTING TYPE _ _ _ _ _ _ _ _ _ _ _ Opportune; e.g. during unscheduled plant shutdown
TESTING DETAILS _ _ _ _ _ _ _ _ _ _ Valves closed on every plant shutdown

EXPERIENCE (CALENDAR TIME)

AVERAGE PER ITEM _ _ _ _ _ _ _ _ _ 2.50 years

EXPERIENCE (OPERATING TIME)

AVERAGE PER ITEM _ _ _ _ _ _ _ _ _ 2.10 years

NUMBER OF FAILURES _ _ _ _ _ _ _ _ 6

FAILURE MODE	FAILURE CAUSE	FAILURES
Leakage - External	Human error - Casting porosity	1
Fail to open - After plant shutdown	Damage - Bent Spindle	1
Leakage - Internal	Erosion - By-pass valve seat & disc	1
Leakage - External	Component failure - Stem packing	3

FAILURE RATE (CALENDAR TIME)

MEAN _ _ _ _ _ _ _ _ _ _ _ _ _ _ _ _ _ 0.600 failures/year per Valve

FAILURE RATE (OPERATING TIME)

MEAN _ _ _ _ _ _ _ _ _ _ _ _ _ _ _ _ _ 0.714 failures/year per Valve

PERFORMANCE DATA

REPAIR TIME
MEAN _ _ _ _ _ _ _ _ _ _ _ _ _ _ _ _ 1.00 day
MINIMUM VALUE _ _ _ _ _ _ _ _ _ _ _ 12.0 hours
MAXIMUM VALUE _ _ _ _ _ _ _ _ _ _ _ 2.00 days

OUTAGE TIME
MEAN _ _ _ _ _ _ _ _ _ _ _ _ _ _ _ _ 12.0 hours

COMMENTS

Power Station Evaporator Inlet/Outlet Isolation Valves.
See DSN 12557 for main valve actuators & DSN 12558 for by-pass valve actuators.
Note that only one failure event (Fail to Open) caused plant outage.

Fig. 6—*contd.*

Waste of Time? If the definition of 'Foe' is applicable, then the collection of the data is usually a waste of time, and any analysis would be meaningless.

We are often asked to justify our data collection activities; usually by those who are about to pay for the work, frequently by those who are operating the plants, sometimes by those with difficult data requirements. As we have already stated, the actual benefits of data collection are not always predictable; they depend upon the particular site problems and the ability of the site staff to use the information generated.

One point is clear. If the operators of a plant keep accurate records of their equipment, and what happens to it, and use that information to improve plant output, then that plant is likely to stay in operation. These records will also provide the raw material for safety/reliability analysts who are going to check the design of the firm's next plant.

REFERENCES

1. EuReDatA Project Report No. 1—Reference Classification concerning Components' Reliability. Report SA/1.05.01.83.02. CEC Joint Research Centre, Ispra (VA), 1983.
2. *Component Event Data Bank Handbook*, Vol. 1. *General Description of the CEDB and General Guide of the CEDB Handbook*. Report TN/1.05.C1.84.66. CEC Joint Research Centre, Ispra (VA), 1984.
3. Humphreys, P., Games, A. M. & Smith, A. M., Progress towards a better understanding of dependent failures by data collection, classification and improved modelling techniques. *Reliability '87*, Birmingham. The Institute of Quality Assurance, London and The National Centre of Systems Reliability, Cheshire, Paper 2C/4.
4. Walls, L. A. & Bendell, A., The structure and exploration of reliability field data; what to look for and how to analyse it. *Reliability '85*, Paper 5B/5.
5. Daniels, B. K. & Stevens, B., Management Report for PERA/NCSR Joint Project on Integrated Manufacturing Systems—Availability & Reliability. NCSR Rep. ASG/35902/0.

14

Developments

A. Bendell

Department of Mathematics, Statistics and Operational Research,
Nottingham Polytechnic, Burton Street, Nottingham NG1 4BU, UK

14.1 INTRODUCTION

The previous chapters have attempted to describe the status quo in relation to both the principles of data base construction, management and use in reliability applications, and the particular ramifications associated with particular important data bases. This chapter, in contrast, briefly identifies some of the areas in which developments have taken place which will in turn have implications for reliability data bases.

Reliability practice itself is affected by changes in methodology, technology, education and professional practice.[1] In a background of continuous and accelerating change, developments in reliability practice, and hence in reliability data bases, should be accepted as part of progress. On the other hand, there are, of course, many false claims and false starts, and a careful analyst should find it advantageous to retain an iota of scepticism.

The sections of this chapter concentrate upon changes in data handling, changes in methodology and technology, the emergence of new reliability data bases, and changes in education and attitude.

14.2 CHANGES IN DATA HANDLING

There are, perhaps, four particular aspects of this topic. First and second, there are changes in computer technology, sub-divided into hardware and software changes. Third, there are changes in data base software, which is of major importance for all reliability data bases, and, fourth, there is the emergence of automatic data acquisition with its consequent problems. To predict developments in any of these over the next few years is extremely difficult. However, some attempt to do this was carried out by Bendell.[1,2]

The rapid speed of development in computer technology, partly because of the major British and European research projects (Alvey, Esprit, Race, etc.), means that the gains here are likely to be major. The recent years have perhaps seen movement away from on-line data bases to the distribution of data base material on floppy disks to remote micro-computers. The opportunities now available in networking microcomputers, however, imply that some of the advantages of networked PCs could be incorporated within future data base organisational structure. Developments in computing technology, particularly perhaps parallel processing, mean that the sophistication of the analysis routines available as standard within data base systems can be greatly extended. The user-friendliness and the extent of diagnostic and graphical aids will be enhanced. Developments in artificial intelligence are providing the potential for intelligent support to the semi-intelligent user. There is, however, a long way to go in this last area, and claims for achievements are perhaps typically optimistic. A weakness of all data base systems is that they rely upon the reliability of the software elements of which they largely consist, as it is acknowledged that software failures are one of the major remaining causes of system failure.[3] The amount of work being undertaken in the area of formal methods offers great promise for avoiding this inherent limitation by coding automatically from the systems specification or by proving the correctness of such a code.

Progress in all these area, however, will rely greatly upon the educational base of reliability practitioners, if they are to be incorporated in the reliability data bases of the future.

14.3 DATA BASE SOFTWARE

It is particularly dangerous to speculate on developments in this area, as they rely greatly upon commercial decisions outside the scope of this book. What data base software is to be commercially developed in the future and hence available to support the quick and easy establishment of reliability data bases must be a subject for speculation. However, one would expect to see incorporation of aspects of intelligence as well as the commercial availability of more specialised data bases and those more integrated with the task for which they are intended. All data bases have a particular purpose, and if that purpose may be captured in a broad enough perspective then commercial products can be made available which integrate the data base requirement with the function for which they are intended. In this we may expect to see an increase, particularly, in project management software/data bases.

14.4 METHODOLOGY AND TECHNOLOGY LED CHANGES

To date, there have been two major methodology led changes in the structure of reliability data bases. These are the realisation that the traditional constant fault-rate methodology will not be appropriate in all circumstances (for instance, if deterioration is present) and that accordingly additional parameters needed to be recorded, rather than constant fault rate or a single figure such as a mean lifetime. This has led to movement towards the recording of time-to-failure information rather than window-type data. The second methodological change is associated with the realisation that, even if deterioration is present, replacement items may not experience the same time-to-failure characteristics, and that repairable systems may have different inter-failure behaviour following repair or replacement of individual sub-assemblies.

It is, of course, extremely difficult to predict the advances that will be made in methodology in the next few years. However, methodological changes now have implications for the data bases about to be established, and the emerging interest in the inclusion of covariate information or additional explanatory factors in the description of system and failure characteristics is likely to be reflected in future data base structures. To some extent, this is already happening, and is referred to below in the section on new data bases.

Technology led changes, other than those associated with the computer storage of the data base itself, are harder to predict. In a conceptual sense, the reliability data base faces a problem in that its only reason for existence is the lack of information about the reliability of new technologies, as the reliability of old technologies tends to be reasonably well understood. It is, however, for these new technologies that the availability of reliability data are very limited. It takes time to extract and to build up such data, and to decontaminate from the early design problems which may swamp the more systematic failure characteristics in the data.

Many of the new data bases being established are associated with new technologies, but these tend to be in their infancy, despite having accumulated considerable amounts of data, as the incidents of failure are often very infrequent, and data validation acts to remove the much more frequent causes of failure associated with design and fabrication. The point, however, is that where information is most required, such as in the emerging software and electronic technologies, and in the as-yet little-understood areas such as human factors and common cause failures, data are least available.

14.5 NEW DATA BASES

Reliability data bases are now not only an established aspect of the reliability and engineering field world-wide, but also are a growing one. The area has seen a new vitality overtaking its more staid past. A need to find answers now to immediate technological problems both in design and operation of systems has meant that the benefits of data collection and organisation come to the fore.

One particular new data base designed to produce this type of usable information is the data base at Loughborough University of Technology on the field failure of electronic components. This base aims to provide information about the main trouble-making components in electronic systems. It is funded by the UK Ministry of Defence (MOD), and represents a collaborative project between the MOD,

Loughborough University of Technology, Nottingham Polytechnic, the Danish Engineering Academy, STC, Plessey, GEC and two Danish companies.

14.6 R&M 2000

One aspect of the new impetus to reliability data collection and data base development is the R&M 2000 programme established by the US Air Force. The document both leads and follows the trend towards reliability achievement rather than reliability prediction, as a reaction to the excessive use of methodologies such as MIL-HDBK 217 to 'predict' notional reliability figures for electronic systems. The implications of R & M 2000 may well be that the requirement and use of reliability data bases for all stages of manufacture through to field use becomes much more important and commonplace. The R & M 2000 documents are likely to have a major impact on reliability procedures throughout the world, for non-military as well as military systems.

14.7 CHANGES IN ATTITUDE

Although reliability studies have made major progress in recent years, they are still subject to criticism. Rarely do we see sensitivity analysis, both of the data and of the assumptions of models, being systematically applied in evaluating a system's reliability characteristics, logistic support requirements, etc. Frequently too, results of reliability analysis are misinterpreted by inexperienced analysts. There is a particular danger of this with graphical methods, particularly where these do not include confidence bounds or simulation bounds to quantify departures from linearity or other forms of norm. The limitations of reliability education currently available world-wide must be seen as one contributor to this problem. In the long term, changes in education may perhaps be the major factor in changing attitudes and professional practice in the reliability area. In turn, this will lead to changing conceptions of data requirements and use of the data. It was for this reason, for example, that the Post-Graduate Diploma in Reliability Analysis at Nottingham Polytechnic was established, on a short-course basis, to make it available to reliability practitioners in European industry, without disrupting their normal industrial work patterns.

REFERENCES

1. Bendell, A., Assessing the future of reliability; II. Towards the year 2000. *Safety Reliab.* (1986).
2. Bendell, A., Assessing the future reliability; I. The basis for growth. *Safety Reliab.* (1985).
3. Bendell, A. & Mellor, P. (eds.), *Software Reliability State of the Art Report, 14: 2.* Pergamon Infotech, Oxford, 1986.

15

Overview; Into the Future

A. Bendell

Department of Mathematics, Statistics and Operational Research, Nottingham Polytechnic, Burton Street, Nottingham NG1 4BV, UK

15.1 FORTY YEARS OF ALWAYS BEING WRONG AND ALWAYS BEING RIGHT

The reliability analyst's job is not a pleasant one. Isolated from the rest of the organisation by artificial barriers, regarded as not being a 'proper' engineer and being in a position, by a figure, to dam a development project or a contract tender, the reliability engineer has usually drifted into the role by promotion or as a response to an 'opportunity' having been pointed out. This is not to say that it is not a rewarding role, although perhaps the rewards come largely in rather subtle ways.

There have been many major errors in reliability prediction in the last 40 years, and there have been many more less major and less publicised errors, but broadly the methodology and the approach have brought structure and rigour to an area which previously was largely unstructured and ignored. Problems of unreliability do not dissipate because you pay no attention to them. The progress that has been made in methodology, approach and acceptance of the discipline in the last 40 years is major and should not be ignored. The increasing awareness in the outside world of the principle of risk will make the propagation of reliability analysis easier in the future. With determination for success, reliability analysts and reliability data bases could become as established a part of organisations as accountants. By their nature, reliability predictions are always wrong and always right.

15.2 THE NEXT FORTY YEARS

The way to gain accuracy in prediction is by being vague; even better is to avoid the issue.

However, an indisputable influence over the next few years must be the major impact of the *computer*. The continuation of general trends in computing since the inception of the industry imply a movement towards more on-line, more user-friendly systems to undertake much of the tedious work of present-day computer use. Thus, the reliability analyst and data bank user will see a movement towards more visual techniques and the implementation of numeric solution methodologies, as an alternative to analytic ones for which the advancing computational ability will make little difference. Further, developments in algebraic manipulation packages, such as Macsyma, will enable reliability theorists and modellers to study the simplification and implications of their models without recourse to numerical illustration. Perhaps most important of all, we will see a movement towards expert systems, and, more immediately, the provision of assistance within the programs themselves. Given the current slow pace of educational and computing developments in reliability technology, it is likely that it will take a few years to produce satisfactory expert systems for reliability application; the reasons were discussed by Bendell.[1] However, what would be of immediate use, and is technically feasible now, would be the introduction of reliability computer programs in which different program sequences are followed, based on the results obtained. Such software could assume a lower level of user understanding and judgement than is necessary to work safely with many of the current reliability packages.

As well as the movement towards more friendly, more visual and less stop-gap programs, and the associated advantages of algebraic manipulation languages, developments in communications will allow easier access to data bases, both current ones and those being established. The area of data bases is itself a major aspect of development over the next 10–15 years, both in terms of the limitations and upgrading of existing data bases and the establishment of new reliability data bases. There are a number of areas where this is taking place. Data bases represent a long-term investment for the reliability community. The early reliability bases, with which we live today, were established at an early stage of reliability methodology, and in consequence have sharp limitations, which affect the input format and hence the contents of these bases. In consequence, the present value of the computer records held must be regarded as limited. What is important about the developments taking place in establishing reliability data bases now, and in the future, is that they represent the concept and the methodology of the time, rather than the past. This implies more detailed data collection, more careful validation, more extensive storage, and easier data handling, than existed previously.[2]

The movement to, and development of, work-stations is taking place at an amazing rate. The use of networked work-stations will, in the long term, have a major impact upon many industrial work patterns, as well as upon the education of reliability engineers. The high level of interaction that will be available by this means will itself alter approaches to dealing with problems. Nor must one forget the development of electronic mail facilities, with the immediate potential for data updates, and automatic data collection which, when the current teething problems are eliminated and the data collection is properly designed, may facilitate a near semi-automatic system from collection to analysis.

However, there are boundaries to such development. Undoubtedly the major barrier is one of education. Initial education for reliability engineering is still largely absent. Some in-service training for those who do find themselves pulled into the field is available via short courses organised by various bodies. The provision, however, is haphazard and largely backward-looking. There is so much basic methodology to come to grips with, and in such a short time, that emphasis has to be placed in such courses on the 'black-box' application of 'established' reliability methodologies that have been well tried over many years of practical application. Little emphasis can be given to the changing nature of statistical methodology and the technology available for analysis. The problem is aggravated because the nature of reliability engineering frequently implies isolated cells of reliability engineers within companies. The movement towards professionalisation that the British Safety and Reliability Society and other bodies world-wide represent should assist in the long term in mitigating against this, but in the short term we are left with an isolated and heterogeneous industrial reliability community without a sound basis in the methodologies they need to use or an overview of developments in the field, and without systematic provision to remedy this situation.

What, then, are the sorts of developments in reliability education that we should expect to see in the next few years? Obviously, there is a need for more education for understanding, and less emphasis on a 'how to do it' training approach. The black-box concept of 'education' is embedded in much of the current probability plotting and hazard plotting training, as well as in the use of more advanced techniques, such as the Laplace test for trend (e.g. reliability growth) where it is taught algorithmically without explanation. In short, a higher level of statistical *understanding* will be required of the entrant. It is this aspect which the current courses do not yet deal with. There are, however, some promising signs in this respect, not least at Nottingham Polytechnic, in the UK, where such an approach is being developed in the Post-Graduate Diploma in Reliability Analysis.

Another essential element of the education issue is directly related to the comments above on computing. At this stage in the development of computing technology, it is surprising that reliability education, with its intrinsic emphasis upon data analysis and modelling, has not yet centred around a *computer-based approach*. Rather, basic methodologies are presented often in a 'back of an envelope' way, with little, haphazard and disunified guidance on computer implementation. This state of affairs cannot continue; the penalty for society would be too great. There must be movement here, as elsewhere, towards a personal work-station approach.

The developments in education and in computing themselves have implications for the new statistical methodologies, in addition to the trends which have been emerging independently in these respects. The last few years have seen a renewed emphasis upon the *exploration* of reliability data rather than black-box modelling, and it is to be hoped that the new attention given to this area by Ascher and Feingold in the USA, and Bendell and Walls in the UK, will continue to spread.[3–5]

Rather than making any prior assumptions about the nature of the reliability problem and of the reliability data, exploratory data analysis (EDA) techniques allow the analyst to try several competing methodologies, to identify appropriate structure and/or abnormality in the data, on the basis of which appropriate models may be built for analysis. The emphasis is therefore upon relatively simple analytic and graphical techniques. In reliability data, aspects such as trend, serial correlation, lack of homogeneity, common-cause failures, rogues or outliers, cyclical behaviour, etc., must be looked for. The methodologies are described in the above references. These techniques are by their nature highly interactive and visual, and fit in well with the developments in computing described above. In consequence, one would expect to see major implementation of these approaches over the next years.

As well as the most simple EDA techniques, there are related areas of statistical methodology which have a good record in other areas of application, but which have not yet established themselves within the reliability community. The signs are, however, that interest in them will continue to grow. Perhaps foremost amongst these is proportional hazards modelling. In his seminal paper which introduced the technique, Cox[6] identified the areas of application of the technique as being 'in industrial reliability studies and in medical statistics'. Alas, and typically, although the technique has generated a great amount of interest, until very recently this was mainly in the medical field. The familiar lack of trained statisticians working in reliability has severely restricted its development in this field. There are signs that this is changing.[7]

Proportional hazards modelling is an efficient means for more automatically incorporating the effect of additional explanatory factors or covariates which may have an effect on reliability. Factors such as temperature, pressure, operating conditions, design changes, etc., may be incorporated. Repairable as well as non-repairable systems may be studied. Data may be censored or uncensored. The technique is an efficient method for decomposing the variation in life lengths into orthogonal factors, identifying the significant ones, and then reconstituting the model for prediction purposes. Further, it allows the analyst to work with sparse non-homogeneous data which would otherwise be non-analysable.[8] A major feature of the model is that it makes virtually no assumptions, the exception being that it assumes that the effects of the covariates upon the hazard are multiplicative or proportional; this gives the technique its name. The initial assumption may be violated, in which case this can be identified from the data and the remedial steps can be taken.

Two other essentially exploratory approaches which are only beginning to be employed in this area, but which will be used much more during the coming years, are multivariate techniques and time series analysis. Multivariate methods were suggested for reliability applications 10 years ago by Buckland,[9] in the context of the reliability of nuclear power plants. The actual implementation of these methods in the reliability area, however, has been virtually non-existent, although Libberton et al.[10] provided an interesting application in the context of automatic fire-detection systems on a large industrial site. The results were promising, but this area of application is in its infancy. In general terms, multivariate methods are based upon the recognition that the true physical circumstances of failure information are multivariate in nature, with environment, operating conditions, weather and many other factors influencing and being influenced by failures. Multivariate methods, then, are concerned with identifying the pattern in a multivariate space of failure information, and simplifying and modelling that pattern.

In contrast, time series methods in reliability applications have largely been associated with Nozer Singpurwalla and his co-workers at the George Washington University in the USA.[11-13] Time series methods are concerned with identifying a pattern in the serial ordering of events in time, modelling this pattern, and using it for forecasting purposes. As well as aspects such as trend, cyclical behaviour (which may occur because of weather effects, minimal repairs upon failure, correction of errors at the end of test phase in software, etc.,) can be identified. Despite the claims of the current literature, it would appear that the methods employed in standard statistical time series analysis are not well suited to reliability data, which contain must greater inherent variability than data in many other applications. Modifications of methods will thus be necessary in the next few years.[14]

Another area of continuing development will be in maintenance and replacement optimisation. This will partly occur as a result of the developments in computing technology which facilitate more realistic replacement scenarios. Thus, attention is likely to be increasingly given to the sequential replacement policies arising out of optimum replacement decisions over finite time horizons, rather than relying upon the simplified theory associated with unrealistic infinite time horizons.[15]

In a similar way also, developments in computing will facilitate the movement towards the non-Markovian modelling of systems, as the Markov assumptions (exponential distributions) for failure and repair distributions are known to be in error, and in certain circumstances to cause serious distortion.[16] It is reassuring to find a movement already in this direction, although, at present, largely based on simulation.[17]

A connected development that one would expect to see is a movement towards less confusion and indeed less approximation (often inappropriate approximation) in the construction and analysis of fault-trees and Markov models. Some aspects of the current state of affairs were discussed by Bendell and Ansell.[18]

Another highly important development, and most relevant of all to the theme of this book, is in the area of the design of data collection and of experiments. Although well developed in biological and medical contexts, the statistical approach to experimental design has been very neglected in the industrial context generally.[19] The resultant move in Western society towards Taguchi methods (adapted from Japan) to optimise product and process designs for reliability and quality is overdue.[20]

Having discussed developments in computing, education and techniques, what are the outstanding technical problems associated with the development of reliability assessment over the next few years? In the author's opinion these are not as serious as the barriers to information flow and the correct use of methods, and potential methods, within the reliability engineering community. Thus, the importance of the developments in education are paramount, as is, perhaps, the elimination of the amateur reliability computer programs. Apart from this, it must be said that some of the analysis methods outlined above would, if generally used, remove many of the current technical problems associated with reliability data analysis. For example, the use of proportional hazards modelling would remove the difficulty experienced in the reliability analysis of data with heavy censoring and sparse data matrices.

There still remain a number of problems to be solved. These include the inherent difficulties of design-stage reliability prediction; the need for further information on the power of various reliability methods, and on the robustness of the methods; the need for improvement in the design of lift tests, accelerated tests, etc.; the intrinsic modelling problems associated with common-mode and common-cause failures, human factors and software reliability; the need for a clear understanding of the implicit assumptions and physical applicability of certain models, such as MIL 217, fault-tree formulations, etc.; and, perhaps most fundamentally, the need to develop purpose-built exploratory methodologies suitable for the particular data patterns that arise within reliability data.

In conclusion, then, the next 40 years are seen as critical ones in the development of reliability engineering. Methodologies and data bases will certainly move forward in this period, but to what extent this will be matched by professional practice will depend upon the extent to which more honesty and more openness can be developed. In the author's opinion, developments in computer technology and software, in education and in methodologies must, and will, converge to produce better reliability engineering practice.

15.3 USING EXTERNAL DATA SOURCES AND MAKING UP DATA

There are, of course, a number of areas where it is unrealistic to expect to obtain adequate field or test data for analysis. This is clearly the case at the stage of early system design, but it may also be true where an existing system has run for insufficient time to obtain failure data on relatively rarely failing components. This is particularly a problem if these components are of new design or production. The problem faced is how to substitute for the data that cannot be collected, or how to circumnavigate the lack. The possibilities include the use of *data from elsewhere* (i.e. from other products or plants or from other *data banks*) or, more formally, *Bayesian* techniques. Neither of these is a very satisfactory approach, as data transferred from elsewhere, or from other data banks, may not be appropriate to the operating regime or the plant in question. However, they may provide ball-park figures. Often in practice there is little recourse but to use subjective estimates obtained by those allegedly knowledgeable in the field. Bayesian methods help to formalise this procedure, but add little extra.

Thus, one turns to the question of the *comparability of reliability data* associated with different products and plants. This is strongly related to the question of the level of aggregation, as the plants and their operating conditions represent additional explanatory variables to those such as component specifications, immediate stress of system, etc. A major development in the methodology for dealing with such explanatory variables is proportional hazards modelling, as described above.

However, the process of interrogating sources and tracking down suitable external data remains difficult and requires experience.

Particular areas in which satisfactory data are currently very hard to obtain are *common-cause or common-mode failures, human factors* and *software reliability.* These are all aspects of systems for which it is extremely difficult to obtain reliable data, so that recourse is often made to arbitrary and unsubstantiated models. These areas appear to have the common feature that each is of critical importance to system's reliability and its assessment, yet is insufficiently known at present to incorporate it effectively into the data collection and analysis programme. These are all areas also where it is to be hoped that major progress will be made in the next few years. For example, in software reliability a number of developments are taking place.[21] These include work under the European ESPRIT and British Alvey programmes, and in particular an Alvey project on Software Reliability Modelling at Nottingham Polytechnic in collaboration with the UKAEA, British Aerospace, STC, Logica, and City and Newcastle universities.

15.4 JUSTIFYING A RELIABILITY DATA BASE

It is to be hoped that this book will provide the ammunition to justify the construction, establishment and use of reliability data bases in general. In a specific case, the question is much more complicated. Apart from the immediate advantages that are planned at the data base construction, it is likely that new advantages will come to light once the data base is established.

Now it is up to you.

REFERENCES

1. Bendell, A., Assessing the future of reliability. I: The basis for growth. *Safety Reliab.* (1985).
2. Bendell, A., Assessing the future of reliability. II: Towards the year 2000. *Safety Reliab.* (1986).
3. Ascher, H. E. & Feingold, H., *Repairable Systems Reliability: Modelling, Inference, Misconceptions and their Causes.* Marcel Dekker, New York, 1984.
4. Bendell, A. & Walls, L. A., Exploring reliability data. *Quality Reliab. Engng Int.*, **1** (1985) 37–52.
5. Walls, L. A. & Bendell, A., The structure and exploration of reliability field data; what to look for and how to analyse it. *Proc. 5th Nat. Reliab. Conf.*, 5B/5/1-17, 1985.
6. Cox, D. R., Regression models and life-tables (with discussion). *J. R. Statist. Soc.*, B, **34** (1972) 187–202.
7. Wightman, D. W. & Bendell, A., The practical application of proportional hazards modelling. *Reliab. Engng*, **15** (1986) 29–55.
8. Bendell, A., Walley, M., Wightman, D. W. & Wood, L. M., Proportional hazards modelling in reliability analysis—an application to brake disks on high-speed trains. *Quality Reliab. Engng Int.*, **2** (1986) 45–52.
9. Buckland, W. R., Reliability of nuclear power plants; statistical techniques for analysis. Task Force on Problems of Rare Events in the Reliability of Nuclear Power Plants, JRC, Ispra, 8–10 June 1976, CSNI Rep. 10, 1976.

10. Libberton, G. P., Bendell, A., Walls, L. A. & Cannon, A. G., Reliability data collection and analysis for automatic fire detection systems on a large industrial site. *Proc. Seminar Data Collection and Analysis for Reliability Assessment.* I.Mech.E., London, 1986.
11. Singpurwalla, N. D., Estimating reliability growth (or deterioration) using time series analysis. *Naval Res. Logistics Q.*, **25** (1978) 1–4.
12. Singpurwalla, N. D., Analysing availability using transfer function models and cross-spectral analysis. *Naval Res. Logistics Q.*, **27** (1980) 1–16.
13. Crow, L. H. & Singpurwalla, N. D., An empirically derived Fourier series model for describing software failures. *IEEE Trans. Reliab.*, **R-33** (1984) 176–83.
14. Walls, L. A. & Bendell, A., Time series methods in reliability. *Proc. 9th ARTS*, Bradford, April 1986. (To appear in *Reliab. Engng.*)
15. Ansell, J. I., Bendell, A. & Humble, S., Age replacement under alternative cost criteria. *Mgmt Sci.*, **30** (1984) 358–67.
16. Edgar, J. & Bendell, A., The robustness of Markov reliability models. *Quality Reliab. Engng Int.*, **2**(2) (1986).
17. Argent, S. J. & Ryan, S. G., An analysis of supergrid transmission fault data in a specific area of England and Wales. *Proc. 8th Advances in Reliab. Technol. Symp.*, Bradford, A2/3/1-10 (1984).
18. Bendell, A. & Ansell, J. I., Practical aspects of fault-tree analysis and the use of Markov reliability models. *Proc. 5th Nat. Reliab. Conf.*, Birmingham, Vol. 2, 4B/2/1-8 (1985).
19. Baines, A., Industrial statistics and operational research (with discussion). *J. R. Statist. Soc., A*, **147** (1984) 316–26.
20. Bendell, A. & Disney, J., Quality attainment by Taguchi optimisation methods for product and process design. *Proc. 19th Int. Symp. Automative Technol. and Automation*, Vol. 35-44, ISATA, 1988.
21. Bendell, A. & Mellor, P. (eds), *Software Reliability State of the Art Report, 14: 2.* Pergamon Infotech, Oxford, 1986.

Index